Battle of Britain

Battle of Britain

LEN DEIGHTON

CM&G

Library of Congress Cataloging in Publication Data
Deighton, Len,
   Battle of Britain.

1. Britain, Battle of, 1940.   I. Title.
D756.5.B7D43   940.54'21   80-11663
SBN 0-698-11033-1

This book was designed and produced in Great Britain by
George Rainbird Limited
36 Park Street
LONDON W1Y 4DE, England
Designer: Adrian Field
Picture Researcher: Tom Graves

Text set by SX Composing Ltd, Rayleigh, England
Printed and bound by Dai Nippon Printing Company Ltd, Tokyo, Japan

Half-title page: Bf 109s over the English Channel
Title page: A Hurricane still flying today (*Photo by Tony Howarth*)

Contents

Foreword

It would be neither wise nor true for any writer to declare that one picture is worth a thousand words. Perhaps that was something I believed when I was a photographer, or when I was a student at St Martin's School of Art in London, because my whole life was devoted to visual images. I enjoyed being an illustrator but could not resist the pleasures, of orchestrating visual ideas, that an art director's job provides. My sketchbooks reveal the same sort of direction. They begin with pages of drawings but as the years went past there was more and more description scribbled into the margins. By the time I graduated from the Royal College of Art I was convinced that a picture is only as good as the context in which it is displayed. A flattened Coca Cola tin in a Bond Street gutter is worthless garbage; moved into an art gallery and spotlit, it might fetch a thousand pounds.

The truth of this becomes even more apparent for anyone who can look through a large photo archive with an expert ready to help. A blurred smudge – corners bent, and caption lost – is hardly worth wasting time with, until someone who can analyze the picture begins to explain what was happening.

The wonderful graphic material – posters, paintings and all manner of ephemera – that I had seen since first beginning serious research into the 1940 battles strongly reawakened my interest in illustration. Soon I began to experiment with the idea of telling the story of the Battle of Britain using text that was embodied in the visual material.

It was soon evident that if done properly, and there was really no point in doing it any other way, it would be costly and time absorbing. There could be no question of using other publishers' material. Every drawing and coloured illustration must be designed and created for this book. Similarly every diagram and map must be specially drawn for this text. A really big hunt must be mounted to find unfamiliar archive material.

I could never have achieved my aim working alone. My publishers in London and New York responded to the idea with enthusiasm. I was doubly lucky in finding the Rainbird organization – which had long been producing exactly the sort of illustrated book I most admired – ready to put all their resources of experience and talent at my disposal. The confidence and resource they have shown makes me deeply grateful. Added to this I cannot help but remember that it was George Rainbird himself who gave me advice and encouragement and paid work too while I was still a student at the Royal College of Art.

Elsewhere I have undertaken the most hazardous task of attempting to remember those who have helped me create this book, but it is appropriate that I single out my good friend Max Hastings who brought to it the immense fund of knowledge he had built up while writing his magnificent history book *Bomber Command*. I believe it is not just coincidence that we both came to the subject of the Battle of Britain having spent some time studying the RAF bombing raids over Germany. This book is an attempt to look at the Battle within the context of history, separated from the high-powered propaganda from both sides much of which still distorts current beliefs about what actually happened.

Very small in scale, the Battle of Britain was the last of the gentlemen's wars. After this the air forces of both sides resorted to the area bombing of civilians in town centres. The war in the Pacific was a portent of wars to come. Hitler sent his armies into the Russian wastelands.

And yet the more I study the Battle of Britain the more convinced I become that it was a pivotal point of the history of this century. To anyone who says that it was not one of the most important battles of the Second World War I ask, without it what other battles would there have been?

Len Deighton

Strategic air power:

For most of the First World War, air forces were organized as branches of their nations' armies and navies. The British Army was served by the Royal Flying Corps (RFC), the Royal Navy by the Royal Naval Air Service (RNAS). The pioneer airmen fought a long struggle against entrenched naval and military prejudice, to prove that aircraft could make a critical contribution to warfare. By 1917, they had made their point. Few sensible soldiers or sailors denied the value of aircraft for providing reconnaissance and tactical support on the battlefield and over enemy lines of communication. Enthusiasm for the new dimension carried many British airmen a stage further: they wanted their freedom from military and naval hierarchies to wage war as an independent service.

The airmen's dream

Left: All that early ground-attack aircraft like this Russian two-seater could do was to harass trenches and lines of communication. But air power had one great advantage over artillery, argued airmen: almost unlimited range. Bombers could reach far behind the battlefields to attack the vulnerable urban and industrial centres of the enemy. Already in Spain in 1936 (see above), civilians were suffering severely at the hands of the apostles of air power

It was the development of the bomber that gave them their chance. Bombing, they argued, provided a revolutionary new means of launching an offensive against an enemy that had nothing to do with the dreary stalemate at sea or the bloody deadlock between the armies. There was now a new method of attacking an enemy at will, of striking devastating blows at his industrial and military centres against which he had no effective defence.

The airmen might never have got their way in the face of opposition from the established services (and from the RFC's commander, General Trenchard) but for two factors: the first was that the British Prime Minister, Lloyd George, was ill-disposed towards his generals after their terrible failures in France, the second was that the Germans launched a series of attacks on south-east England by Gotha bombers in the summer and autumn of 1917. The RFC could do nothing to stop them.

The nation was already war weary, and the Gotha attacks were the last straw. They provoked uproar among the public, in the press and the House of Commons. Lloyd George needed an immediate panacea. He appointed himself and the Imperial hero, General Smuts, as a two-man committee to examine the organization of Britain's air forces. In the event, Smuts did most of the work. After a hasty survey, he delivered his report. In a few weeks' study of air warfare, the General had become seized by the airmen's vision of the future. He dramatically endorsed their claim to offer an independent, revolutionary means of waging war.

Britain's air defences were quickly strengthened, and the Gotha attacks dwindled. But, under the impetus of the Smuts Report, on 1 April 1918 the Royal Air Force was brought into being as an independent service. The RFC and RNAS merged under the command of General Sir Hugh Trenchard, who now became a leading advocate of independent air warfare.

Top: Air raid damage in Southend, Essex, 1917.
The novelty of an air attack at first caused alarm
and disruption out of all proportion to the material
effect but civilians became astonishingly resilient
Above: One of Germany's Gotha bombers
Above right: Guernica shrouded in smoke after
bombardment: symbol of horror from the air

Right: Until the early 1930s, successive British
governments were assured by the RAF that the only
effective counter against air attack was to bomb the
other side but in the last years before the Second
World War, the Government spent millions on
strengthening Civil Defence organizations though other
European countries were still much better prepared

SERVE TO SAVE

' A nation which has command of the air...'

General Jan Smuts
'An air service can be used as an independent means of war operations. . . . As far as can at present be foreseen, there is absolutely no limit to the scale of its future independent war use. And the day may not be far off when aerial operations with their devastation of enemy lands and destruction of industrial and populous centres on a vast scale may become the principal operations of war, to which the older forms of military and naval operations may become secondary and subordinate.'
1917

General Giulio Douhet
'A nation which has command of the air . . . can bomb the interior of an enemy's country so devastatingly that the physical and moral resistance of the people would also collapse . . . An aerial fleet capable of dumping hundreds of tons of bombs can easily be organized; therefore, the striking force and magnitude of an aerial offensive, considered from the standpoint of either material or moral significance, are far more effective than those of any other offensive yet known. . . .
'. . . All this is a present possibility, not one in the distant future.'
1921 *The Command of the Air*

**Marshal of the RAF
Sir Hugh Trenchard**
'It is not . . . necessary for an air force, in order to defeat the enemy nation, to defeat its armed forces first. Air power can dispense with that intermediate step, can pass over the enemy navies and armies, and penetrate the air defences and attack direct the centre of production, transportation and communication from which the enemy war effort is maintained. . .'

'It is on the destruction of enemy industries and, above all, in the lowering of morale of enemy nationals caused by bombing that the ultimate victory lies. . . .'
1928

Brigadier William Mitchell
'Air Power holds out the hope to the nations that in the future air battles taking place miles away from the frontiers will be so decisive and of such far-reaching effect that the nation losing them will be willing to capitulate without resorting to a further contest on land or water. Aircraft operating in the heart of an enemy's country will accomplish their object in an incredibly short space of time once the control of the air has been established, and the months or even years of contest of ground armies with a loss of millions of lives will be eliminated in the future. . .'
1925 At the hearings of the President's Aircraft Board

Captain Basil Liddell Hart
'A modern state is such a complex and interdependent fabric that it offers a target highly sensitive to a sudden and overwhelming blow from the air. . . . Imagine for a moment London, Manchester, Birmingham and half a dozen other great centres simultaneously attacked, the business localities and Fleet Street wrecked, Whitehall a heap of ruins, the slum districts maddened into the impulse to break loose and maraud, the railways cut, factories destroyed. Would not the general will to resist vanish, and what use would be the still determined fractions of the nation, without organization and central direction?'
1925 *Paris, or the Future of War*

Stanley Baldwin
'I think it is well for the man in the street to realize that there is no power on earth that can protect him from being bombed. Whatever people may tell him, the bomber will always get through. The only defence is offence, which means that you have to kill more women and children more quickly than the enemy if you want to save yourselves. I just mention that . . . so that people may realize what is waiting for them when the next war comes.'
1932 The former and future British Prime Minister speaking in the House of Commons

Pilots of the London Air Defence at Kenley, 1928

'The Bomber will always get through'

From the beginning, the thinking of the RAF's leaders was dominated by the memory of what the German raids on England had achieved: hundreds of casualties, a dramatic drop in munitions production in the London factories, and a major political crisis. If a handful of ill-equipped bombers could achieve these results in a few raids in the Great War, the airmen reasoned, was there any limit to what they might achieve in the next?

In the decade after the war, many military prophets around the world became equally bewitched by this vision. The Italian, General Douhet, wrote a book in 1920 entitled *The Command of the Air*, which Hitler was quoting enthusiastically in conversation in 1931. Brigadier Billy Mitchell in America urged the cause of air power, and sought to prove his point by sinking an obsolete battleship

at anchor with air-dropped bombs. Britain's foremost military thinkers, Liddell Hart and JFC Fuller, although they later became opponents of strategic bombing, were at this time fervent believers.

In Britain, Sir Hugh Trenchard and his young disciples were fighting for the very existence of the RAF against generals and admirals who wanted it divided again under their commands. The concept of an independent strategic bomber offensive became the basis of the airmen's creed. To justify their independence, they had to have a function that made them more than flying artillery for fleets and armies. So with the paltry budgets available through the 1920s and early 1930s, Trenchard built a mainly bombing air force although he devoted very little thought to what it was going to do, or indeed what it was really capable of.

As the professional airmen forecast Armageddon

Alcock and Brown take off from Newfoundland on 14 June 1919. The epic transatlantic flight dramatically revealed the potential of air technology. Their flight, in a standard twin-engined Vickers Vimy bomber, took 16.5 hours and ended near Clifden, Ireland

from the skies, politicians and the public became infected by their prophecies. Scores of books were published, most of them fantastic, predicting vast casualties and limitless destruction from air bombardment. The airmen assured the politicians that since the fighters of the day were only a few mph faster than the bombers, there was no hope of creating an effective defensive system against bomber attack; the only chance of safety lay in creating a strategic deterrent by building one's own force of bombers.

Stanley Baldwin's gloomy prognosis in 1932 (based on Trenchard's advice) that 'the bomber will always get through' provided a new rallying cry for the pacifists, and ironically strengthened the hand of those who thought rearmament was futile.

From 1917 to the outbreak of the Second World War, there was always a body of sensible and thoughtful men – Winston Churchill prominent among them – who believed that the threat from the air was exaggerated, and that a society that defended itself vigorously could survive and defeat an air attack. But it was the pessimists whose view prevailed. Reports of the Italian bombing of Abyssinia,

of the great Japanese air attacks in Manchuria and, above all, of the Condor Legion's operations over Guernica and other Spanish towns in the Civil War, increased public alarm.

British and French airmen warned their governments of the prospect of thousands, even hundreds of thousands of casualties in the first weeks of an air attack. The threat from the air became as dominant a fear between the wars as the atomic bomb has been since 1945, with the important difference that the power of conventional bomber attack on a modern industrial society had never been tested.

'Air power . . . Its mystery is half its power'

Senior British airmen of the period did not see themselves simply as service officers but as apostles of a new form of warfare which excited them almost as much as it appalled the public. 'Air power has its dreams', wrote one of the RAF's foremost public advocates, a civil servant at the Air Ministry named JM Spaight. 'It knows that its qualities are unique. The armoury of the invincible knight of old held no such weapon as that which it wields. It dreams of victory achieved perhaps by a swift, sudden, overwhelming stroke at the heart and nerve centre of a foe . . . Its mystery is half its power.'

At the root of all the airmen's hopes was a conviction that whether or not bombing physically destroyed the enemy's industry (and they did very few sums to work out whether this was even possible) civilian morale would collapse when missiles rained around workers' homes and offices. It was the terror of being bombed which was expected to be decisive.

'In air operations against production', wrote Group Captain John Slessor, a future Chief of Air Staff, in 1936 'the weight of attack will inevitably fall upon a vitally important, and not by nature very amenable, section of the community, the industrial workers, whose morale and sticking power cannot be expected to equal that of a disciplined soldier.'

It was against this background of the airmen's vision that the air forces of Europe and especially the RAF evolved between the two World Wars. It was these theories that would be put to their first decisive test in the blitz and the Battle of Britain.

Air technology 1918-1939:

In the First World War, combat aircraft evolved very rapidly. The most important breakthrough was the Fokker team's development of an interrupter gear that enabled a machine-gun to fire through a propeller, and thus allowed a pilot to attack an enemy simply by aiming his aircraft at it. Designers learnt how to build highly manoeuvrable fighters, and bombers capable of carrying a 1,800 lb bombload to a target 250 miles away. In 1918, service development stopped dead. The defeated powers were disarmed, and the victors retrenched. The RAF entered the 1930s with aircraft that were only improved models of those used in the First World War.

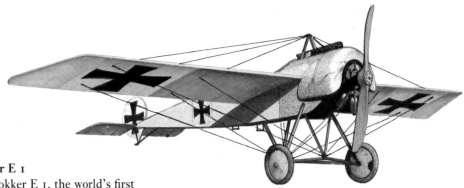

Fokker E 1
The Fokker E 1, the world's first aircraft to carry interrupter gear which prevented its Parabellum machine-gun from firing when the barrel was in line with the propeller blades. Anthony Fokker's design team rushed through the invention in July 1915 when the Germans captured Roland Garros's French fighter, fitted with deflector blades on the propeller to minimize damage from bullets striking it. For a few weeks 'the Fokker scourge' overwhelmed the Allied air forces, until the designers matched the interrupter system

Sopwith Triplane
The Sopwith Triplane introduced in November 1916; a supremely manoeuvrable aircraft with a top speed of 113 mph. Its weakness was that it could stand little structural damage

Combat aircraft

Fokker D VII
The Fokker D VII, perhaps the outstanding fighter of the First World War. Introduced in May 1918, its maximum speed was 116 mph, but its very high power-weight ratio enabled it to 'hang on its prop' to make a vertical attack from below. It achieved a ceiling of almost 23,000 ft, although, like the German jet Me 262 in the Second World War, it was never in sufficient quantity to be decisive

Handley Page
The Handley Page O/400 twin-engined bomber, a remarkable manufacturing achievement of its generation. It could carry 1,800 lb of bombs over 500 miles at a speed of 97 mph

Bristol Bulldog
The Bristol Bulldog, the backbone of Britain's fighter defence between 1929 and 1936. The air-cooled radial engine by which it was powered, like that of so many British aircraft between the war, made very high speeds aerodynamically impossible

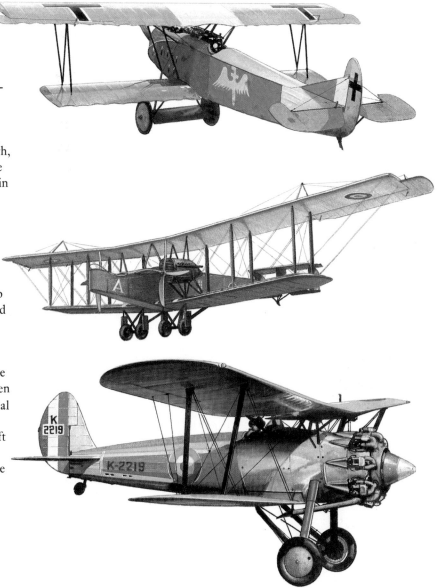

The problem of speed
The speed of service aircraft improved very slowly. The First War designers had never conquered the problem of speed – the best 1918 types were capable of only 120–140 mph. Yet the RAF's first-line Bristol Bulldog could manage only 174 mph in 1936. Even if money for re-equipment had been available, the British Air Staff showed little inclination to look ahead towards new technology. Throughout the interwar years, civilian designers were developing new materials, new methods of building airframes, above all new engines. It was the British Supermarine S 6B that took the world air speed record past 400 mph in 1931. The servicemen were slow to understand that a revolution was taking place around them.

Airframes and undercarriages

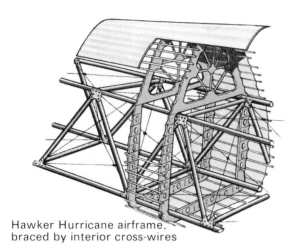

Hawker Hurricane airframe, braced by interior cross-wires

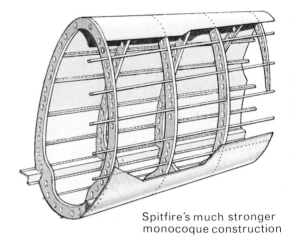

Spitfire's much stronger monocoque construction

Early aircraft were constructed of a wooden frame, with wooden struts to give shape, and a canvas covering overall. Even after painting, the resulting structure was very poorly streamlined. The development of light alloys such as Duralumin during the First World War gave the post-war designers the opportunity for tremendous advances in the shape and finish of their aircraft. It became possible to build monoplanes with only light bracing wires to support the wings, and soon with no external bracing at all. The covering of the new metal wings could itself bear part of the structural weight, unlike its canvas predecessor. The new metal monocoque fuselage structures were much simpler to build and lighter in the air. So great was the advance of streamlining that it has been estimated that a 1950 aircraft required a quarter of the power to move the same weight as a 1920 biplane. By the 1930s, designers understood the vital importance of reducing exterior bulges on their aircraft to a minimum. Above all, this influenced landing gear. Design advanced from the fixed undercarriages of the First World War (and of most inter-war service types) to the spatted, streamlined models of the 1920s civil aircraft, and then to the fully retractable undercarriage as on the advanced Heinkel *Blitz*.

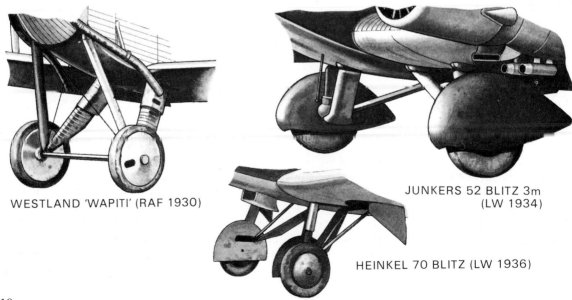

WESTLAND 'WAPITI' (RAF 1930)

JUNKERS 52 BLITZ 3m (LW 1934)

HEINKEL 70 BLITZ (LW 1936)

Fighters developed for the RAF in Britain compared against fighters developed in other countries during the 1930's

Manufacturers' designation	Biplane/Monoplane	In series production year	Design history status [1]	Undercarriage type [2]	Maximum output horsepower	Power Plant	Classification [3]	Maximum speed miles per hour	Service ceiling feet	Loaded weight lb	Wing span feet inches	Number of guns [4] Calibres
CZECHOSLOVAKIA												
Avia B-534 IV	B	1936	L	F	860	Hispano-Suiza 12Y	IL	249	34 800	4,365	30 10	4 x 7.7
Avia Av 135	M	1939	E	R	860	Hispano-Suiza 12Y	IL	332	27 900	5,430	35 7	1 x 20/2 x 7.7
FRANCE												
SPAD 510	B	1936	E	F	690	Hispano-Suiza 12X	IL	236	34 400	3,705	29 0	4 x 7.7
Dewoitine D 150	M	1936	L	F	860	Hispano-Suiza 12Y	IL	250	34 500	4,235	39 8	1 x 20/2 x 7.5
GERMANY												
Heinkel He 51 A	B	1934	E	F	750	BMW VI	IL	205	25 360	4,180	36 1	2 x 7.9
Heinkel He 112B	B	1937	E	R	680	Junkers Jumo 210E	IL	317	27 890	4,960	29 10	2 x 20/2 x 7.9
ITALY												
Fiat C R 42	B	1939	L	F	840	Fiat A74 RC 38	RA	267	34 450	5,060	31 9	1 x 12.7/1 x 7.7
Fiat G 50	M	1938	E	R	840	Fiat A74 RC 38	RA	293	32 480	5,970	36 1	2 x 12.7
JAPAN												
Kawasaki Army Type 95 Model 1	B	1936	E	F	800	Kawasaki Ha-9	IL	246	32 800	4,000	33 0	2 x 7.7
Mitsubishi Navy Type 96 Model 21	M	1937	E	F	610	Kotobuki 2-KAI-3	RA	265	14 030	3,550	35 6	2 x 7.7
NETHERLANDS												
Fokker D XVII	B	1933	L	F	600	Rolls-Royce Kestrel II S	IL	208	28 710	3,260	31 6	2 x 7.9
Fokker D XXI	M	1938	E	F	830	Bristol Mercury VIII	RA	285	33 130	4,520	36 1	4 x 7.9
USA												
Curtiss Export Hawk III	B	1936	L	R	750	Wright R-1820 F-53	RA	240	25 800	4,320	31 6	2 x 0.30 in
Curtiss P-36A	M	1937	E	R	1,000	P & W R-1830-13	RA	313	33 000	6,010	37 4	1 x 0.50 in/1 x 0.30 in
USSR												
Polikarpov I-153	B	1939	L	R	1,000	Shvetsov M-62R	RA	249	33 100	4,430	32 10	4 x 7.62
Polikarpov I-16 Type 4	M	1935	E	R	725	M-25 (Wright R-1820)	RA	282	30 450	3,135	29 6	2 x 7.62
ROMANIA												
SET-XV	B	1934	E	F	550	Gnome-Rhône 9K	RA	211	13 120	3,410	30 10	2 x 7.7
POLAND [5]												
PZL P 24 F	M	1938	L	F	970	Gnome-Rhône 14N	RA	267	34 450	4,230	35 2	2 x 20/2 x 7.7
YUGOSLAVIA [6]												
Ikarus IK-2	M	1937	E	F	860	Hispano-Suiza 12Y	IL	266	34 450	4,255	37 5	1 x 20/2 x 7.9
ROYAL AIR FORCE												
Bristol Bulldog IIA	B	1930	E	F	490	Bristol Jupiter VIIF	RA	174	27 000	3,530	33 11	2 x 0.303 in
Hawker Demon	B	1932	L	F	580	Rolls-Royce Kestrel VDR	IL	182	27 500	4,670	37 3	3.4 x 0.303 in
Gloster Gauntlet I	B	1934	L	F	645	Bristol Mercury VIS	RA	228	35 500	3,950	32 9	2 x 0.303 in
Hawker Fury II	B	1936	L	F	640	Rolls-Royce Kestrel VI	IL	223	29 500	3,610	30 0	2 x 0.303 in
Gloster Gladiator I	B	1936	L	F	840	Bristol Mercury IXS	RA	253	33 000	4,750	32 3	4 x 0.303 in

1 E – Early stage of development
  L – Later stage of development
2 F – Fixed main undercarriage
  R – Retractable undercarriage
3 IL – Inline-Vee, liquid-cooled
  RA – Radial, air-cooled
4 Gun calibres expressed in milli-metres except where indicated

5 Poland was unique as its military aircraft industry, dating from 1929, never produced a biplane fighter and was technologically ahead of bigger national industries (in all-metal construction, for example)

6 Yugoslavia, although with one of the smallest aircraft industries in Europe, possessed some bright, French-educated design engineers. Compare Poland's lengthily-developed P 24F with the modest design history of Yugoslavia's IK-2.

Engines

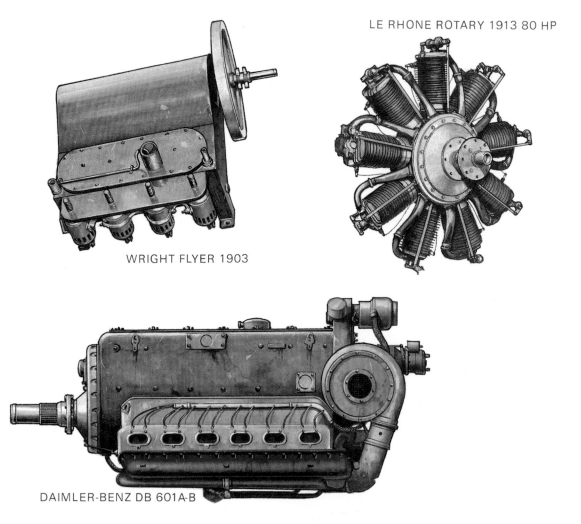

WRIGHT FLYER 1903

LE RHONE ROTARY 1913 80 HP

DAIMLER-BENZ DB 601A-B

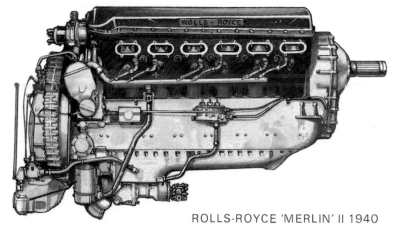

ROLLS-ROYCE 'MERLIN' II 1940

The Wright Brothers' first powered flight was made possible by Charles Taylor, their assistant, who made a lightweight petrol engine in six weeks from scratch. He was more important as a pioneer of powered flight than the brothers. First World War aircraft development was dominated by the rotary engine, but in 1918 the immensely successful American 'Liberty' engine showed what a vee-shaped twelve cylinder design could achieve. Henceforth, it was this type that engineers strove to improve, the British aiming for an engine that would give one horsepower for every pound of weight against the Wright Brothers' Flyer 3's 9.5 lb, and the 'Liberty's' 2.1 lb.

The Rolls-Royce Merlin engine, which powered the RAF's best aircraft of the Second World War, evolved from the company's PV 12 design – the PV denoting 'Private Venture'. Fuel development – most of it done in the USA – resulted in the discovery that tetraethyl lead suppressed detonation, the isooctanes in 1925, and the blending agents that raised most military aircraft fuel from 87 to 100 octane by 1939. Improved fuel led to improved superchargers, using the aircraft's hot exhaust gases and especially important at high altitude. Sodium-cooling and stellite valve seatings vastly improved performance. A duralumin crank-case weighed only one tenth of its aluminium alloy counterpart, and was twice as strong. Chromium, nickel, manganese, tungsten and silicon all contributed to the alloys that made the new high performance engines possible.

The Daimler-Benz DB 601A engine which would power the Messerschmitts in the Battle of Britain was even more advanced than the Merlin, thanks to its fuel injection system. Carburettors are subject to the changes of temperature inevitable in air combat, and could miss beats owing to centrifugal effect as the aircraft dived. The DB 601A's fuel injection system put a measured amount of fuel into each cylinder according to temperature, engine speed, etc.

Aero-engines 1848–1960

POWER UNIT	YEAR	HORSE-POWER	WEIGHT LBS	WEIGHT PER HP	REMARKS
Stringfellow: *steam*	1848	25	600	24	Unmanned
Manly radial: *Langley*	1903	52.4	200	3.8	Crashed on take off
Wright Bros' *Flyer 1*	1903	12	152	12.7	The first heavier-than-air, sustained, powered flight
Wright Bros' *Flyer 2*	1904	16	180	11.4	Longest flight 5 minutes 4 seconds
Wright Bros' *Flyer 3*	1905	19	180	9.5	The first aircraft to fly more than half an hour
Wright Bros' *Flyer 32*	1908	35	182	5.5	Enabled Flyer 3 to take a passenger
Gnome Rotary	1909	50	165	3.3	French engine. Later powered Camel/Fokker
Liberty V 12	1918	420	882	2.1	The first designed for mass production
Rolls-Royce Condor	1920	650	1310	2.6	
Daimler-Benz *601A*	1937	1100	1344	1.2	
(Bf 109E)	1938	1030	1335	1.3	
R R Merlin Series II *Spitfire/Hurricane*	1960	6000	2000	0.3	NB Jets and turboprops cannot be accurately compared with piston engine performance
R R Tyne: *Turboprop*					

The Schneider Trophy

One of the most important forces in encouraging the development of high-speed aircraft between the wars was the Schneider Trophy. It was awarded to the victor in an international race for floatplanes over a course of 150 nautical miles, and had been instituted in 1912 by Jacques Schneider of the French armaments family, who believed, like many other men of his time, that the future of aviation lay with planes that could take off on water.

In 1919, the Royal Aero Club staged the first post-war race at Bournemouth. Three British, one French and one Italian aircraft entered. It was apparent from their choices of design that the familiar rotary engine was now eclipsed by the in-line watercooled models developed during the war. A very young designer named RJ Mitchell was responsible for one entry, the Supermarine Sea Lion, but on this occasion his creation performed without distinction. Indeed, after a series of accidents to all the other entrants, the Italian had only to complete the course to win a walkover, and the race ended in fiasco when he flew the wrong course.

In 1922 the Mitchell-designed Sea Lion II won the contest at Naples at an average speed of 146 mph. The 1923 race was won by the American Curtiss CR-3 at 177 mph. In the next race in 1925, Mitchell's new Supermarine S 4 crashed in the trials, and the American R3C-2 won at a speed of 233 mph.

By now, the Schneider Trophy had become a matter of immense international prestige, with competing nations devoting hundreds of thousands of pounds to building their entries. The technology of the high-speed seaplane had outstripped that of its land-based counterpart, although of course the wheeled aircraft profited from the experience gained. The Trophy had provoked a remarkable creative competition among the designers of the day, and most useful of all, an exchange of ideas. The Italian Macchi M 39 which won the 1926 race at a speed of 246 mph was strongly influenced in design by the American Curtiss. It was now generally appreciated that streamlining was more important than brute strength in building a really fast aircraft.

The 1929 race saw the birth of the great partnership of Mitchell's S 6 airframe with the Rolls-Royce engine, whose ultimate achievement would be the Spitfire. Rolls-Royce aero engines had been eclipsed by those of Napier and Bristol since 1918, but when Mitchell was looking for a new engine to power his latest creation, he consulted Hawker's Chief Test Pilot, Major George Bulman. Bulman recommended Rolls-Royce. After some initial hesitation the project was launched. After many teething troubles, the Rolls-Royce 'R' was fitted to Mitchell's airframe. Against an Italian team, which had put huge effort into the race, the Supermarine S6 won at an astonishing 328 mph. Mitchell had almost single-handed brought the monoplane into the forefront of British aircraft design.

If, in 1931, Britain won the race for the third time, she would become permanent holder of the Schneider Trophy. Yet the socialist Prime Minister Ramsay Macdonald announced that there would be no government money to support this bid. There was a public outcry. In January 1931, Lady Houston, the widow of a shipping magnate, put up £100000 from her own pocket to ensure that Mitchell's S 6B could race. There were no other entrants. On 12 September 1931, the S 6B flew the course at a speed of 340 mph, and secured the Trophy forever. Two weeks later, the aircraft took the world air-speed record at 407 mph. The foundations had been laid for British high performance aircraft and their engines in the Second World War.

Above: Sir Henry Royce, whose company built the engines that won the Trophy
Left: Bournemouth, setting for the first post-war Trophy race, in 1919
Top left: The Supermarine S 6 seaplane which achieved victory for Britain in 1929
Top right: Schneider Trophy

The evolving bomber

In 1919, the British Vickers Vimy bomber was capable of carrying a 2,500 lb bombload for 300 miles. It was the first true heavy bomber. Yet in the 1920s and into the 1930s, despite the RAF's commitment to strategic bombing, the shortage of cash drove Trenchard's air force to depend upon a succession of light bombers for its front line, the best of which was the Hawker Hart, introduced in 1930. It was left to others – notably Russians, Italians and Americans – to advance bomber design into the mid-1930s, when Germany dramatically entered the field.

Vickers Vimy

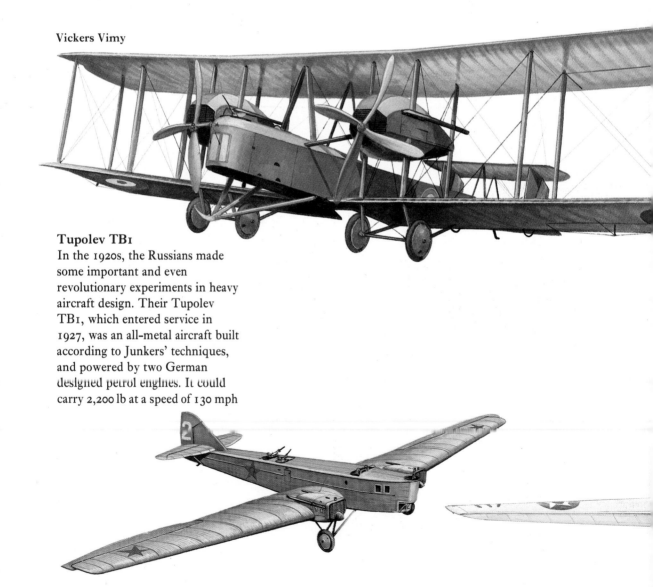

Tupolev TB1
In the 1920s, the Russians made some important and even revolutionary experiments in heavy aircraft design. Their Tupolev TB1, which entered service in 1927, was an all-metal aircraft built according to Junkers' techniques, and powered by two German designed petrol engines. It could carry 2,200 lb at a speed of 130 mph

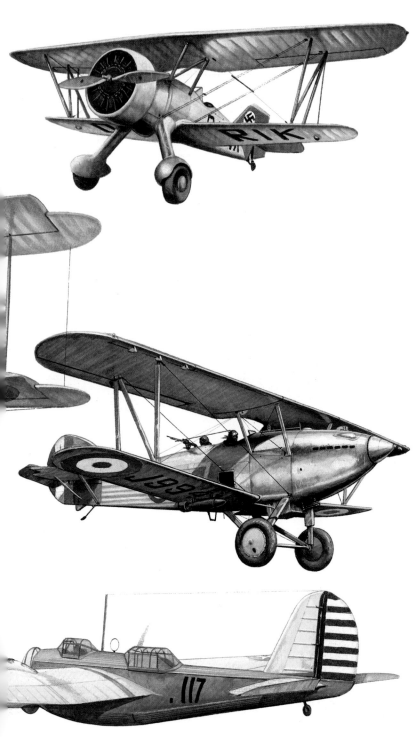

Export Hawk II

The Export Hawk II design preceded the US Navy F 11C-2. Ernst Udet was so impressed by Al Williams' (Gulf Oil Company's aviation manager) demonstrations of dive-bombing with 'Gulfhawk' that he had the German Air Ministry buy two Hawk IIs to introduce dive-bombing tactics in Germany

Hawker Hart

The Hawker Hart, introduced in 1930, was beloved of the RAF men of its period. It carried a bombload of only 550 lb – scarcely sufficient to wage the strategic bombing campaign to which the RAF was committed – but it was a delight to fly and, at 184 mph, could outrun the RAF's front-line fighter, the Bulldog. It was a measure of the airmen's muddled thinking about the possibilities of all-purpose aircraft that, in the light of the Hart's success, they called for a fighter version, the three-gun Demon, which entered service in 1931 and outpaced the Hart by only 3 mph

Martin B-10

The American Martin B-10 introduced in 1934, showed the shape of the streamlined heavy aircraft of the future. It could carry a 2,260 lb bombload, and outpaced the US pursuit fighters of its day

The rise of Hitler's Luftwaffe:

When Germany collapsed in 1918, almost a hundred of her aircraft companies found themselves without work. AEG, who had built the Gotha twin-engined bomber, was one of the few with the foresight to have prepared for peace. In 1917, they had formed the world's first civil aeroplane line, Deutsche Luft-Reederei, and by early 1919 they were operating a service between Berlin, Leipzig, Weimar and Hamburg. AEG was not the only firm to keep Germany in the aviation business: on 25 June 1919, Professor Hugo Junkers' new all-metal cantilever monoplane the F-13 flew for the first time. It was a revolutionary breakthrough in design, and was soon bringing in orders, even in a world flooded with surplus combat aircraft.

Erhard Milch

Ernst Udet

Junkers and Milch

Professor Junkers was a pacifist scientist from an old Rhineland aristocratic family. He was sixty in 1918, a white-haired man with a large forehead and clear blue eyes. Some of his most brilliant design achievements were still before him.

The most formidable of Professor Junkers' young post-war protégés was a twenty-seven-year-old former Army Air Service Observer named Erhard

Milch. Milch was supposedly a naval apothecary's son: 'Loyalty to the Kaiser and loyalty to my country were the only political doctrines I received either as an officer or earlier in my parents' home'.

Top right: Crowds flocked from all over Germany to watch and join the gliding craze that began in the late 'twenties

Opposite: Milch with British 'brass' at Mildenhall bomber station during his 1937 visit to the RAF

The men of the new air force

Throughout his life, he was troubled by a secret which he sought to suppress to the end: his mother Clara had fallen in love with her uncle. Since marriage was forbidden by Church law, she reluctantly married another man, Anton Milch, on condition that she was not required to have his children. Instead, she had her children by her uncle. Young Erhard Milch only discovered in 1933 that the wealthy visitor whom he had called 'uncle' was in fact his father. Even then, he learned the truth only because an investigation had been started into his background as malicious rumours that he was Jewish had been circulated in the hope of getting him dismissed from his key job with the Nazi regime.

Milch was a brilliant organizer. In the war, he had commanded a fighter squadron even though he could not pilot an aircraft. When the German Government pressured thirty-eight independent German airlines into forming a single national company in 1926, Milch was brought from Junkers to be one of its bosses. By 1929 Milch was Chief Executive of Lufthansa and a secret Nazi. He had formed a close alliance with Hermann Goering, paying the former fighter ace a regular 'consultancy fee', and enlisting his help when Lufthansa was threatened with government financial cutbacks in 1927. Milch was also organizing the air transport for the Nazi leaders whose campaign relied heavily on fast travel – they flew 28 000 miles in 1932 alone.

It is not true that Lufthansa provided the cover for the development of a German bomber force under the guise of a civil airliner fleet, although the immensely successful Junkers Ju 52/3m later became a military transport. But Lufthansa built up a corps of highly trained aircrew and established Germany as one of the foremost air nations of the world: by 1930 her civil aviation operations in Germany were bigger than the worldwide networks of Britain and France combined. Meanwhile, membership of Germany's air sports clubs had increased from 20 000 in 1926 to 50 000 in 1929. Germany and Austria held every gliding record worth mentioning. The experimental twelve-engined

The Luftwaffe in Spain

At the outbreak of the Spanish Civil War in July 1936, Hitler provided twenty Ju 52s and a fighter escort of six He 51s to convoy 10,000 Moorish soldiers from North Africa to Spain for General Franco. In November 1936, the first German pilots of the 'volunteer' Condor Legion arrived in Spain. In the next two years, Germany cynically rotated thousands of her aircrew and dozens of

aircraft types, in service with the Condor, to distribute battle experience as widely as possible. By May 1937, the Condor was operating 200 aircraft, including fifty Ju 52s in a bomber role, up to fifty fighters, and various ground-attack and reconnaissance types. Later the Messerschmitt Bf 109B fighter and the new He 111 bomber were tested. There was never a shortage of volunteer

pilots from the Luftwaffe, who received extra pay and a step up in rank for serving with the Condor.

The Germans perfected ground-attack techniques in Spain, often turning around their aircraft so fast that each completed six or seven sorties in a day. The Luftwaffe's first generation of 'aces' in the Second World War, including 'Dolfo' Galland and 'Vati' Mölders, had their first taste of action with the Condor. But the Germans also made some serious errors on the strength of their Spanish experience. They muddled through the war with scarcely any provision for ground-to-air or air-to-air radio communication, and made no effort to improve their equipment in this field before 1940. They also found that their Do 17 and He 111 bombers were faster than the Republicans' biplane fighters, and rashly regarded this as proof of the effectiveness of the self-supporting bomber formation, especially after Milch and Udet visited the RAF airfield at Hornchurch, covering London, in September 1937 and found it equipped with Gladiator biplanes which were also outpaced by the Heinkels and Dorniers.

Above: Wolfram von Richthofen, commander of the Condor Legion, tours the front with Franco
Above left: Ju 52's, Germany's superb civil and military transport, were available to move men from North Africa to Spain
Left: 1939. Men of the Condor Legion march to the dockside. Hitler now had urgent work for them

Ernst Udet

A self-portrait by Udet

Goering was always happiest in the company of the old style 'seat of the pants' fliers like himself, rather than modern 'nuts and bolts' technicians. Ernst Udet, who in June 1935 was given the key job as Head of the Luftwaffe's Technical Department, was just such a man. A careless, high-living bohemian wit who lived only for flying, Udet had been second to von Richthofen among Germany's aces in the First World War. He believed passionately in the concept of 'knights of the air' and liked to tell how he had gone balloon-busting alone one day when he was a flight commander with Jagdstaffel 15, and found himself dog-fighting with a single machine. As he looped and circled, looking for an opening, he saw the words 'Vieux Charles' painted on the fuselage, and knew that he was fighting the French ace, Guynemer. Then his guns jammed. The Frenchman flew over him upside down, waved, and broke away. Udet would never accept the suggestion that Guynemer's guns had also jammed – he was convinced that this was an example of the chivalry still possible in air warfare.

After the war, Udet lent his name to an aircraft factory and a stunt-flying circus – once, on an expedition filming African wildlife, he flew so low that his plane was damaged by a lion jumping at it. It was Udet who first saw the military possibilities of dive-bombers and gliders for Germany. In the early years of Hitler's air force, even as a civilian Udet kept in close touch with design and development, and gave his advice freely to Goering and Milch.

He was thirty-nine when he became Head of Technical Development – some believed that Goering recruited him as a deliberate counterpoise to Milch's influence. In any event, he was an unfortunate choice for the job, chronically casual and undisciplined. Milch despised him, and disliked having to consult the over-manned and chaotic department Udet controlled. There is no doubt that the cheerful little ace's influence on the development of the Luftwaffe combat aircraft for the second stage of World War II was disastrous.

Dornier Do X had crossed both the North and South Atlantic, and a German pilot had made the first east–west crossing of the North Atlantic. The *Graf Zeppelin* airship had circumnavigated the world. Pilots were a new German elite: exams for entry to Lufthansa's Air Transport School lasted ten days, and in 1932 when the young 'Dolfo' Galland applied, eighteen applicants were accepted out of 4,000.

Milch was marked for high office when the Nazis gained power in 1933. The former First World War ace, Hermann Goering, became Air Minister because Hitler valued him as a symbol of the old, victorious German forces and 'The Fat Man' had been with the Party since its earliest days. But while Goering was figurehead, it was Milch who was appointed to do the work, as Secretary of State for Air.

The Building of the new Luftwaffe

The nature of the new Luftwaffe, dominated by Goering and Milch, was dictated by some curious accidents and decisions. General Wever, the first Chief of Staff, was a keen advocate of the strategic heavy bomber. But when he was killed in an air crash in 1936, neither his successor Kesselring nor Goering thought it worth persevering with these big, expensive aircraft. What the Nazis wanted were quickly-built medium and light bombers in large quantities. The prototypes of the Ju 89 and the Do 19 heavy bombers, which Germany would miss so desperately in the Second World War, were broken up in their factories.

When the Luftwaffe came to choose the fighter that would be its front-line interceptor from the late 1930s, there were four possibilities. The Arado Ar 80 was eliminated because it had a fixed undercarriage which made its weight problem worse, and the Focke-Wulf Fw 159 prototype was an obsolete parasol-wing design. The Heinkel He 112 was based on the company's earlier beautiful He 70, a robust, open cockpit aircraft only slightly slower

than its remaining rival. Its chief failing was that it was very heavy-handed at the controls.

Finally there was the Messerschmitt Bf 109, whose prototype was powered by an imported Rolls-Royce Kestrel engine for want of anything better. It was incomparably the best aircraft. It was ordered into full-scale production.

By the time of the *Anschluss* with Austria in March 1938, Germany was able to lift more than 2,000 fully-equipped troops into Vienna in 150 transport aircraft. By September 1939, the Luftwaffe possessed 3,750 aircraft, including more than 1,000 Bf 109s, 195 Bf 110s, and 1,270 He 111, Do 17 and Ju 88 bombers. Goering's organization was also responsible for anti-aircraft defences, and could muster the finest heavy and light flak teams in the world, manned by 90,000 men.

Yet there were very important weaknesses in this imposing organization: it was designed principally as a short-range tactical air force; it lacked adequate reserves of aircraft to back up its impressive-looking front line. Its creators had devoted immense energy to giving Germany a force of first-rate modern aircraft for war in 1939–40, but had been very careless about following through, launching designers on the next generation of aircraft for the 1940s. This weakness would become apparent by 1942 when only the Focke-Wulf Fw 190 had come forward to match the new Allied aircraft coming off the production line.

Perhaps most serious of all, once Germany's factories had filled the orders to complete the Luftwaffe's front line according to plan, they were allowed to maintain an absurdly low level of replacement production for a nation embarking on a major war. Already by 1940, Britain was building aircraft faster than Germany, and in 1941–42 the lag would become disastrous for the Axis.

But in 1939, with its corps of very highly trained pilots, many of them with battle experience, with its superiority of numbers, spearheaded by the superb Bf 109 fighter, the Luftwaffe was a formidable weapon of war and a great achievement for its principal creator, Erhard Milch.

Opposite top: Ju 52s at a Nuremberg Rally in the late 1930s. Between the wheels it is possible to see the platform from which, when lowered, a bomb could be dropped or a gun fired

'Salad Days' 1918-1939:

In the two years following the Armistice, the RAF shrank from 188 squadrons to 25. Its budget fell to a low of eleven million pounds in 1922 and never rose above twenty million pounds until rearmament began in 1935. Between the wars, the air force received only an average seventeen per cent of the total defence spending. In accordance with Trenchard's theories of strategic bombing by self-defending formations, the lion's share of this money went to his bombers. In 1940, Fighter Command would become the 'glamour boys' but between the wars it was the bomber men who considered themselves the elite of the RAF. As late as 1936, out of forty-two home-based squadrons in the RAF, only thirteen were fighters, and six of these were equipped with the obsolete Bristol Bulldog.

Trenchard and, after his retirement as Chief of Air Staff in 1930, his successors, believed that money spent on fighter defence was wasted. Yet by the early 1930s, the RAF's morale and popular prestige were very high. Flying had caught the world's imagination in the 1920s, with the exploits of Alcock and Brown, Charles Lindbergh and the barnstormers. The RAF's annual Hendon Air Pageant, staged in north London within reach of a vast urban audience, was a brilliant public relations exercise. Few airmen, far less members of the public, stopped to ask themselves what contribution formation flying with wingtips linked by ribbon could make to building a modern air force.

Trenchard defeated the other services' demands for the RAF's dissolution by another effective public relations ploy: he invented 'Air Control' for policing the distant frontiers of the Empire. Trenchard persuaded the government that the threat and, when necessary, the use of air bombing was a far cheaper method of controlling dissident tribesmen than sending punitive columns of troops. Throughout the interwar years, the RAF gained its only battle experience dropping small bombs on rebel villages, most of them in Iraq and on the north-west frontier of India.

It remained open to question whether this was

effective in administering tribesmen, but it did much to justify the RAF's continued existence in the eyes of the Treasury. In 1934, twenty-five squadrons were deployed overseas, against forty-two in Home Defence. The real cost of 'Air Control' was that it taught the RAF to think of bomber operations in naive terms of low-level daylight sorties against an enemy who shot back with rifles.

Trenchard's chief purpose in the 1920s was to make the RAF an established institution, entrenched beyond any possibility of being broken up at the behest of the other services. He devoted much of his slender budget to building solid brick stations, and an impressive mansion to house Cranwell, the RAF's training college that sought to match Sandhurst and Dartmouth. An elaborate full dress uniform complete with busby and sword was designed for RAF officers to wear at parades and mess 'Dining-in nights'. The new service was always self-consciously determined that its officers should look and behave like gentlemen, sensitive to jibes from their army and naval counterparts that RAF men were 'motor mechanics in uniforms'.

But to the public in the 1920s and 1930s, the air was a thrilling new dimension, and pioneer pilots were glamorous figures. The RAF entered the 1930s having created the atmosphere of the finest

The air force that Trenchard built

Even after his retirement, Trenchard remained a dominant force in the RAF. Here, he was opening the new headquarters of 604 Squadron, in 1934

flying club in the world – not fashionable, but intensely exciting. Its officers lived in elegant comfort, being paid to fly when half the world's young men were willing to pawn a week's salary for the privilege of getting into the air. They flew only in good weather, and learned little about the difficulties of blind or night flying, of navigation and bomb-aiming under battle conditions. The Air Ministry did little scientific study of the problems either of destroying large structures with bombs, or of destroying modern aircraft by gunfire, and thus selected armament for its aircraft by more or less arbitrary decision. In the annual Air Exercises of June–July 1934, the Vickers Virginia night bombers of the 'attackers' cruised through the defences almost undetected, at 80 mph.

It was an age of innocence. It was fortunate for Britain that with the coming of Sir Edward Ellington as Chief of Air Staff in 1933, and Sir Hugh Dowding as Commander-in-Chief of the newly-created Fighter Command in 1936, men reached the top of the RAF who not only disputed that 'the bomber would always get through', but also understood that it was vital to ensure that it did not. They would be only just in time.

Top left: A flamboyant public relations exercise: the RAF's strength deployed for the admiring public at the 1931 Hendon Pageant.

Top right: The RAF's views on bomber operations were more romantic than realistic. This was a demonstration at the 1921 Hendon Air Pageant, but techniques had not advanced greatly by 1939

For an adventurous young man in search of travel, comfort, glamour and excitement, the Royal Air Force between the wars was close to paradise.

Middle: The Officers' Mess offered the gentlemanly pleasures of company, servants and a sort of gracious living

Opposite: The RAF's role carrying out 'Air Control' on the fringes of the Empire gave pilots the chance of a foreign posting (at the risk of being castrated if they were captured by the villagers they bombed)

SEE THE
WORLD
WITH THE
Royal Air Force
Apply: INSPECTOR OF RECRUITING.
4 HENRIETTA ST, COVENT GARDEN, LONDON, W.C.2.
Or any R.A.F. Unit or Depôt.

L (S)

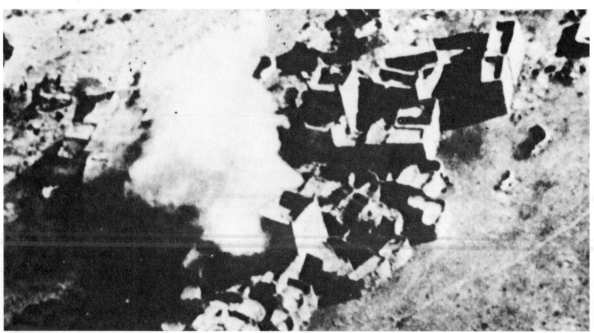

Above: The Hendon Air Pageant

Below: 'Air Control' in action: bombs from RAF Bristol Fighters bracket the fort at Darwa, Aden, during operations against tribesmen in 1925

Where the RAF found its men

Between the wars, the RAF recruited officers and men from a wide variety of backgrounds.

◄ **The Auxiliary Air Force** *was conceived in 1924 as a reserve air force parallel to the army's Yeomanry Regiments. Young men from comfortable backgrounds were recruited to form part-time, locally-based squadrons such as 600 (City of London), 602 (City of Glasgow), and so on. Initially the Auxiliary squadrons were equipped with obsolescent aircraft but by 1939, so great was Fighter Command's need that the fourteen squadrons of the 'weekend fliers' had almost all been given Hurricanes and Spitfires*

The RAF College Cranwell *was the normal entry* ► *route for eighteen-year-old school-leavers who set out to make a career as regular RAF officers. In the 1930s, as rearmament created the need for hundreds of extra officers, suitable applicants with the right educational qualifications – many of them Colonials – were granted RAF Short Service Commissions without passing through Cranwell*

◄ **Halton Apprentices' School** *was created by Trenchard to provide a corps of highly skilled ground and maintenance staff for the RAF. Halton took boys from secondary school at fourteen or fifteen and gave them three years' intensive technical training before they were sent to squadrons. Notorious for its tough discipline, Halton graduates created a tradition of 'bull' and 'brass' at many pre-war RAF stations that would not have disgraced the Brigade of Guards. Thousands of 'Direct Entry' NCOs found themselves scorned by the old hands, 'Trenchards Brats'. They had not been through the mill*

The Royal Air Force Volunteer Reserve *was* ► *created in July 1936, in an attempt to build up a reserve of qualified pilots to match that of fighter aircraft which was being created under the rearmament programme. Young men were paid to take a part-time flying course and be available to join the aircrew pool at the outbreak of war. By the summer of 1939, some 200 pilots had completed flying training, although not operational training*

Rearmament:

'Germany is already well on her way to become, and must become, incomparably the most heavily-armed nation in the world and the nation most completely ready for war. . . . We cannot have any anxieties comparable to the anxiety caused by German rearmament.'
Winston Churchill to the House of Commons, 21 October 1933

If Winston Churchill overstated Hitler's readiness for war between 1933 and 1936, he judged rightly the scale of the threat that was to come. Gradually, grudgingly, the British Government responded. Spending on the RAF rose from a pathetic £17.5 million in 1934 to £27.6 million in 1935, £50.7 million in 1936, £56.5 million in 1937, £73.5 million in 1938.

With the appointment of Air Chief Marsal Sir Edward Ellington as Chief of Air Staff in April 1933 and of Air Marshal Sir Hugh Dowding as Air Member for Supply and Research, at last men reached the top of the RAF who believed that the bomber could and must be stopped. Nevertheless, the lion's share of the air budget continued to be lavished on the RAF's bomber squadrons.

From 1934 onwards, a succession of RAF rearmament plans overtook each other in rapid succession. By Scheme A, approved in July 1934, Home Defence strength would rise from 316 to 476 bombers, and from 156 to 336 fighters by April 1939. The more ambitious Schemes C, F, and H followed in 1935, 1936 and February 1937 respectively.

Then in December 1937, Scheme J was suddenly checked. Sir Thomas Inskip, Minister for the Coordination of Defence, argued that it would cost too much and provided too few fighters. After prolonged argument, in April 1938 the Cabinet accepted Scheme L, by which the RAF would reach a strength of 1,352 bombers and 608 fighters by April 1940. Airmen claim that Inskip was a poor minister who forced these measures through at the cost of severe delays in creating a heavy-bomber force – merely for financial and political reasons, because

*Top left: Ellington Top right: Inskip
Below: Left to right: Milch, Goering and
SA chief Viktor Lutze admiring the new
Luftwaffe, 20 April 1935*

fighters cost less than bombers. But in reality, it was Inskip's insistence on higher priority for fighter production that gave Fighter Command the tiny margin of strength by which it was able to achieve victory in 1940. Inskip deserves to be remembered as one of the true victors of the Battle of Britain.

The new age of air warfare

❝ I tell the House . . . frankly . . . neither I nor my advisers had any idea of the exact rate at which production could be, and actually was being, speeded up in Germany in the six months between November and now. We were completely misled on that subject. . . . There has been a great deal of criticism . . . about the Air Ministry as though they were responsible for possibly an inadequate programme, for not having gone ahead faster, and for many other things. . . . I only want to repeat that whatever responsibility there may be . . . it is the responsibility of the Government as a whole, and we are all to blame.

Prime Minister STANLEY BALDWIN to the House of Commons, 22 May 1935

If the aerial bombardment of our cities can be restricted or prevented, the chance . . . that our morale could be broken by "frightfulness" will vanish, and the decision will remain in the long run with the armies and navies. The more our air defences are respected, the greater will be the deterrent upon a purely air war

WINSTON CHURCHILL, 23 July 1935 ❞

Between 1935 and 1937, the combined strength of the RAF and Fleet Air Arm rose from 91 squadrons to 169, and from 1,020 aircraft to 2,031. But eighty per cent of these machines were obsolescent. The real struggle in these years was to create the new Hurricanes and Spitfires in time to match Germany's new generation of combat aircraft.

A similar race began to reorganize the air defences of Britain and to train the men to fly the new fighters. The Commonwealth contingent in the RAF was expanded, 1,700 Short Service Commissions were granted, 800 more NCO pilots were accepted, and the number of Flying Training Schools was increased from six to eleven. But it took

a year to teach a man to fly a fighter, let alone to fight in one, and time was pressing. The refusal of the Canadian Prime Minister, Mackenzie King to allow RAF training to be carried out in Canada was a serious blow. It was evident that among fighter aircrew especially, much of the burden of war would fall upon the part-timers of the Auxiliary Air Force, and the Royal Air Force Volunteer Reserve.

In 1936, the old Air Defence of Great Britain organization was abolished, and replaced by four functional Commands: Fighter, Bomber, Training and Coastal. One July day, a tall, thin, rather frail-looking middle-aged man arrived unannounced and alone at Bentley Priory, an old Gothic house north-west of London which had been nominated as Fighter Command's headquarters. After some difficulty persuading the Orderly Room sergeant to let him in, the visitor wandered through the empty rooms until he found one with a southerly view, and instructed the sergeant to put his name on the door. Then he thanked him and left. Air Marshal Sir Hugh Dowding, newly appointed Commander-in-Chief of Fighter Command, had chosen his office.

Dowding divided Britain into four Group areas for defence purposes, and with his staff set about the creation of a new direction system for the control of his fighters in the face of enemy attack. Dowding planned on the brave assumption that the primitive radar then under development would work. It would be supported by the civilian volunteer Observer Corps, tracking enemy aircraft across Britain, whose organization was expanded and strengthened through the 1930s.

Shortly before Christmas 1937, the first of Dowding's squadrons was equipped with the new Hawker Hurricane, a few months before the Luftwaffe staged the acceptance trials of the revolutionary new Messerschmitt Bf 109. On both sides, the weapons with which the Battle of Britain would be fought were now reaching the air forces.

Spitfire

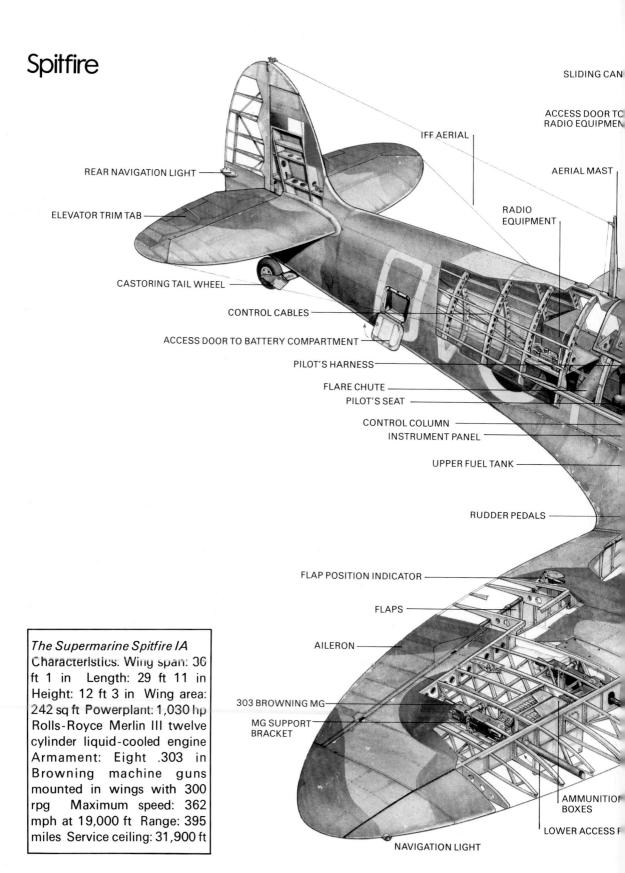

SLIDING CAN

ACCESS DOOR TO RADIO EQUIPMEN

AERIAL MAST

IFF AERIAL

REAR NAVIGATION LIGHT

RADIO EQUIPMENT

ELEVATOR TRIM TAB

CASTORING TAIL WHEEL

CONTROL CABLES

ACCESS DOOR TO BATTERY COMPARTMENT

PILOT'S HARNESS

FLARE CHUTE

PILOT'S SEAT

CONTROL COLUMN

INSTRUMENT PANEL

UPPER FUEL TANK

RUDDER PEDALS

FLAP POSITION INDICATOR

FLAPS

AILERON

303 BROWNING MG

MG SUPPORT BRACKET

AMMUNITIO BOXES

LOWER ACCESS

NAVIGATION LIGHT

The Supermarine Spitfire IA
Characteristics. Wing span: 36 ft 1 in Length: 29 ft 11 in Height: 12 ft 3 in Wing area: 242 sq ft Powerplant: 1,030 hp Rolls-Royce Merlin III twelve cylinder liquid-cooled engine Armament: Eight .303 in Browning machine guns mounted in wings with 300 rpg Maximum speed: 362 mph at 19,000 ft Range: 395 miles Service ceiling: 31,900 ft

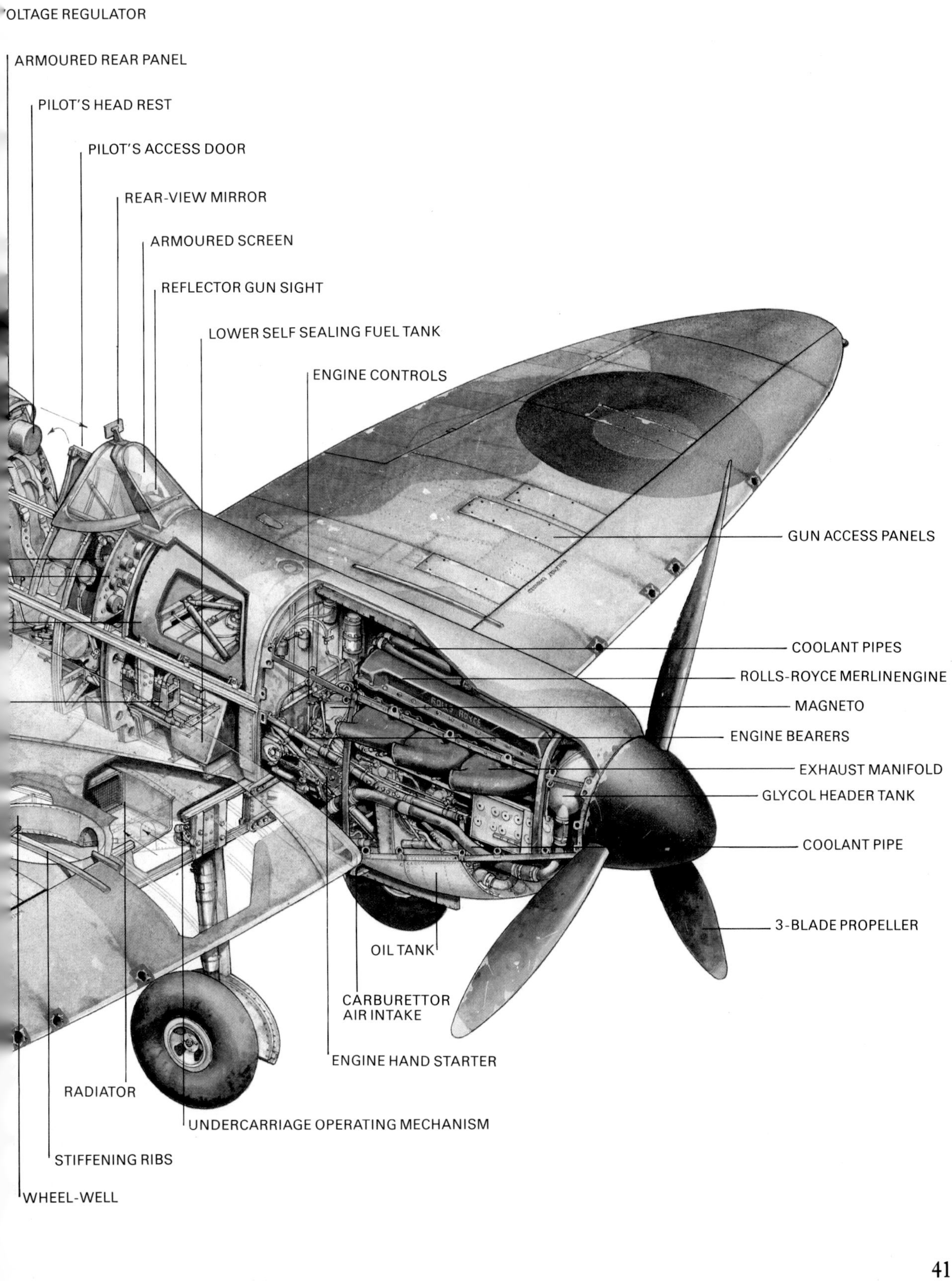

VOLTAGE REGULATOR

ARMOURED REAR PANEL

PILOT'S HEAD REST

PILOT'S ACCESS DOOR

REAR-VIEW MIRROR

ARMOURED SCREEN

REFLECTOR GUN SIGHT

LOWER SELF SEALING FUEL TANK

ENGINE CONTROLS

GUN ACCESS PANELS

COOLANT PIPES

ROLLS-ROYCE MERLINENGINE

MAGNETO

ENGINE BEARERS

EXHAUST MANIFOLD

GLYCOL HEADER TANK

COOLANT PIPE

3-BLADE PROPELLER

OIL TANK

CARBURETTOR AIR INTAKE

ENGINE HAND STARTER

RADIATOR

UNDERCARRIAGE OPERATING MECHANISM

STIFFENING RIBS

WHEEL-WELL

The Supermarine Spitfire

Reginald Mitchell, chief designer for the Supermarine company which had become part of the huge Vickers concern in 1928, created the seaplanes which won three Schneider Cup races, and which ultimately achieved a speed of 407 mph, using special chemical fuels. With this remarkable achievement behind him, Mitchell turned to the more mundane Air Ministry specification F7/30 and began to consider plans for a new fighter, to embrace the virtues of his Trophy winners but capable of being flown by average pilots and in March 1932, the Air Ministry agreed to the manufacture of a prototype.

In 1933, the prototype was under construction when Mitchell went into hospital for a cancer operation. Although only thirty-eight, he was a very sick man and took a continental holiday to convalesce. In Europe, he met and talked to some young German pilots. He came home convinced that a war was inevitable, and that his new fighter could play a decisive role in it. With the vision and compulsive dedication that is sometimes given to the very sick, he refused all advice to rest, and went back to his drawing-board to devote his life to his aircraft.

The prototype was a gull-winged monoplane with a fixed undercarriage and open cockpit. When it first flew in February 1934, its Goshawk II engine gave it a maximum speed of only 238 mph. Mitchell knew that it was not good enough. He started again. While the Air Ministry ordered production of the Gloster Gladiator fighter in the midst of a new flirtation with biplanes, Mitchell began to redesign around the prospect of the new Rolls-Royce PV12 engine. In January 1935, work started on a new prototype. The airframe was ready before Rolls-Royce completed the engine. The Spitfire flew for the first time on 5 March 1936.

Mitchell's aircraft was revolutionary in a way that Camm's was not. Every feature of the Spitfire called for new and complex manufacturing techniques. The fuselage was in three sections: a tubular case for the engine, a monocoque centre part, and a detachable aft section, of which the last two formers extended upwards to become the tail fin. The spar

on which the wings were built was made up of girders that fitted one inside the other. Each was of different length, so that the spar was thickest where most strength was needed at the wingroot, and hollow at the wingtip. It resembled a huge leaf spring. The leading edge of the wing was covered with heavy gauge metal that gave the wing immense strength, while aft of the spar it was thinly clad. The end product was a balance of lightness and strength.

Supermarine lacked the resources to build even the Air Ministry's initial order of 310 aircraft, so manufacture of Spitfire components was farmed out among a bevy of subcontractors, and the sections were brought to Supermarine for assembly. Its revolutionary design caused a succession of headaches for the factories, but it is remarkable that the production system worked as well as it did.

Like Camm, in the spring of 1935, Mitchell was compelled to vary his design to take account of the new Air Ministry requirement for an eight-gun armament. Where Camm grouped his Hurricane's guns close to the wing root, Mitchell spaced the Spitfire's Brownings along the wing, now reshaped to give the aircraft its classic elliptical silhouette.

Mitchell's beautiful thin wings, reducing air resistance and thus increasing speed while still providing maximum area for a given span, were the greatest design achievement in his Spitfire. Pilots have a saying about aircraft: 'If it looks right, it is right.' The Spitfire looked magnificent. From the outset, it delighted every pilot who flew it, although it could be lethal for a novice in a spin and on landing. Its big bubble canopy gave exceptional visibility, particularly by comparison with the Messerschmitt Bf 109. It was delightfully light to fly, although at high altitude it could become hard work. It was a match for the Bf 109 at every point except high altitude performance above 20,000 feet where the German fighter excelled.

Nine Fighter Command squadrons were equipped with Spitfires by September 1939, and nineteen squadrons by 7 July 1940. Some Spitfire Ibs, mounting two 20 mm cannon in addition to four Brownings, became available in time for the Battle of

Britain, but teething troubles with the cannon were not cured in time for it to play a significant role.

The two Supermarine test pilots who worked in the Spitfire from Eastleigh airfield in Hampshire in the early summer of 1936 often noticed Reginald Mitchell's old Rolls-Royce parked by the hangars as they took off. He enjoyed watching his creation take to the air. But he never lived to see its great

Manufacturing the Spitfire at Castle Bromwich. The wing sections caused many problems before satisfactory assembly techniques were devised

moment in 1940. He died in 1937, at the age of forty-two. When they told him that his aircraft would keep the name given to his earlier gull-wing prototype – the Spitfire – he said it was 'just the sort of bloody silly name they would choose'.

Hurricane

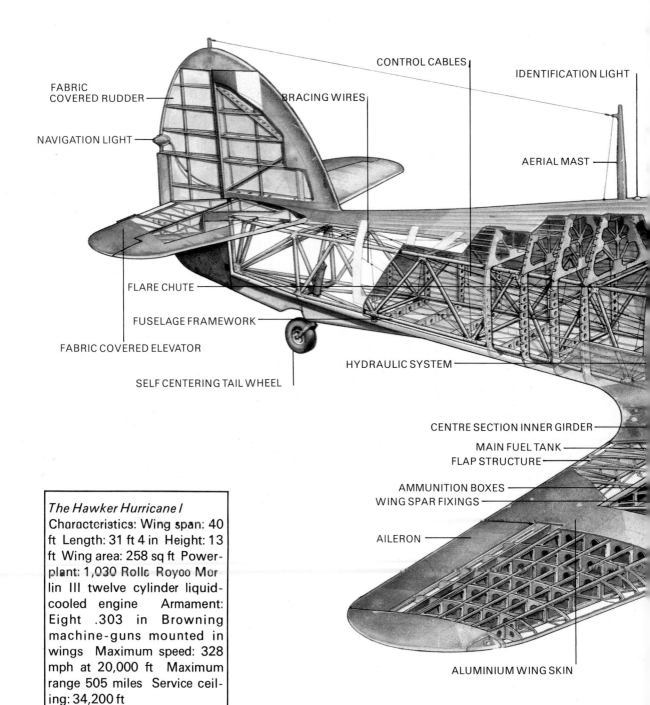

CONTROL CABLES

IDENTIFICATION LIGHT

FABRIC COVERED RUDDER

BRACING WIRES

NAVIGATION LIGHT

AERIAL MAST

FLARE CHUTE

FUSELAGE FRAMEWORK

FABRIC COVERED ELEVATOR

HYDRAULIC SYSTEM

SELF CENTERING TAIL WHEEL

CENTRE SECTION INNER GIRDER

MAIN FUEL TANK

FLAP STRUCTURE

AMMUNITION BOXES

WING SPAR FIXINGS

AILERON

ALUMINIUM WING SKIN

The Hawker Hurricane I
Characteristics: Wing span: 40 ft Length: 31 ft 4 in Height: 13 ft Wing area: 258 sq ft Power-plant: 1,030 Rolls Royce Merlin III twelve cylinder liquid-cooled engine Armament: Eight .303 in Browning machine-guns mounted in wings Maximum speed: 328 mph at 20,000 ft Maximum range 505 miles Service ceiling: 34,200 ft

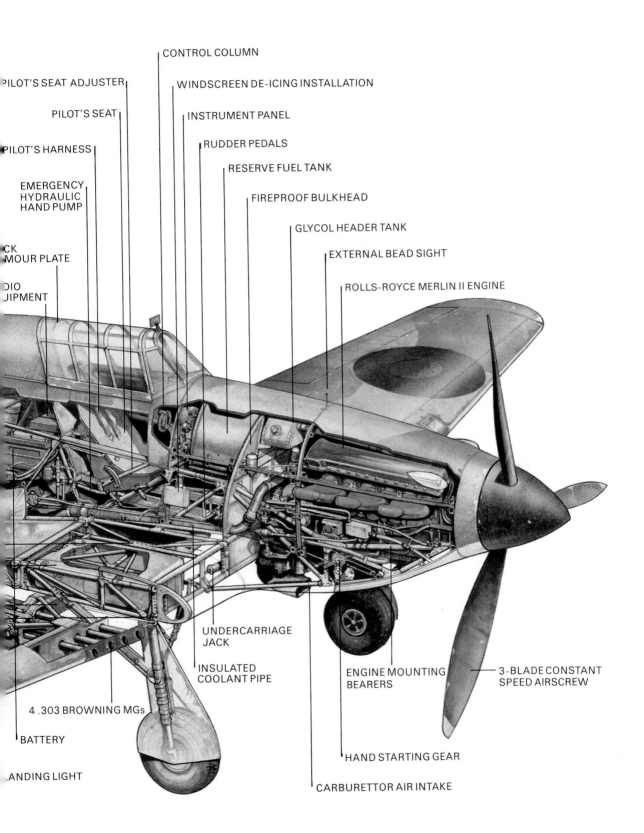

CONTROL COLUMN

WINDSCREEN DE-ICING INSTALLATION

INSTRUMENT PANEL

RUDDER PEDALS

RESERVE FUEL TANK

FIREPROOF BULKHEAD

GLYCOL HEADER TANK

EXTERNAL BEAD SIGHT

ROLLS-ROYCE MERLIN II ENGINE

PILOT'S SEAT ADJUSTER

PILOT'S SEAT

PILOT'S HARNESS

EMERGENCY
HYDRAULIC
HAND PUMP

CK
MOUR PLATE

DIO
UIPMENT

UNDERCARRIAGE
JACK

INSULATED
COOLANT PIPE

4 .303 BROWNING MGs

BATTERY

ANDING LIGHT

ENGINE MOUNTING
BEARERS

3-BLADE CONSTANT
SPEED AIRSCREW

HAND STARTING GEAR

CARBURETTOR AIR INTAKE

45

The Hawker Hurricane

The Hawker Hurricane I, which in terms of numbers of aircraft engaged would make the most important contribution to Fighter Command's defence of Britain in 1940, was born out of Air Ministry specification F7/30, a fighter to replace the Bristol Bulldog. Sydney Camm, who had become Hawkers' chief designer at the age of thirty-two in 1925, submitted plans for a biplane and a monoplane. Both were rejected. The monoplane, it was said, was 'too orthodox even for the Air Ministry'.

The tall, stooping, angular Camm returned to his drawing-board. Tearing up the Air Ministry specification, he began to conceive a fighter as a private venture for Hawker. He knew the promise of the new PV12 engine under development by Rolls-Royce, which later became the legendary Merlin.

He also tried to create an aircraft that could be constructed by using as many as possible of Hawkers' existing tools and jigs, for economy reasons.

The new aircraft was in effect a monoplane version of Hawkers' existing, highly successful Fury biplane, also designed by Camm. Its design was almost complete in 1935 when Camm received a more advanced Air Ministry specification which called for the mounting of eight machine guns. He had new wings made to carry the extra guns. In November 1935 the prototype of the Hawker Hurricane, the F36/34, powered by the Rolls-Royce Merlin C, flew for the first time.

In many ways the Hurricane was a traditional aircraft, constructed of wood and fabric stiffened by a metal-tube framework. But in battle, the Hurricane fuselage proved much more resistant to exploding

Left: The early Hurricanes were fabric- not metal-covered. Both varieties proved able to take an extraordinary amount of punishment in air combat, and the sliding hood (in contrast to the hinged canopy on the Bf 109) was very popular with pilots who often flew with it open, to keep cool and to have a better chance of escape in an emergency
Right: The Hawker Hurricane

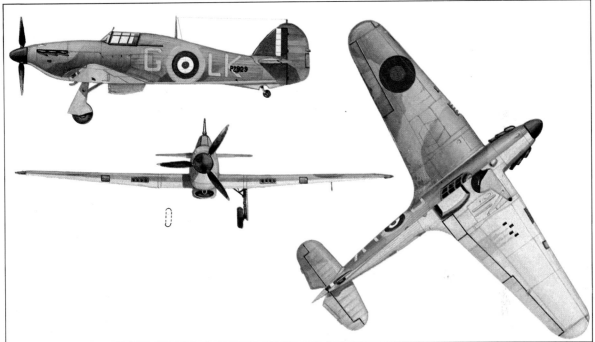

cannon shells than the metal Spitfire. Remarkable repairs could be improvised in squadron workshops. For a first-generation retractable undercarriage fighter, the Hurricane with its inward-folding landing gear proved extraordinarily robust. After early teething troubles with the engine, the fitting of constant-speed propellers early in 1940 and the development of stressed metal-skin wings completed the Hurricane's emergence as an outstanding high performance aircraft and a delight to fly.

Hawker appreciated its promise before the Air Ministry did. Their directors authorized tooling for production of 1,000 aircraft in March 1936, three months before the Government placed a contract for 600 aircraft. By September 1939, 497 aircraft had been completed against orders of 3,500, and 18 Fighter Command squadrons had been equipped.

Despite Britain's desperate needs, several dozen Hurricanes were exported to 'sympathetic' nations including Belgium and Yugoslavia.

The Hurricane was a half-way house between the biplanes of the early 1930s and the Spitfires of the 1940s. It was outclassed by the Messerschmitt Bf 109, yet experience in the Battle of Britain showed that in the hands of skilled pilots, it could achieve remarkable success. Between July and October 1940, 1,715 Hurricanes took part in the Battle, and claimed eighty per cent of the German aircraft credited to Fighter Command. From 1941 onwards, the Hurricane would be relegated to a fighter-bomber role and obsolete as an interceptor in fighter to fighter combat. But in 1940, the critical moment came just in time for Camm's creation to be decisive.

The second line

Boulton Paul Defiant I
Delays in production caused the first Defiants to enter squadron service only in December 1939. With their relatively long endurance and powerful turret armament, they were intended to fly standing defensive patrols, and indeed packed a formidable punch when intercepting bombers. On their first appearance in the Battle of France, they scored some surprise successes against Messerschmitts caught unawares by rear-firing guns. But once the Germans had got their measure, Defiants became deathtraps for their unfortunate crews: incapable of dogfighting or rapid fire at unexpected angles, too slow to get away, difficult even to bale out of. After some disastrous losses early in the Battle, they would become inadequate night fighters

The Gloster Gladiator II
The Gladiator was a development of the Gloster company's successful Gauntlet fighter and was introduced to fill the gap that opened in the mid-1930s between the old biplanes and the new generation of eight-gun monoplanes. The first aircraft entered squadron service at Tangmere in 1937. By 1938 the Gladiator was already being relegated to overseas service as the Hurricane took over Home Defence. But two squadrons were heavily engaged and suffered crippling losses in the Battle of France. Barely adequate against bombers, the Gladiator was hopelessly outclassed against modern monoplane interceptors. During the Battle of Britain, 247 Sq Fighter Command and 804 Sq Fleet Air Arm operated Gladiators

Bristol Blenheim IF

This unfortunate aircraft was an attempt to operate a long-range heavy fighter variant of the Blenheim light bomber. Equipped with four Brownings in a ventral pack under the fuselage, one gun in a rear turret and one in the port wing, it was hopelessly slow and clumsy in action against German fighters. Even when transferred to a night fighter role, it proved too slow to catch most German bombers to which it was vectored. The seven Blenheim squadrons in Fighter Command on 1 July 1940 could play little useful part in the Battle. Their fate showed the futility of the Air Ministry doctrine that it was better to put anything into the air than nothing

The Defiant
Characteristics: Wing span: 39 ft 4 in   Length: 35 ft 4 in   Height: 12 ft 2 in   Wing area: 250 sq ft   Powerplant: 1,030 hp Rolls-Royce Merlin III twelve cylinder liquid-cooled engine   Armament: Four .303 Browning machine-guns with 600 rpg mounted in electrically-operated turret   Crew: two   Maximum speed: 304 mph at 17,000 ft   Range: 465 miles   Service ceiling: 30,350 ft

The Gladiator
Characteristics: Wing span: 32 ft 3 in   Length 27 ft 5 in   Height: 11 ft 7 in   Wing area: 323 sq ft   Powerplant: 840 hp Bristol Mercury VIII AS nine cylinder air-cooled engine   Armament: Four .303 Browning machine-guns, two in nose with 600 rpg, two under lower wing with 400 rpg   Maximum speed: 257 mph at 14,600 ft   Range: 444 miles   Service ceiling: 33,500 ft

The Blenheim
Characteristics: Wing span: 56 ft 4 in   Length: 39 ft 9 in   Height: 9 ft 10 in   Wing area: 469 sq ft   Powerplant: Two 840 hp Bristol Mercury VIII nine cylinder air-cooled engines   Armament: One .303 Browning machine-gun in port wing, four Brownings in central fairing, one .303 Vickers K machine-gun in dorsal turret   Maximum speed: 285 mph at 15,000 ft   Maximum range: 1,125 miles   Service ceiling: 27,280 ft

Messerschmitt

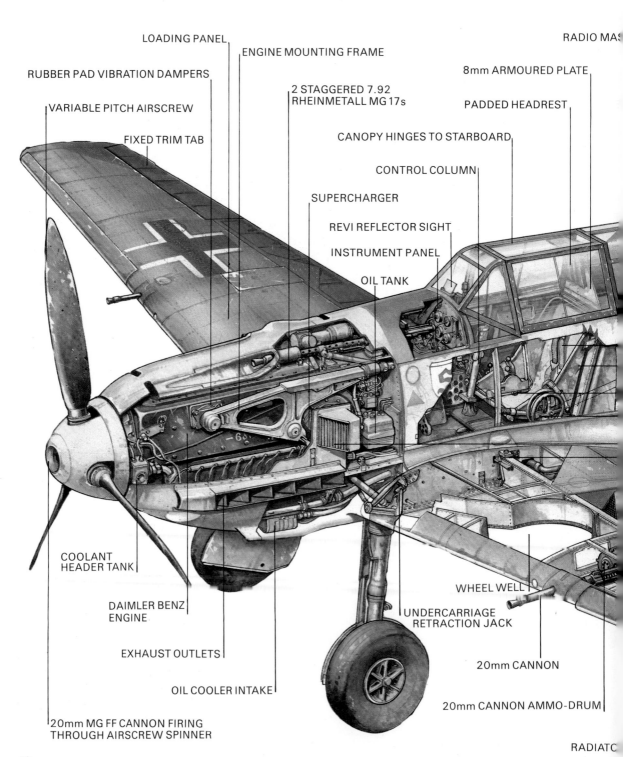

LOADING PANEL

ENGINE MOUNTING FRAME

RUBBER PAD VIBRATION DAMPERS

2 STAGGERED 7.92
RHEINMETALL MG 17s

VARIABLE PITCH AIRSCREW

FIXED TRIM TAB

RADIO MAS

8mm ARMOURED PLATE

PADDED HEADREST

CANOPY HINGES TO STARBOARD

CONTROL COLUMN

SUPERCHARGER

REVI REFLECTOR SIGHT

INSTRUMENT PANEL

OIL TANK

COOLANT
HEADER TANK

DAIMLER BENZ
ENGINE

EXHAUST OUTLETS

OIL COOLER INTAKE

20mm MG FF CANNON FIRING
THROUGH AIRSCREW SPINNER

WHEEL WELL

UNDERCARRIAGE
RETRACTION JACK

20mm CANNON

20mm CANNON AMMO-DRUM

RADIATC

VARIABLE INCIDENCE
METAL SKIN TAIL PLANE

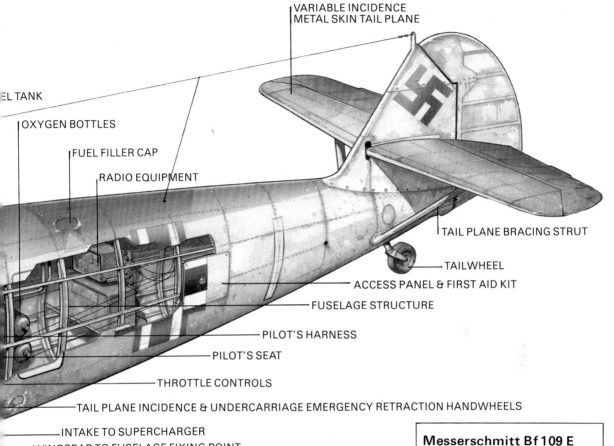

EL TANK

OXYGEN BOTTLES

FUEL FILLER CAP

RADIO EQUIPMENT

TAIL PLANE BRACING STRUT

TAILWHEEL

ACCESS PANEL & FIRST AID KIT

FUSELAGE STRUCTURE

PILOT'S HARNESS

PILOT'S SEAT

THROTTLE CONTROLS

TAIL PLANE INCIDENCE & UNDERCARRIAGE EMERGENCY RETRACTION HANDWHEELS

INTAKE TO SUPERCHARGER
WINGSPAR TO FUSELAGE FIXING POINT

SLOTTED FLAP

SLOTTED AILERON

AUTOMATIC LEADING-EDGE SLOTS

ADIATOR FLAPS SHOWN FULLY DEFLECTED

Messerschmitt Bf 109 E
Characteristics: Wing span:
32 ft 4½ in   Length: 28 ft 8 in
Height: 11 ft 2 in   Wing area:
174 sq ft   Powerplant:
1,150 hp Daimler-Benz
DB 601A twelve cylinder
liquid-cooled engine
Armament: Two 7.9 mm MG
17 machine-guns on engine
crankcase, with 1,000 rpg;
two 20 mm MG FF cannon in
wings, with 60 rpg (or two
further MG 17s on some
aircraft)   Maximum speed:
357 mph at 12,300 ft
Range: 412 miles   Service
ceiling: 36,000 ft

Messerschmitt Bf 109 E

Willy Emil Messerschmitt, creator of Germany's foremost single-engined fighter of 1940, was born the son of a Frankfurt wine merchant in 1898, three years after Reginald Mitchell. A passionate air enthusiast from his childhood, he was lucky enough to become friendly with one of Germany's earliest air pioneers, Friedrich Harth. By the age of sixteen, he had built a glider to Harth's plans. At eighteen, Messerschmitt joined the Schleissheim military flying school, and worked on aircraft design in partnership with Harth until the older man was badly injured in a crash. Eventually, with financial help from his wife, Messerschmitt was able to buy the Bavarian Aircraft Works at Augsburg.

He proved one of the great, if erratic geniuses of aircraft design. In the 1920s he pioneered a succession of record-breaking gliders, although they established a tradition of frailty which continued even to his 1940 fighter. Messerschmitt designed the disastrous Me 210 fighter, the Giant six-engined transport, the rocket-powered Comet fighter, and the superb Me 262 jet.

His relationship with the Nazis was ambiguous. He was on easy terms with Hess, the Deputy Party Leader, but Milch had been an implacable enemy since one of his closest friends was killed in the crash of some Messerschmitt-designed planes in 1931. In the first years of the Luftwaffe, Milch exerted himself to exclude Messerschmitt from every possible contract. When he was finally compelled to give the factory work, he inflicted the final humiliation of ordering them to build Heinkel biplanes under licence.

It was Ernst Udet who chose the Messerschmitt Bf 109 against the Heinkel He 112 when the Luftwaffe ordered its new generation fighter in October 1935. It was a bold decision, for Messerschmitt had never before built a combat aircraft. Just as Camm developed the Hurricane from his earlier Fury, so Messerschmitt used his Bf 108 civil tourer as the basis for the Bf 109.

Germany's great weakness at this time was lack of a first-class engine, and the prototype Bf 109 was powered by an imported Rolls-Royce Kestrel. In 1936, the Rolls Merlin was pushed from 720 to 990 hp, but even in 1938 the German Jumo 210D could achieve only a miserable 670 hp.

Messerschmitt had always sought to create lightweight, low-drag, simple monoplanes. Now he designed the smallest, lightest, and most aerodynamically efficient airframe that would fit the Jumo engine. To offset the inevitable high wing-loading, he employed Handley Page leading-edge slots for extra lift (an unprecedented device for a fighter) as well as slotted ailerons interconnected to the flaps.

The German Air Ministry demanded two machine-guns, and Messerschmitt mounted these above the engine. There was also space for a 20 mm cannon firing through the airscrew hub, where the engine mass would supposedly buffer the recoil. In this way, Messerschmitt left his very thin, frail wings free of guns. It was a major blow when the Luftwaffe learned of the RAF's new eight-gun monoplanes. The Bf 109's wing would *have* to carry guns. A new wing was designed with bulges for the ammunition boxes of the 20 mm MG FF cannon now mounted on each side.

In 1938, Messerschmitt started to produce the Bf 109 E, known to Luftwaffe men as the Emil. This was fitted with the Daimler Benz 601 A engine that generated 400 extra horsepower for its 400 extra pounds of weight. Further strain was put on the wings, which now had to carry the engine's ducted radiators.

Because the Bf 109 was such a fine aircraft, it could stand the strains placed on its airframe by constant redesign. But all its life, it was plagued by armament problems: on later models the wing guns were removed. The Emil's airscrew hub cannon was never satisfactory. The Bf 109 had a very narrow undercarriage, so that the fuselage rather than the wing carried the weight of the aircraft. It was ingenious but five per cent of all Bf 109s built were destroyed in landing accidents.

Messerschmitt's enemies said that he still thought he was designing gliders when he built the Bf 109.

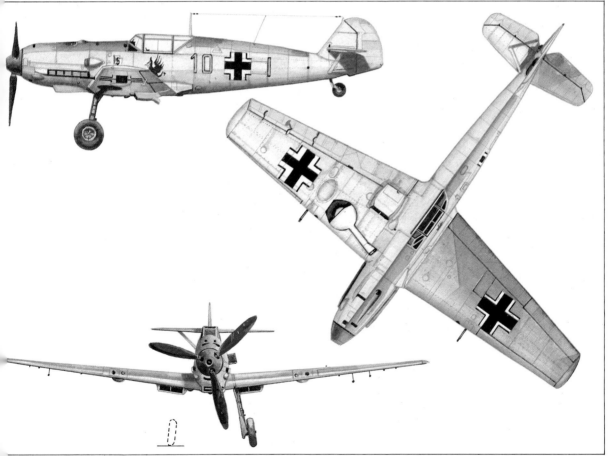

Top left: Messerschmitts under construction

Top right: The Messerschmitt Bf 108

Certainly its lightweight airframe and high-lift wings are also basic elements of sailplanes, and the fighter was always a delicate aircraft in contrast, for instance, to the Hurricane. But in the air, the Bf 109's performance made it a formidable match for Mitchell's Spitfire. By September 1939, the Luftwaffe possessed 12 Gruppen of 850 Bf 109 Es. By August 1940, 23 Gruppen were in action on the Channel front. By 1945, the Bf 109 had become the most widely produced combat aircraft of the war.

Germany's second line

The Messerschmitt Bf 110

In 1939, the Luftwaffe was the only air force in the world which had tried to face the problem of creating an escort fighter with the range to accompany bomber attacks. The best pilots in Germany were posted to Goering's elite Bf 110 *Zerstorer* (destroyer) units. Historians have under-rated the Bf 110s. Their poor acceleration and wide turning circle made them no match for the Spitfire in the Battle of Britain, and indeed gave the overworked Bf 109s an extra role protecting them. But by any standards, the Bf 110 was a fast aircraft – 40 mph faster than most Hurricanes – and its formidable nose armament could be deadly. When a Bf 110 had the chance to dive from high level for a single attacking pass before breaking away, it could be very effective. It later became a first-class night fighter, and performed well against daylight bomber formations.

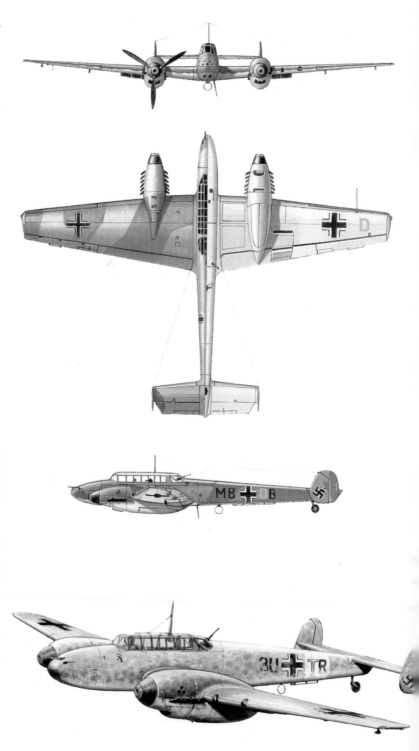

Messerschmitt Bf 110C
Characteristics: Wing span: 53 ft 4¾ in Length: 39 ft 8½ in Height: 11 ft 6 in Wing area: 413 sq ft Powerplant: Two 1,150 hp Daimler Bonz DB 601A twelve cylinder liquid-cooled engines Armament: 4 x 7.9 mm MG17 machine guns with 1,000 rpg and 2 x 20 mm MG FF cannon with 180 rpg in nose; one rear-firing MG 15 machine gun with 750 rpg in cockpit Maximum speed: 349 mph at 22,960 ft Normal range: 530 miles Service ceiling: 32,000 ft

Junkers Ju 87 B

The Stuka's operations in Poland in 1939 made it the very symbol of *Blitzkrieg* in the eyes of the world. With its massive cranked wings, spatted undercarriage and screaming sirens, it was the only purpose-built German dive-bomber, with a line inscribed on the canopy to enable the pilot to judge his angle of dive, and a window in the floor to spot the target. The German propaganda machine glamorised the Stuka so that aircrew clamoured to join Ju 87 units. But its low speed, short range, small bombload and lack of armour made it a hopelessly inadequate aircraft against any kind of ground or air defences. After a few weeks very heavy losses in the Battle of Britain, the Ju 87s were reserved for operations against lighter opposition.

Junkers Ju 87B
Characteristics: Wing span: 45 ft 3¼ in Length: 36 ft 1 in Height: 13 ft 10½ in Wing area: 343 sq ft Powerplant: 1,100 hp Junkers Jumo 211 A-1 twelve cylinder liquid-cooled engine Armament: 2 x 7.9 mm MG 17s in wings, 1 x 7.9 MG15 in rear cockpit mounting Bombload: 1 x 1,100 lb bomb on crutch mounting under fuselage, 4 x 110 lb bombs under wings Maximum speed: 232 mph at 13,500 ft Range (1,100 lb bombload): 370 miles Service ceiling: 26,500 ft

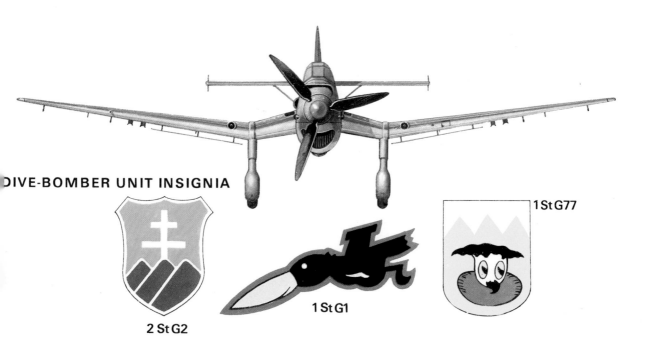

DIVE-BOMBER UNIT INSIGNIA

2 St G2

1 St G1

1 St G77

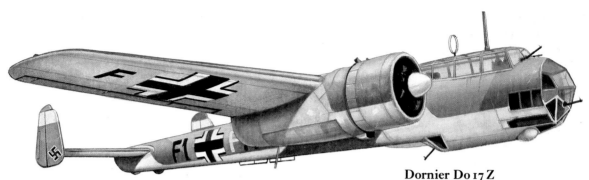

Dornier Do 17 Z

The Do 17 'Flying Pencil', originally conceived as an air mail carrier in 1934, was obsolescent by 1939, but equipped about a quarter of the German bomber and reconnaissance units deployed in the Battle of Britain. Unarmoured and underpowered (Willy Messerschmitt had cornered the best engines for his fighters), it was highly vulnerable to fighter attack and carried a poor bombload. Its chief merits, in the eyes of its crews, were strength, stability and reliability.

The Junkers Ju 88 A

The Ju 88 was the Luftwaffe's only really satisfactory bomber, directly comparable with the later RAF Mosquito, and produced at astounding speed, from drawing board to first flight in 1936. Later versions of the Ju 88 suffered from official insistence that it possessed dive bombing capability, and a vendetta against Junkers by Erhard Milch. But in 1940, when the aircraft made its large-scale operational debut, high speed gave the Ju 88 a far better chance of survival than the Do 17 or He 111 against Fighter Command. It proved one of the most versatile aircraft of the war.

Heinkel He 111

The He 111 carried almost double the Dornier's bombload, but suffered the same lack of power and speed, only partly compensated by heavy armour and defensive armament. The German free-mounted guns were far less effective than the British power-operated turrets. By mid-September 1940, the He 111 had been relegated to night-bombing on the Channel front, and later to anti-shipping and transport work.

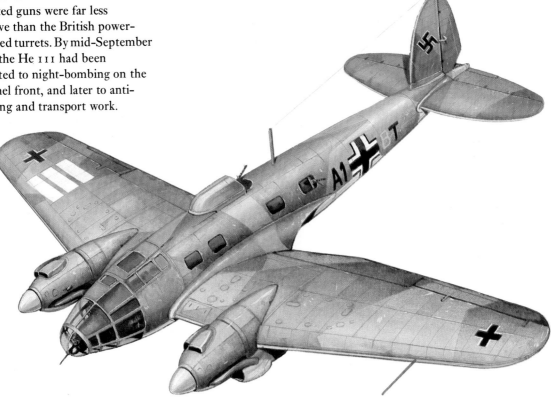

Dornier Do 17Z
Characteristics: Wing span: 59 ft 0¾ in Length: 52 ft Height: 14 ft 11½ in Wing area: 592 sq ft Powerplant: Two 1,000 hp Bramo 323P nine cylinder air-cooled engines Armament: Up to eight 7.9 mm MG 15s in front, rear and beam cockpit and ventral positions Bomb-load: 2,200 lb Maximum speed: 265 mph at 16,400 ft Normal range: 745 miles Ser-vice ceiling: 26,400 ft

---

Heinkel He 111
Characteristics: Wing span: 74 ft 1¾ in Length: 53 ft 9½ in Height: 13 ft 1½ in Wing area: 942.9 sq ft Powerplant: Two 1,100 hp Daimler-Benz DB 601A-1 engines Armament: 3 x 7.9 mm MG 15 guns in nose, dorsal and ventral positions Bombload: 4,410 lb Maximum speed: 247 mph at 16,400 ft Maximum range 1,224 miles Service ceiling: 26,250 ft

---

Ju 88
Characteristics: Wing span: 59 ft 10¾ in Length: 47 ft 1 in Height 15 ft 5 in Wing area: 540 sq ft Powerplant: Two 1,200 hp Junkers Jumo 211B-1 twelve cylinder liquid-cooled engines Armament: 3 x 7.9 mm MG15s in front and rear cockpit mounting and ventral gondola Bombload: 3,968 lb on four underwing pylons Maximum speed: 286 mph at 16,000 ft Range: 1,553 miles Service ceiling: 26,500 ft

The aircraft builders

Professor Hugo Junkers, Milch's benefactor, and the creator of a fine series of all-metal monoplanes, became an outspoken critic of the Nazis. Milch had him arrested and he was forced to sign over control of his companies to the State. The Professor died six months later and Milch sent a wreath. Milch's treatment of Junkers made him intensely disliked by many of his colleagues.

Willy Messerschmitt, the son of a Frankfurt wine merchant, was born in 1898. His contribution to aviation was immense, beginning with designs for record-breaking gliders and ending with the most effective fighter of the war: the Me 262 jet. His relationship with the Nazis was ambiguous. Milch was an implacable enemy but Hess, the deputy leader of the Nazi Party was a life-long friend.

Reginald Mitchell, born in 1895, won the 1931 Schneider Cup with the S6B seaplane but then turned to the development of a new fighter which eventually became the Vickers-Supermarine Spitfire. He died in 1937 before his fighter began to come off the production line but his contribution to the winning of the Battle of Britain was immeasurable.

Sydney Camm, chief designer of the Hawker company (1925), was born in 1893. He was responsible for the Hawker Hurricane, half-way house between the old biplane and the new Spitfire. (His last work was on what became the revolutionary jumpjet of the 1970s – the Harrier.) He died in 1966.

Guns

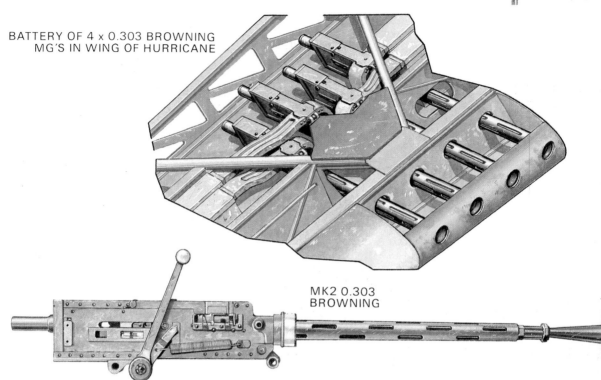

BATTERY OF 4 x 0.303 BROWNING
MG'S IN WING OF HURRICANE

MK2 0.303
BROWNING

Between the two Wars, neither side did enough scientific calculation about the weight of gunfire necessary to destroy a modern aircraft, and the vital need for high-velocity fighter cannon rather than traditional rifle-calibre machine-guns. The cannon the Luftwaffe possessed were of too low velocity to be really effective, and it was astonishing how often an RAF fighter could riddle a German bomber with 0.303 gunfire, and yet have to watch it escape home if the bullets had missed vital weak spots.

But one of the unsung victors of the Battle of Britain was an Air Ministry officer named Squadron Leader Ralph Sorley, who in the early 1930s when the Spitfire and Hurricane were still under design conceived the need for them to carry an unprecedented eight machine-guns rather than the traditional two or four. It was Sorley who foresaw that at modern battle speeds, it was the weight of fire a

fighter could deliver in two or three seconds that would be decisive, and impressed his view on his commanders. Camm and Mitchell were asked to redesign their embryo fighters with eight guns and, after tests in 1933–34, the American Colt machine-gun was chosen to equip them. By 1939, it had been extensively modified and was being manufactured in Britain as the Browning.

At the eleventh hour, in January 1939, the De Wilde incendiary bullet patent was purchased by Britain from its Belgian inventor for £30,000, just in time to be effective in the Battle of Britain. In 1940, RAF tests on an old Blenheim proved decisively that cannon were far more effective than machine-guns in destroying aircraft, and that summer the first cannon Spitfires came into service. But their teething troubles were not solved until after the Battle of Britain. The Colt-Browning was the

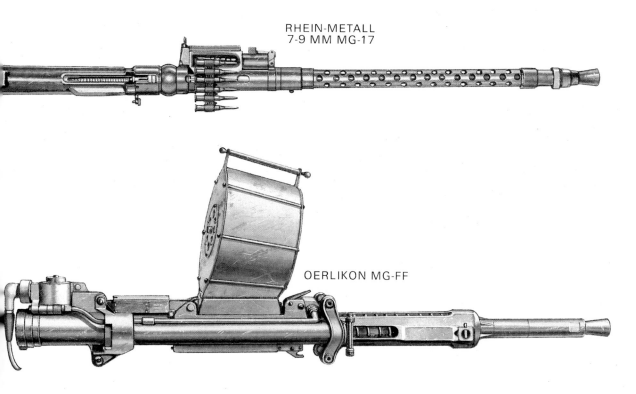

RHEIN-METALL
7·9 MM MG-17

OERLIKON MG-FF

Royal Air Force's key weapon in 1940.

A three-second burst from a Luftwaffe Bf 109's two 20 mm cannon and two 7.9 mm machine-guns weighed 18 lb, against the 10 lb of a Spitfire's gun-fire. But when the Germans modified the Swiss Oerlikon cannon to make it lighter and faster-firing for aircraft use, they had to reduce the amount of powder in its charge, and thus the gun's muzzle velocity. This proved a serious weakness; again and

again, badly hit British fighters got home, because German cannon shells exploded on impact and failed to do fatal damage. The Bf 109 also suffered from carrying less than seven seconds' ammunition in its wing drums. In the early stages of the war, both sides suffered difficulties with guns freezing at high altitude. The RAF partly solved the problem of wet cold by sealing the gun muzzles with fabric patches, protecting them until they fired.

Guns	Calibre	Supply carried (rounds)	Gun weight (lb)	Gun length (in)	Muzzle velocity (ft/second)	Rate of fire (rnds/minute)	Projectile weight (ounces)
Browning (RAF)	7.7mm (0.303in)	300	22	44.5	2,660	1,200	0.344
Oerlikon MG-FF	20mm	60	53	52.8	1,800	520	4.82
Rheinmetall-Borsig MG17	7.92mm	1,000	28	47.2	2,450	1,100	0.45

Radar

In October of 1937, a Luftwaffe delegation, headed by Milch and Udet, visited Britain. According to Milch, in the ante-room of the Officers' Mess at Fighter Command, he addressed a question to the assembled officers: 'Now, gentlemen, let us all be frank,' he said. 'How are you getting on with your experiments in the detection by radio of aircraft approaching your shores?'

Milch claimed that 'more than one glass was dropped to the floor with a crash'. There was embarrassed laughter, and an attempt to change the subject. But Milch persisted. 'Come, gentlemen, there is no need to be so cagey. We've known for some time that you were developing a system of radio location. So are we, and we think we are a jump ahead of you.'

The British had begun their experiments in 1935, and had since been developing radar in deadly secrecy, under the cover title of RDF – radio direction-finding. It never occurred to them that, as so often with scientific advances, parallel experiments were going on elsewhere. Dr Rudolf Kühnhold, Chief of the German Navy's Signal Research department, had created a workable radar set by 1934, and by 1939 Germany possessed gun-laying and early warning radar in advance of anything Britain had built.

But in the practical application of radar, Germany fell badly behind. It has been said that the motto of the British radar scientists was 'second best tomorrow'. Between 1935 and 1939, in close co-operation with Dowding and the great scientific civil servant Henry Tizard, British scientists created the radar network that made victory possible in 1940.

The creation of radar totally transformed the ability of the defence to anticipate and thus defeat a bomber attack. The days of 'the bomber must get through' had ended. It is difficult to exaggerate the dominance that radar would achieve over war in the air (and at sea) by 1945.

Sir Henry Tizard   *R A Watson-Watt*

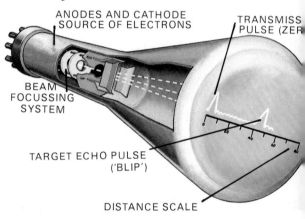

ANODES AND CATHODE
SOURCE OF ELECTRONS

TRANSMISS
PULSE (ZER

BEAM
FOCUSSING
SYSTEM

TARGET ECHO PULSE
('BLIP')

DISTANCE SCALE

A blip appeared on the tube as the transmitter released its pulse of energy. This either disappeared for ever – if the sky ahead was empty – or was bounced back to the receiver towers, making a second blip. The time elapsed between the blips enabled the operator to gauge the range of the aircraft. Direction-finding was much less reliable, but Fighter Command's Filter Room could assess this by taking cross-bearings from two neighbouring radar stations The huge, undisguisable radar masts were clearly visible from the French Channel coast. At the base of

Long before radar was discovered, the phenomenon of radio waves re-radiating from distant aircraft had been noticed, not least by irritated radio listeners suffering interference on their sets. But this was regarded as a problem rather than a breakthrough.

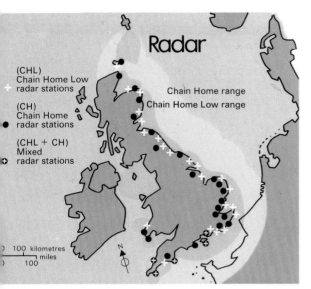

Radar

(CHL)
Chain Home Low
radar stations

(CH)
Chain Home
radar stations

(CHL + CH)
Mixed
radar stations

Chain Home range
Chain Home Low range

100 kilometres
miles
100

the twin sets of transmitter and receiver towers was a 'receiver hut' where the operators, often WAAFs, watched the cathode tubes
Top: Britain's radar chain in July 1940. The shorter range Chain Home Low stations operated on a 1.5 metre waveband, against the 10 metre waveband of the Chain Home stations. Once an aircraft had crossed the British coast, it could no longer be plotted by radar – all of whose stations faced seawards – and Fighter Command relied on the Observer Corps for visual tracking of enemy formations

In 1934, amidst the intense government alarm about the threat from the air, a committee was set up, under the chairmanship of Tizard, to consider possible means of defence against the bomber. Grasping at straws, they asked Robert Watson-Watt, a scientist at the National Physical Laboratory, if there was any future in a 'death ray' to destroy aircraft. Watson-Watt replied on 27 February 1935. His inspired memorandum discounted the death ray, but identified three vital areas for research and investigation: the re-radiation of radio waves, to detect aircraft, radio-telephone communication between a ground controller and defending fighters to direct them to the aircraft thus located, and a coded signal transmitted from friendly aircraft, essential to identify friend from foe.

With great courage, Tizard and his committee decided to stake everything on supporting Watson-Watt's research. By May 1935, 70 ft masts had been erected and tests begun.

In 1936, the researchers moved into Bawdsey Manor on the coast of Suffolk. Here, in a uniquely informal country house atmosphere, the academic physicists mingled with visiting civil servants and RAF officers, exchanging ideas in what became known as the Bawdsey 'soviets', working and talking at all hours of day and night.

Bawdsey produced a marriage of scientific invention and practical service experience that was never achieved in Germany. In 1936, Tizard presided personally over a vital series of practical tests of radar, based on an RAF fighter station, which became known as 'the Biggin Hill Experiment'. With Dowding's full support, the scientists and staff officers explored the problems of linking the radar warning of attacking aircraft to a successful interception by defending fighters, using ground controllers and plotting tables, and a vital quick calculation of their converging courses which became known as 'the Tizzy angle', after its originator.

After Bawdsey's successes in the 1937 Air Exercises, the Air Ministry authorized a further seventeen radar stations. To supplement the 'Chain Home' stations that were the backbone of the network, more sophisticated 'Chain Home Low' sets, of shorter range but with rotating aerials and much more precise direction-finding, were installed to track low-flying aircraft. These were largely the work of an Australian War Office scientist, named Butement.

Eleventh hour

It was the fear of air bombardment by high explosive and gas that made September 1939 such a sombre moment for the British, in sharp contrast to the exuberance of August 1914. One and a half million women and children were evacuated from the major cities to the country (though many of them came back a few weeks later). On 1 September, the day Poland was invaded, the black-out that was to continue for more than five years descended on Britain. Air raid trenches and shelters had already been dug in the open spaces of London and other large towns.

Outbreak of war

At Fighter Command, deliveries of Spitfires and Hurricanes were proceeding smoothly, but six months behind schedule. Sir Hugh Dowding was now to lead in battle a force in whose creation he had played a unique part, from encouraging the development of its aircraft and armament to supporting the development of radar and the fighter direction system. His overwhelming concern was lack of numbers. He was deeply concerned about the RAF's responsibility to provide aircraft to support the British Expeditionary Force (BEF) in France when he still lacked the fifty-two fighter squadrons considered essential to defend Britain.

Sir Henry Tizard was fishing on the river Wye when he heard of the invasion of Poland. He decided that the traffic and confusion between Shropshire and London would be impossible that day, and returned to the river where he caught several good trout.

The Luftwaffe's campaign in Poland cost Germany 285 aircraft and exhausted half its total bomb stock-pile in twenty-two days. A few weeks later, on a visit to the Heinkel factory, Ernst Udet took the owner aside and murmured unhappily: 'I never really thought there would be war with Britain.'

After Erhard Milch had played a prominent part in enabling the Wehrmacht to recover from initial setbacks and occupy Norway, Hitler awarded him the Knight's Cross, and said that only a man like Milch could have done it: 'And why? Because here was a man like me, who just did not know the word "impossible"!'

British, French and German air strength, September 1939	British First Line	British Reserves	French First Line	French Reserves	German First Line	German Reserves
Bombers	536	1,450	—		1,750	1,700
Light Bombers	—	—	463		380	700
Fighters	608	320	634	1,600	1,215	1,700
Long-range Reconnaissance	—	—	444	of all	360	200
Army co-operation	96	105	—	types	310	300
Coastal Reconnaissance	216	125	194		305	300
Fleet Air Arm	204	200	—		—	—
Total	1,660	2,200	1,735	1,600	4,320	4,900

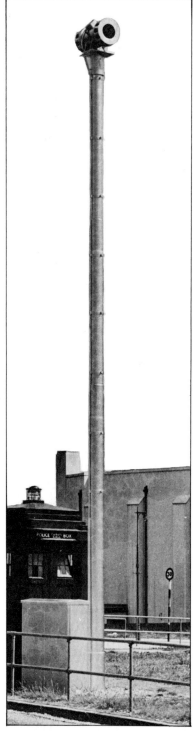

Top: Gas masks being distributed at Munster Road school, Fulham, 1939
Right: Street corner air-raid siren
Above: Digging shelters in Lincoln's Inn Fields

The fall of France:

The RAF's war began in earnest on 10 May 1940, with the German invasion of France. During the winter of 1939–40, Bomber Command had carried out a series of disastrous daylight raids against the German fleet and Fighter Command had fought spasmodic engagements with Luftwaffe reconnaissance and fighter patrols and sent two squadrons to support the British Army in Norway. With the opening of the war in the West, the full power of the Luftwaffe revealed itself. Some 1,400 German aircraft were committed in support of the invasion. The Dutch and Belgian air forces were virtually wiped out in the first hours. Many of the French air force's available 275 day fighters and 70 bombers were destroyed on the ground. The RAF's Advanced Air Striking Force of some 400 obsolescent bombers and fighters entered a struggle against devastating odds.

The German invasion May 1940

NETHERLANDS

GERMANY

BELGIUM

FRANCE

French VII Army (Giraud)

Belgian Army (Leopold III)

British Expeditionary Force (Gort)

French I Army (Blanchard)

French IX Army (Corap)

French II Army (Huntzinger)

French III Army (Condé)

River Meuse

German XVIII Army (Küchler)

Army Group B

German VI Army (Reichenau)

German IV Army (Kluge)

Army Group A

German XII Army (Kleist)

German XVI Army (Busch)

Army Group C

N

0   50   100 kilometres
0   25   50 miles

The battle of France

Far left: Sir Hugh Dowding
Left: Sir Arthur 'Ugly' Barratt
Above: The Fairey Battle light bomber
*Below: Dowding spells out the price of reinforcing
failure: his letter to the Chief of Air Staff*

-2-

9.   I must therefore request that as a matter of paramount urgency the Air Ministry will consider and decide what level of strength is to be left to the Fighter Command for the defence of this country, and will assure me that when this level has been reached, not one fighter will be sent across the Channel however urgent and insistent the appeals for help may be.

10.   I believe that, if an adequate fighter force is kept in this country, if the fleet remains in being, and if Home Forces are suitably organised to resist invasion, we should be able to carry on the war single handed for some time, if not indefinitely. But, if the Home Defence Force is drained away in desperate attempts to remedy the situation in France, defeat in France will involve the final, complete and irremediable defeat of this country.

                I have the honour to be,
                        Sir,
                Your obedient Servant,

                H.C.T. Dowding
                Air Chief Marshal,
                Air Officer Commanding-in-Chief,
                Fighter Command, Royal Air Force.

1

HEADQUARTERS, FIGHTER COMMAND,
ROYAL AIR FORCE,
BENTLEY PRIORY,
STANMORE,
MIDDLESEX.

Reference — FC/S.19048.

16th May, 1940.

Sir,

                I have the honour to refer to the very serious calls which have recently been made upon the Home Defence Fighter Units in an attempt to stem the German invasion on the Continent.

2.   I hope and believe that our Armies may yet be victorious in France and Belgium, but we have to face the possibility that they may be defeated.

3.   In this case I presume that there is no-one who will deny that England should fight on, even though the remainder of the Continent of Europe is dominated by the Germans.

4.   For this purpose it is necessary to retain some minimum fighter strength in this country and I must request that the Air Council will inform me what they consider this minimum strength to be, in order that I may make my dispositions accordingly.

5.   I would remind the Air Council that the last estimate which they made as to the force necessary to defend this country was 52 Squadrons, and my strength has now been reduced to the equivalent of 36 Squadrons.

6.   Once a decision has been reached as to the limit on which the Air Council and the Cabinet are prepared to stake the existence of the country, it should be made clear to the Allied Commanders on the Continent that not a single aeroplane from Fighter Command beyond the limit will be sent across the Channel, no matter how desperate the situation may become.

7.   It will, of course, be remembered that the estimate of 52 Squadrons was based on the assumption that the attack would come from the eastwards except in so far as the defences might be outflanked in flight. We have now to face the possibility that attacks may come from Spain or even from the North coast of France. The result is that our line is very much extended at the same time as our resources are reduced.

8.   I must point out that within the last few days the equivalent of 10 Squadrons have been sent to France, that the Hurricane Squadrons remaining in this country are seriously depleted, and that the more squadrons which are sent to France the higher will be the wastage and the more insistent the demands for reinforcements.

The Under Secretary of State,
Air Ministry,
LONDON, W.C.2.

/I....

Air Ministry policy in the last years of peace had been to increase the RAF's numerical strength with any aircraft that could be put into production, however, inadequate, rather than wait passively for the new generation of fighters and bombers. The Battle of France proved that outclassed aircraft could contribute nothing on the battlefield. They simply served as 'flying coffins' for hundreds of experienced Regular aircrew, who would be desperately missed.

The Battle and Blenheim bombers sent to France in support of the BEF in September 1939 were known to be at the mercy of any German fighter. But the Air Ministry had no intention of sending the much more effective Wellingtons, Whitleys or Hampdens, which were earmarked for its cherished strategic offensive, from English bases.

The bombers in France were supported by six squadrons of ninety-six Hurricanes and a handful of Gladiator fighters. But no effective air-ground co-ordination procedures had been developed. More critical, there was no fighter direction system of the kind that existed for the defence of Britain, to enable Sir Arthur Barratt, the RAF's AOC in France, to make good use of what aircraft he had.

The Luftwaffe's attack was not only in overwhelming strength, but brilliantly co-ordinated. Henschel and Storch reconnaissance aircraft roamed the front, reporting targets for the Do 17, He 111 and Ju 87 bombers. Messerschmitt Bf 109s and 110s strafed Allied airfields and troop concentrations, and provided blanket cover for the German advance, in tandem with the Luftwaffe's superb light flak teams on the ground.

On the first day of the German advance, thirteen of thirty-two Battles put into the air were lost, and most of the remainder damaged. Of six 600 Squadron Blenheim fighters sent to patrol Waalhaven from Manston, only one returned. On 12 May, 12 Squadron's Battle pilots were asked for volunteers to attack the vital Maastricht bridges. Five took off and all were lost. On 14 May, seventy-one Battles were dispatched and forty were lost. By 15 May, Barratt had lost 205 aircraft without checking the German army's advance by a single hour.

From the moment that the campaign began, the War Cabinet in London was under intense pressure from France to reinforce the RAF's fighters at the front. On 12 May four more squadrons of Hurricanes flew to the continent. A further thirty-two aircraft followed the next day. But as the front crumpled and France's morale staggered, her Prime Minister, Paul Reynaud, appealed personally to Churchill: 'If we are to win this battle, which might be decisive for the whole war, it is necessary to send at once . . . ten more squadrons.'

Dowding's intervention

Winston Churchill was still totally committed to saving the Battle of France. All his energies were directed towards supporting the BEF and the French Army. But Air Chief Marshal Sir Hugh Dowding, Commander-in-Chief of Fighter Command, was the man entrusted with the air defence of Britain. As France crumbled, Dowding anticipated his fighters becoming overnight the front line in the struggle with Germany. The RAF had long ago concluded that the minimum force with which this front line could be manned was fifty-two squadrons. Already, Fighter Command had been reduced to thirty-six squadrons to reinforce the continent. Now there were even more drastic demands. Dowding asked for permission to talk to the Cabinet.

In the event, in the Cabinet Room at 10 Downing Street on the afternoon of 15 May, Dowding talked to Churchill, Sinclair (the new Air Minister), Beaverbrook (just appointed Minister of Aircraft Production), and Sir Cyril Newall (Chief of Air Staff). He produced a simple graph, showing Hurricane losses since the Battle of France began, and projecting inexorable progress to disaster if these were allowed to continue at the same rate.

Above right: A British Hurricane squadron 'scramble' in France
Above left: A German light flak gun: they were brilliantly deployed in co-ordination with the Luftwaffe's fighters to cover vital objectives from air attack as the Wehrmacht advanced
Right: German columns advancing through France, May 1940: a snap from Rommel's personal album

'After that it was chaos'

Sgt Arthur Power, a veteran Observer of thirteen years' service, was stationed with 88 Battle Squadron at Auverieve, a few miles east of Rheims, when the German attack began.

❛ The Germans strafed us on the first day without doing much, because all our aircraft were dispersed. But on the big French airfield a few miles away at Mourmelon-le-grand everything was lined up in rows, parade ground style, and there wasn't much left when the Luftwaffe had finished.

We were ordered to attack the advancing German columns around Sedan. On 11 and 12 May, everybody got back all right. Then on 13 May, five of our aircraft went again on exactly the same course for the third day running. Only one came back. After that it was chaos. We did some leaflet-dropping at night. Those of us who were left moved from field to field, half a dozen times in a fortnight. A lot of prople just got lost. We ended up with two other Battles from squadrons we didn't know, alone on a field in central France, about the time of Dunkirk. There was so little information. We'd take off and see troops and transport, with no way of knowing if they were even French or German. We'd have a look, and if they threw things at us, we threw them back and then buzzed off at a rate of knots.

On our last day we had flown five times and were just getting ready to go again when we were ordered to jettison bombs and scarper. Our aircraft had been damaged a good bit by then, but we found another that was only missing a tailwheel, put our tailwheel on it, pushed the groundcrew in the back, and took off. All I had was a cycling map of northern France. The French fleet blasted off at us as we flew over them, then we were clear. We finally staggered down at Middle Wallop in Hampshire. It was some sort of training station, and while we were getting something to eat, some bastards swiped everything in the aircraft down to our souvenirs and the gear of the people who had been lost. Then we were grudgingly given some maps and told to push off. We were posted to Belfast "pending re-equipment". ❜

The next day, 16 May, Churchill flew to Paris to hear another impassioned appeal for help from Reynaud. He telephoned London to ask the Cabinet to agree to dispatch yet another six Hurricane squadrons. He would later claim that Dowding had informed him that the minimum force for the defence of Britain was only twenty-five squadrons, and thus that a margin of safety remained. It is impossible to accept that Dowding so grossly misstated his own position. In the high emotion of the moment, Churchill seems to have responded to the French appeals much as he would do in 1941 to those from Greece, in the face of his service chiefs' opposition.

In Downing Street that 16 May, emboldened by Churchill's absence, Newall told the Cabinet of Dowding's great fears. They compromised. Six further Hurricane squadrons were committed to operate from forward airfields in France, returning each night to England.

Dowding's effective strength had been reduced to twenty-six squadrons, precisely half the force that he thought vital to protect Britain.

Yet at the full Cabinet meeting which followed, Dowding was a silent spectator. Neither Churchill, Sinclair nor Newall made any further reference to Dowding's bleak forecast. A further four Hurricane squadrons were ordered to France.

Left: The wreckage of a British Spitfire. This picture was taken by a German photographer on the beaches of Dunkirk in June 1940

Dunkirk

By the time of the French surrender on 22 June, the RAF had lost 959 aircraft in the West and a further 66 in Norway, 509 of these being fighters. Home defence was reduced to 331 Spitfires and Hurricanes, supported by 150 'second-line' fighters – Blenheims, Defiants, and Gladiators. Valuable battle experience had been gained, but at the cost of 435 pilots lost, killed, missing or captured. Only 66 of the 261 Hurricanes dispatched to France had returned. Dowding's fears had been realized, but the best efforts of the Luftwaffe had not been able to prevent the British from evacuating 338 226 British and Allied solders from Dunkirk.

In the last days of May and the first of June, as the Royal Navy evacuated the remains of the BEF from Dunkirk, the prestige of the RAF sank to its lowest ebb in the eyes of the army. For weeks they had been strafed and bombed by the Luftwaffe, apparently without opposition. Now 'the Brylcreem boys' were abused and often physically attacked everywhere that soldiers and airmen met.

In reality, Dowding's squadrons were shuttling continuously between their airfields and the Dunkirk perimeter, attempting to break up German air attacks before they reached the beaches. But operating at extreme reach across the Channel, each squadron had only around fifteen minutes' fuel endurance at combat speeds before being compelled to turn back. The troops suffered terribly.

'Al' Deere, the New Zealand ace who flew with 54 Squadron, had experience of the army's bitterness. He was shot down by the reargunner of a Dornier 17 in the morning of 29 May, and crashlanded his Spitfire 'Kiwi One' on a beach fifteen miles from Dunkirk. Thumbing a lift and stealing a bicycle, he forged his way through the throng of refugees, and finally walked the last miles to the causeway. As he ran towards one of the evacuation destroyers, he was stopped by an angry army major.

'I am an RAF officer,' said the bedraggled, roughly bandaged Deere. 'I am trying to get back to my squadron which is operating over here.'

'I don't give a damn who you are', shouted the major. 'For all the good you chaps seem to be doing, you might as well stay on the ground.' Deere escaped him and made his way to the wardroom of the destroyer, to be greeted by stony silence from a throng of army officers.

'Why so friendly?' asked Deere. 'What have the RAF done?'

'That's just it', said one of the 'brown jobs'. 'What have they done?'

Deere and his colleagues, bitterly conscious of their own exhaustion and losses, were understandably aggrieved.

Left: Two views of Dunkirk: Withdrawal from Dunkirk, *a painting by Charles Cundall, and a photograph of troops awaiting evacuation*

June 1940: Hitler triumphant

By the end of June 1940, Hitler ruled all Western and Northern Europe from Tromsö to the Pyrenees. The Wehrmacht High Command prepared a memorandum outlining a 'river crossing on a broad front' – the invasion of Britain. But Hitler hesitated. The seizure of France, Norway, Denmark and the Low Countries had achieved his foremost aims, removing the threat to his western flank and securing access to raw materials. Britain was reduced to impotence. Was it really necessary to carry out a hazardous full-scale invasion and occupation before turning to his central strategic purpose – the eastward expansion of the German empire?

As early as 2 June, Hitler told Field Marshal von Rundstedt: 'Now that Britain will presumably be willing to make peace, I will begin the final settlement of scores with bolshevism.'

The original text of the German government communiqué announcing Italy's entry into the war on 10 June proclaimed: 'German and Italian soldiers will now march shoulder to shoulder and not rest until Britain and France have been beaten.' In his own handwriting, Hitler amended this to read '. . . and will fight on until those in power in Britain and France are prepared to respect the rights of our two peoples to exist.'

Hitler in triumph

Hitler's attitude to the British was always ambivalent. He was torn between admiration for their Empire and anger at their political hostility, sympathy for them as fellow Aryans and contempt for them as decadent bunglers. Throughout June as he enjoyed his triumph in France, he awaited news from his intermediaries in Sweden and Switzerland that the British were ready to make a peace based on recognition of his conquests.

Even when Britain's obstinacy became apparent, Hitler remained uncertain about invading her. He was frustrated by Franco's determination to remain neutral, which denied him the opportunity to close the western Mediterranean by seizing Gibraltar. He was profoundly alarmed by Russia's move into Lithuania on 12 June, Estonia and ▶ *page 76*

June 1940: Churchill defiant

The British saw any possibility of a German adventure in the East as being dwarfed by the towering reality of the Wehrmacht on the Channel coast. The British public and most of their politicians were convinced that they faced imminent invasion and the threat of destruction. The German triumphs in France and Norway had convinced them that the Wehrmacht possessed almost mystical powers. Even senior British officers were haunted by fear of a sudden German invasion spearheaded by paratroops and Fifth Columnists. They did surprisingly little cool analysis of the problems invasion posed for the German army and navy.

Lack of clear thinking extended to the British intelligence departments. At the end of June, the Joint Intelligence Chiefs reported that they could not promise the Home Defence Executive the three-day warning of invasion that it had demanded. On 2 July, they reported that there was little doubt that invasion would be Germany's next move.

'Ultra' decrypts of German signals, which were anyway scanty at this stage of the war, provided little help since the Wehrmacht in France communicated with Germany almost entirely by landline. The Secret Intelligence Service's stations in Western Europe had been crippled by the German Occupation. Diplomatic intelligence was conflicting, but generally pessimistic.

RAF reconnaissance of the Channel ports monitored the build-up of German shipping, but even the Royal Navy was mesmerized by the possibility that the Germans might have devised a miraculous system for a blitzkrieg sea crossing: 'We cannot . . . assume', reported the Chief of Naval Staff early in July, 'either that special craft will not have been provided, or that past military rules as to what is practicable and what is impracticable will be allowed to govern the action undertaken.' He concluded that Hitler might be able to land 100 000 men on the coast of England without any significant warning.

One man, almost alone, continued to doubt whether the Germans would land in Britain: the Prime Minister. With his remarkable ▶ *page 77*

‘ With regard to an invasion . . . The Führer had not so far uttered any such intention, as he is fully aware of the extreme difficulties inherent in such an operation. That is also why the High Command had as yet undertaken no studies or preparations (the Commander-in-Chief, Luftwaffe, has put certain things in hand, e.g. the activation of a parachute division).
17 June 1940: GENERAL JODL'S ASSISTANT to the the German Naval Staff

The Führer has no intention of mounting an invasion . . . There won't be any invasion, and I have no time to waste on planning one.
25 June 1940: GENERAL HANS JESCHONNEK, Luftwaffe Chief of Staff

Naturally, it matters a lot what the British expect the Führer's purpose to be in fighting their country . . . Can the British . . . swallow their envy and pride enough to see in him not the conqueror but the creator of the new Europe? If they continue to wallow in their present pigheadedness then God help them.
30 June 1940: WALTER HEWEL, Hitler's Diplomatic Liaison Officer

Perhaps we automatically shy from taking over the immense task of inheriting both Europe and the British Empire. "Conquer Britain – but what then, and what for?" – This question of the Führer's is countered by others, like Herr Von Ribbentrop, with a comparison to two great trees that cannot prosper if they grow up close together.
5 July 1940: BARON WEIZSACKER, State Secretary of the Foreign Ministry.

As England, despite her hopeless military situation, still shows no sign of willingness to come to terms, I have decided to prepare, and if necessary to carry out, a landing operation against her. . . .
16 July 1940: ADOLF HITLER Directive No 16 ‎‎

Latvia on 16 June. On 28 June, the Russians moved into Eastern Rumania. Already Stalin was exploiting Germany's preoccupation in the West.

What if the Russians attempted a major stab in the back against Germany while the Wehrmacht was committed to a campaign in Britain? Hitler was haunted by fear of possible collusion between Churchill and Stalin. Germany's oil supplies could be in peril. What if invasion failed? The Wehrmacht's losses of equipment, not to mention morale and prestige, would drastically restrict Hitler's future options elsewhere. He was faced by two real or prospective enemies, but as he himself put it later, he had only one bullet in the breech.

Hitler's dilemma

Hitler did not immediately resolve his dilemma. He sought to keep his options open. Ever mindful of public opinion at home, he ordered thirty-five divisions to be disbanded and increased production of consumer goods in Germany's factories. On the Channel coast, he proposed to keep the stakes on the table. The British could be threatened, at no substantial cost to Germany.

The German High Command (OKW)'s order *The War Against England*, dated 2 July 1940, began: 'The Führer and Supreme Commander had decided . . . that a landing in England is possible, provided that air superiority can be attained and certain other necessary conditions fulfilled.'

'If they continue to wallow in their present pigheadedness then God help them.'

On 25 June, one of his secretaries wrote: 'The Chief plans to speak to the Reichstag shortly. It will probably be his last appeal to Britain. If they don't come around even then, he will proceed without pity . . . It would obviously be far easier for him if they would see reason themselves. If only they knew that the Chief wants nothing more from them than the return of our own former colonies . . .'

‘ Do you realise that for the first time for a thousand years this country is now in danger of invasion?
1 June 1940: THE CIGS, GENERAL SIR JOHN DILL to GENERAL MONTGOMERY

My reason tells me that it will now be almost impossible to beat the Germans, and that the probability is that France will surrender and we shall be bombed and invaded . . . Yet these probabilities do not fill me with despair. I seem to be impervious both to pleasure and pain. For the moment we are all anaesthetised.
15 June 1940: HAROLD NICOLSON, Under-Secretary at the Ministry of Information

German plans for the invasion of this country will have been worked out in great detail and secrecy.
18 June 1940: *Notes on German Parachutists*, issued by General Headquarters Home Forces

The indications are that it will not be long before Hitler has a go at this country. What kind of can opener he has ready, no one can say. But I will venture to say he will try something new.
24 June 1940: GENERAL RAYMOND LEE, US Military Attaché in London

No news yet of the expected peace terms . . . we are living as people did during the French Revolution — every day is a document — every hour history.

Winston wound up with his usual brilliance and out-of-place levity. His command of English is magnificent; but strangely enough, although he makes me laugh, he leaves me unmoved. There is always the quite inescapable suspicion that he loves war which broke Neville Chamberlain's better heart.
20 June 1940: *'Chips' The Diaries of Sir Henry Channon, MP*

intuitive sense of war, which so often guided him better than his service chiefs, he perceived the dilemma facing Hitler. He anticipated that the Führer might turn elsewhere: '. . . should he be repulsed here or not try invasion,' Churchill wrote to Beaverbrook on 8 July, 'he will recoil Eastward, and we have nothing to stop him . . .'

The Island Fortress
But in the summer of 1940, there was no possible alternative strategy to the creation of the Island Fortress. Churchill set himself to rouse his nation with all the energy and oratory at his command, conscious that the threat of German landings had awakened it with an urgency no more distant peril could achieve.

And whatever the uncertainties of a German invasion by sea, Churchill always anticipated the Luftwaffe's assault from the air. He told Beaverbrook that in the months to come, Britain must build a bomber force with which to defeat Germany, 'without which I do not see a way through . . .' But at the beginning of July, '. . . in the fierce light of the present emergency the fighter is the need, and the output of fighters must be the prime consideration until we have broken the enemy's attack . . .'

'. . . for the first time for a thousand years this country is now in danger of invasion.'

Considering the terrible threat overhanging Britain, Churchill's lack of dismay seemed almost indecent to less robust spirits like Sir Henry Channon. Churchill wrote of his day of taking office in May, as the German armies swept into France: 'As I went to bed at about 3am, I was conscious of a profound sense of relief. At last I had the authority to give directions over the whole scene. I felt as if I were walking with destiny, and that all my past life had been but a preparation for this hour and for this trial . . . I thought I knew a good deal about it all, and I was sure I should not fail. . . .'

'Sealion':

Preparing Hitler's 'river crossing on a broad front'. Along the length of the coast of northern France in in the summer of 1940, German soldiers had to learn how to land men, horses, guns and vehicles from improvised landing-craft under fire. The Wehrmacht had assembled a limited number of genuine landing-craft, but proposed to rely principally on barges with specially-fitted ramps to transport the invasion army. It is not surprising that most German soldiers found the landing exercises bewildering and often farcical. A contrast is inevitable between the Germans' feeble preparations to cross the Channel in 1940 and the vast, highly-trained machine that proved necessary to enable the Allies to do so in 1944.

The German plan for invasion

In the first days after Dunkirk, General Erhard Milch, State Secretary of the Air Ministry, proposed immediate paratroop landings to seize key points in south-east England, paving the way for a full-scale invasion with whatever forces and transport could be assembled. Milch's scheme may not have been as absurd as some historians have thought it. If Hitler wanted to invade and occupy Britain, his best chance was in the traumatic period immediately following the fall of France. Whatever the German army's difficulties in getting ashore and staying there in June, these were far less than they would have encountered with each passing day of the summer and autumn, as Britain mustered her defences. But not until 13 July did the German General Staff lay before Hitler their draft plans for 'Operation Sealion' – the invasion of Britain. On 31 July, the target date for invasion was postponed from mid-August to 17 September.

Admiral Raeder and the navy were doubtful whether they could carry the army across the Channel and then keep open the sea links through the vital first weeks. One of their more fanciful proposals was the creation of screening minefields at the eastern and western ends of the sea corridor, which they thought might keep the Royal Navy out. The landing and supply of the army would depend on 155 transports and 3,000 barges and small boats assembled from the length of the European seaboard, only a handful of them purpose-built landing craft. The naval scheme had the makeshift air of a Dunkirk in reverse, with the difference that there would be no tea waiting on the quayside at the end of the crossing.

Yet if the navy doubted its ability to fulfil its part in the compromise plan, the army was concerned that the landings would be on too narrow a front and carrying too little initial force. Von Rundstedt's Army Group A would provide the main elements. The sixteenth Army under Busch would land on the right, around Ramsgate, while Strauss's ninth Army took the left. Army Group B would launch an independent operation from Cherbourg to Lyme Bay, spearheaded by three divisions from von Reichenau's sixth Army, which would drive north towards Bristol. On Army Group B's beaches, the first wave would be composed of ten infantry divisions – 120 000 men, 4,500 horses – supported by 650 tanks. Their flanks would be secured by paratroop landings. Three armoured and three motorized divisions, a further nine infantry divisions and a final eight infantry divisions would make up subsequent waves. After a week to consolidate the beachhead, on D 7 the army would strike north to seize the high ground on a line from Portsmouth to the Thames Estuary, and in a second movement, advance to cut off London from the west.

When one considers the vast planning, equipment and training machinery that the Allies were later compelled to develop for Combined Operations, the German invasion preparations seem almost as primitive as the British plans to resist them. OKW proposed to carry out at two weeks notice a crossing that the Allies would devote almost two years to preparing in 1942–44. It is not surprising that almost all the German generals and senior naval officers concerned hoped fervently that they would never be called upon to carry out Sealion.

> ✚
> 'We have here the paradoxical situation where the navy is full of apprehension, the airforce is very reluctant to tackle a mission which at the outset is exclusively its own, and OKW – which for once has a real combined operation to direct – just played dead. The only driving force in the whole situation comes from us. But alone we can't swing it.'
> GENERAL FRANZ HALDER, Chief of Army General Staff, on Operation Sealion, 6 August 1940

This does not suggest, however, that Britain was in no danger of invasion. If the Luftwaffe successfully defeated Fighter Command in the air, its bombers could have laid open the ground defences, and left Britain at the mercy of the Wehrmacht. The Battle of Britain would beyond doubt be a vital encounter.

The Luftwaffe was now about to embark on a decisive battle. But its impression of the enemy that it was to fight was extraordinarily ill-informed. Goering's Intelligence staff must bear a heavy responsibility for the disaster that was to come. Their report on the Royal Air Force dated 16 July 1940 reveals that they had failed to penetrate any of the vital secrets of Fighter Command.

German assessment of the RAF

They accurately assessed Dowding's front-line strength, but they were fatally ignorant of the dramatic increase in aircraft output from the factories under Beaverbrook's direction. 'At present the British aircraft industry produces about 180 to 330 first line fighters a month', stated the report. 'In view of present conditions. . . . It is believed that for the time being output will decrease rather than increase.' In reality, fighter production had risen from 446 in June to 496 aircraft in July, and would reach 476 in August.

They had no conception of the brilliant British fighter direction system: 'The command at high level is inflexible in its organization and strategy. As formations are rigidly attached to their home bases, command at medium level suffers mainly from operations being controlled in most cases by officers no longer accustomed to flying (station commanders). Command at low level is generally energetic but lacks tactical skill.'

They grossly underestimated the quality of the Hurricane and Spitfire: 'In view of their combat performance and the fact that they are not yet equipped with cannon guns both types are inferior to the Bf

80

109, while the individual Bf 110 is inferior to skilfully handled Spitfires.'

They were justifiably scornful of the risk to Germany from the RAF's bombers, but recklessly confident that their own would do better: 'In contrast, the Luftwaffe is in a position to go over to decisive daylight operations owing to the inadequate air defence of the island. . . . The Luftwaffe is clearly superior to the RAF as regards strength, equipment, training, command and location of bases . . . .'

These were the beliefs with which the Luftwaffe went to battle and which would lead to so many blunders in the months to come. If the British knew little about German plans to defeat them, the Germans knew still less about their enemy.

…and for the Battle of Britain

10, DOWNING STREET,
WHITEHALL.

On what may be the eve of an attempted invasion or battle for our native land, the Prime Minister desires to impress upon all persons holding responsible positions in the Government, in the Fighting Services, or in the Civil Departments, their duty to maintain a spirit of alert and confident energy. While every precaution must be taken that time and means afford, there are no grounds for supposing that more German troops can be landed in this country, either from the air or across the sea, than can be destroyed or captured by the strong forces at present under arms. The Royal Air Force is in excellent order and at the highest strength it has yet attained. The German Navy was never so weak, nor the British Army at home so strong as now. The Prime Minister expects all His Majesty's servants in high places to set an example of steadiness and resolution. They should check and rebuke expressions of loose and ill-digested opinion in their circles, or by their subordinates. They should not hesitate to report, or if necessary remove, any officers or officials who are found to be consciously exercising a disturbing or depressing influence, and whose talk is calculated to spread alarm and despondency. Thus alone will they be worthy of the fighting men, who in the air, on the sea, and on land, have already met the enemy without any sense of being out-matched in martial qualities.

Winston S. Churchill

4th July, 1940.

While Hitler and his admirals and generals paused before deciding whether to launch the invasion of Britain, Hermann Goering suffered no misgivings about the role of the Luftwaffe. Fresh from its triumphs in France, the Luftwaffe was eager to match itself against the Royal Air Force. On 30 June Goering issued a preliminary instruction: 'As long as the enemy air force is not defeated, the prime requirement is to attack it . . . by day and by night, in the air and on the ground . . .'.

It was understood that Hitler himself would give the word for the major air onslaught against Britain. But in the July weeks that followed Goering prepared to embark on a private war against the RAF over the Channel, independent of the plans or wishes of the army and the Kriegsmarine. By attacking British shipping, he could force Fighter Command into a battle of attrition that must soften them up for the knockout to come. The Luftwaffe stood to win glory and to lose nothing. Hitler and his other service chiefs acquiesced passively. They too saw a battle over the Channel as a cheap, useful demonstration of Germany's might. The orders were given for the overture to the Battle of Britain.

Britain,

'We shall defend our island, whatever the cost may be. We shall fight on the beaches, we shall fight on the landing-grounds, we shall fight in the fields and in the streets, we shall fight in the hills; we shall never surrender . . .'.
Winston Churchill

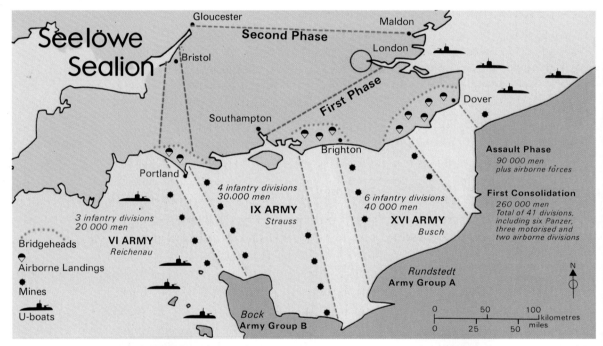

Sir Edmund Ironside, C-in-C Home Forces, May–July 1940

Sir Alan Brooke, C-in-C Home Forces, July–December 1940

summer 1940

It is often with hindsight that men realize that they have seen history made. But in the summer of 1940, almost all English men and women vividly perceived that they were acting out one of the great dramas of all time. Many spoke of the dreamlike quality of the period, as every day the impossible took place alongside the humdrum routine of ordinary living. For once, the aristocrat, Harold Nicolson, echoed a general feeling when he wrote in his diary on 31 July: 'I have always loved England. But now I am in Love with England. What a people! What a chance! The whole of Europe humiliated except us. And the chance that we shall by our stubbornness give victory to the world.'

'We have almost ceased to look forward', mused a *Times* leading article on 3 July. 'The days of looking forward used to pass slowly and heavily because they had merely to be lived through for the sake of others to come, but now the days are all lived through for their own sake.'

A nation which had never much cared for news for its own sake, the British became hypnotized by the ritual of listening to the BBC's 9 pm bulletin. All over the country, soldiers and civilians moved among shoppers and farmworkers in the streets and the fields, making hasty preparations to meet invasion. The popularly mooted date for the coming of the Germans was 15 August. Pillboxes, anti-tank ditches and obstacles – most of them inadequate – mushroomed at road junctions and vital installations, 127 000 people were evacuated from the towns of the East coast, where the invasion was expected and 80,000 people were moved inland from the Kentish coast. General Headquarters Home Forces was established in St Paul's School, Hammersmith. The nation's gold reserves were evacuated to Canada by fast cruiser. On 13 June, the ringing of church bells was prohibited except as a warning of invasion.

Far from being dismayed by their isolation, the British seemed to derive real satisfaction from having shed the uncertain support of France and the Low Countries. 'Personally I feel happier that we have no Allies to be polite to and pamper,' the King wrote to his mother, Queen Mary. His subjects agreed. A Ministry of Information Home Intelligence report noted: 'Many people express relief (of a quite unrealistic kind) that at last "there are no more Allies".'

But there was an ugly, neurotic face of patriotism. Fierce sentences were handed out in courts for spreading demoralizing talk until Churchill himself intervened to stop the prosecutions. Petty officialdom and absurd regulations blossomed, until lighting a cigarette in the black-out was treated as treasonable by some air-raid wardens. A fighter pilot snatching a few hours' leave to see his parents was threatened by a policeman with prosecution for failing to remove the rotor arm from his car in the middle of Glasgow.

'Fifth column hysteria is reaching dangerous proportions', said Home Intelligence on 5 June. Thousands of European refugees who had fled to England from Hitler were rounded up and interned under appalling conditions. Those who remained at liberty required 'Certificates of Reliability'. The Ministry of Information became alarmed by the number of foreigners employed by the BBC.

Amidst the curious unbelieving exhilaration of the summer, Britain's morale remained high. But there was some very real and potentially dangerous class tensions. The upper classes feared that the workers might not have the stomach to continue the fight, particularly under air attack. Equally on the other side, Home Intelligence reports showed that many working people believed that the rich would 'sell out' to Hitler as the French ruling class had done. They had not forgotten the widely-publicized flirtation between the Nazis and some British aristocrats in the 1930s.

As rationing tightened, it was known and bitterly resented that anybody with money could still buy a first-class dinner in a West End restaurant. There was disgust about the manner in which rich Englishmen including Duff Cooper, the Minister of Information, had evacuated their children to the safety of America. Later, when the first bombs fell on the East End leaving fashionable London virtually unscathed, there was a new and potent source of suspicion about who was bearing the cost of the war. It was very fortunate for the British Government that the Luftwaffe soon removed this by bombing the whole city, including Buckingham Palace and the House of Commons, with equal fierceness.

Those in high places devoted a great deal of energy to devising a declaration of war aims that would rally the nation. It was difficult to find tangible sources of encouragement. 'For want of something better', declared a Ministry of Information Planning Committee on 17 June, 'we shall have to plug (1) the Navy, (2) the Empire's strength, and (3) what a hell of a fine race to build up both . . .'. But as Churchill instinctively understood, the British public was not much interested in 1940 in ideas of a crusade to free Europe. The only universally popular call to arms was for the survival of Britain against the German onslaught.

Britain prepares for invasion

Britain's preparations to meet invasion were as inadequate as might be expected after twenty years of military stagnation and the disaster in France. At the end of May, the defences rested on fifteen infantry divisions – all at less than half their 15,500

Top left: Westminster at war: a British propaganda photograph intended to symbolise the national defiance
Top right: Air raid fever: a gas-proof shelter built as a private initiative in a London garden
Left: Old cars block a possible German landing field.
Far left: Evacuees
Centre: A Pont drawing for Punch, *autumn 1940*
'MUST you say "Well, we're still here" every morning?'

establishment – and one incomplete armoured division, under the command of the Commander-in-Chief Home Forces, General Ironside. There were only 963 tanks in the whole of Britain, of which 103 were cruisers capable of countering German armour. The infantry divisions possessed only one-sixth of their complement of field and anti-tank guns. Of the eight divisions entrusted with immediate coastal defence, the First London – responsible for the vital area from Sheppey to Rye – possessed twenty-three field guns, no anti-tank guns, no armoured cars, and no machine-guns.

The weight of the army, such as it was, was concentrated in eastern England where the Germans were expected to land in preference to the south coast. The second armoured division was in Lincolnshire, and General Headquarters' central reserve of three divisions was in the Midlands, from which it would be unlikely to be able to return in the face of heavy air attack during an invasion.

With the return of the BEF from Dunkirk, the man-power problem eased – paper strength increased to twenty-seven divisions. But the shortage of guns and equipment was still appalling. Almost all units depended for transport on buses, driven by civilian drivers who required eight to twenty-four hours' notice to become available. The shortage and quality of heavy coastal guns was particularly embarrassing. When a supercharged naval fourteen inch was installed at Dover – the only weapon capable of engaging German ships and positions across the Channel – it was found incapable of hitting moving targets, and was ordered to hold its fire, since German return shooting was much more effective.

When General Sir Alan Brooke succeeded Ironside on 20 July, he re-deployed the defending divisions for 'mobile offensive action', and moved the reserves forward, much closer to the likely scenes of battle. He cancelled the emphasis – and immense labour – wasted on feeble fixed defensive lines of pillboxes and obstacles across Britain, and concentrated on key road junctions and strategic points. The ageing and often incompetent generals holding

Firing the sea

Among many outlandish schemes devised to meet the invasion threat, the firing of the Channel was the most ambitious. The idea came from Lord Hankey who cherished schoolboy memories of the 'Greek Fire' used in the wars of the Byzantine emperors. In June 1940, a Petroleum Warfare Department was created, and at once began to study means of setting alight the sea and beaches in the path of an invasion. Perforated fuel pipes were laid in a few key positions. Some unencouraging experiments were carried out. But the Government did nothing to discourage rumours that Britain had developed large scale flame-throwing techniques against attackers.

the Home Defence jobs in the spring of 1940 were gradually replaced. The flow of tanks and guns from the factories steadily increased. By autumn, the British army was capable of offering effective resistance at least to the first wave of German invasion. Had the Germans been able to get ashore their proposed forces of armour and artillery, however, the British would have been in desperate straits.

Oddly enough, in one direction the British were over-prepared for invasion in the summer of 1940: the Royal Navy maintained a force of thirty-six destroyers and 1,100 lesser craft on constant invasion stand-by when they were desperately needed elsewhere as convoy escorts. The navy refused to accept that there would be several days' warning of a German landing in which they could concentrate their forces. They continued to be haunted by fear of an overnight invasion.

The Home Guard

In the face of Britain's desperate predicament, the Government resorted to desperate expedients. On 13 May 1940, Anthony Eden appealed on the BBC for civilians to come forward to create a force of Local Defence Volunteers in every town and village in the country. Within a week 250,000 men had joined and a million by August, overwhelming the ability of the authorities to organize, far less arm them. The Local Defence Volunteers, soon renamed the Home Guard, were initially grouped in platoons and companies under the direction of local Territorial Army associations.

There were rifles for only a fraction of the men. The remainder were armed with shotguns, swords, improvised clubs and staves. 'I do not want you to misjudge the shotgun', wrote Ironside hopefully on 5 June. 'I have now coming out over a million rounds of solid ammunition, which is something that will kill a leopard at two hundred yards.'

But it was a surprise landing by German paratroops rather than jungle predators that newspapers were expecting. They dubbed the Home Guard 'parashots'. Contrary to legend, a general issue of pikes took place in 1941, not 1940, but there was a Home Guard cutlass platoon in Essex under the command of a former naval rating, and a mounted troop on Dartmoor raised by the Mid-Devon Hunt.

With hindsight it is easy to be scornful about the value of this army of untrained and feebly equipped old men and invalids. But they were invaluable in taking over endless local guard duties that would otherwise have hamstrung the British army. They provided an organized lookout force to monitor military and airborne activity. Perhaps most important of all, they gave every community a sense of direct involvement in the defence of Britain without precedent in the nation's history.

Above: 'We are arrested by ferocious Home Guards':
the war artist Edward Ardizzone's memory of
a contretemps *at one of the roadblocks that formed*
part of the defence of Britain in 1940

Top left: Anti-aircraft training: one of the more
fanciful inspirations of the Home Guard's leaders in
the summer of 1940

Eve of battle: Dowding

One of the most incredible aspects of the Battle of Britain is that throughout June 1940, Air Chief Marshal Sir Hugh Dowding, C-in-C of Fighter Command, was under notice from the Air Ministry to retire on 14 July. Only on 5 July did the Chief of Air Staff condescend to send him a smooth letter saying that he would be glad if Dowding would stay until October. Understandably irritated, Dowding answered: 'Apart from the question of discourtesy . . . I must point out the lack of consideration involved in delaying a proposal of this nature until ten days before the date of my retirement. I have had four retirement dates given to me and you are now proposing a fifth.'

'A most determined man . . .'

He added a bitter footnote to his brush with Churchill about the Hurricanes sent to France: 'I am anxious to stay because I feel there is no one else who will fight as I do when proposals are made which would reduce the Defence Forces of the Country below the extreme danger point.'

Dowding was treated abominably by the Air Ministry, and he appears to have been unfortunate enough to antagonize Churchill at their first meeting. An eccentric and a loner, he was often at loggerheads with his peers, and his inability to make close friends left him at the mercy of his enemies when the struggle for power within Fighter Command reached a decisive point after the Battle of Britain.

But history has placed Dowding head and shoulders above every other senior British airman of the war, with the possible exception of Tedder. Sir Frederick Pile, the shrewd soldier who commanded Britain's Anti-Aircraft defences throughout the war, wrote of him: '. . . A difficult man, a self-opiniated man, a most determined man, and a man who knew more than anybody about all aspects of aerial warfare.'

Dowding was the eldest son of a successful preparatory school headmaster, with a conventional, dutiful Victorian middle-class background. He followed his father to Winchester, a public school famous for producing inscrutable intellectuals, but

claimed later that he had joined its Army Class because he detested Greek verbs so much. Whatever his real motives, in 1899 he entered the Royal Military Academy, Woolwich. He failed to be accepted as an engineer, but became a gunner. For ten years he served in a succession of British garrisons around the world.

He came home to England in the phase before the First World War when aviation fever gripped the public. Always a keen sportsman, he learned to fly at Brooklands, and had just won his wings when his father heard about it, and forbade him to continue flying because it was too dangerous. At the age of thirty-two, the dutiful Dowding obeyed him.

But a few weeks later war broke out. As a qualified pilot Dowding was at once called to the Royal Flying Corps. By 1915 he was a squadron commander, and by 1918 a brigadier. He transferred to the new RAF, and in the early 1930s became Air Member for Supply and Research. He was one of the first to see the need for metal rather than wooden aircraft. It was on his authority that the first radar experiments with aircraft were carried out. The Spitfire prototype had just flown for the first time when Dowding, aged fifty-four, was taken from planning the technology of air defence to commanding Britain's fighters in the field. In July 1936, he took over at Bentley Priory, and set up house with his sister just along the road from his office.

*Air Chief Marshal Sir Hugh Dowding
(detail from a painting by Sir Walter Russell)*

His great virtues were an instinctive understanding of the essentials of air warfare; the ability to delegate; and the leadership that did so much to build the high morale of Fighter Command. In Keith Park, AOC of 11 Group in the Battle of Britain, Dowding chose the perfect man to command his front line. Dowding was also the chief inspiration of the ground control system, from Bentley Priory to the airfields, that did so much to make victory possible. Once the Battle of Britain began, even with hindsight, it is difficult to fault Dowding's judgement, above all in pacing his commitment of forces to the battle, never losing sight of the need to be able to fight again tomorrow and next week, whatever the temptations and the pressures to risk everything on the battle of the moment.

Goering

Reichsmarschall Hermann Goering, Air Minister and Commander-in-Chief of the Luftwaffe, was the man responsible for gaining control of the air over Britain. As one of Hitler's closest confidants and designated successor, he was by far the most powerful military leader in Germany. The Luftwaffe's triumphs in Poland and the West had greatly increased his prestige and lust for power. At the beginning of July 1940, Goering was at his zenith.

He was the son of a retired government official, and grew up amidst the gothic shadows of Castle Veldenstein near Nuremberg. The castle was owned by his godfather, a Jew named Epenstein, who gave the family house-room because Goering's mother was his mistress. Herr Goering tolerated this arrangement.

The iron man

Goering was badly wounded in the trenches in the First World War. He had always wanted to fly, however and though he could scarcely walk now, this did not prevent him from defying all the rules and persuading a pilot friend named Bruno Lörzer to take him to his squadron, Field Aviation Unit No 25, as his observer. By charm and passionate determination, Goering rode out the subsequent bureaucratic storms, qualified as a pilot, and went on to become one of Germany's most famous fighter pilots. He won the coveted *Pour le Mérite*, and succeeded von Richthofen in command of his celebrated 'flying circus'.

As a war hero with the credentials of a gentleman, Goering was a powerful asset to the Nazi Party when he joined in 1922. Hitler used him as a symbol of responsibility and respectability, and 'the fat man' gained great public popularity, especially among the middle classes who were so nervous of Hitler. As the Nazis rose to power, Goering became President of the Reichstag and Prime Minister of Prussia. In the early 1930s, it was Goering who organized stormtroopers, took over the Prussian Interior Ministry, formed the Gestapo and set up the first concentration camps.

Office and large-scale embezzlement gave Goering a life-style rarely equalled in the twentieth century. He had castles, hunting lodges, town houses; servants in comic opera knee-length coats with rich facings, high gaiters and silver-buckled shoes. A fine horseman and a crack shot, he was a passionate hunter. He had abandoned his youthful womanizing after two contented marriages. He met his first wife, a Swedish countess, after he forced-landed his aeroplane in a snowstorm on a frozen lake, and took refuge in a nearby castle. Karinhall, the great mansion of his heyday, was named in her memory.

The pink, girlish complexion, overweight body and many childish indulgences masked a personality capable of superhuman self-control. Goering cured himself of morphine addiction resulting from treatment given to his stomach wound received in the 1923 putsch. He was a dynamic enthusiast whose apparent directness of manner and speech could pass for honesty, and could be very persuasive.

The regal splendour of Goering's life-style was symbolized by his personal train, code named 'Asia'. It was preceded by a pilot train for his staff, with low-loaders for cars, and freight cars for Goering's shopping. His own carriages were specially weighted to provide a smooth ride, and drawn by two of Germany's most powerful locomotives. There were bedrooms for himself and his wife, a

Goering at Karinhall

study, a cinema, a dining-car and a command post with a map room. There were guest carriages for senior commanders such as Milch, and light flak wagons at front and rear, although whenever possible the train was halted near a tunnel for protection against air attack.

In the spring of 1940, 'the iron man' ordered his train west to Beauvais in France, a suitable command centre for the attack on England which promised to be his greatest triumph.

Yet despite his command of the greatest air force the world had yet seen, Goering had never made

any attempt to understand the real nature and limitations of air power. He was not a fool, but neither was he a 'military thinker'. He took no interest in technology and he saw air combat merely in terms of shooting down as many as possible of the enemy's aircraft. He was an enthusiastic disciple of Douhet's theory of using air forces to win wars while armies and navies merely fought holding actions, yet like the British bomber enthusiasts, he had never subjected these ideas to intellectual scrutiny. Goering's concept of command, and his approach to the Battle of Britain, was crude in the extreme.

RAF's Order of Battle - 1 July 1940

Sector	Squadron	Aircraft	Combat ready	Base airfield
No 11 Group HQ Uxbridge Middlesex				
Biggin Hill	32	H	12	Biggin Hill
	79	H	12	Biggin Hill
	245	H	15	Hawkinge
	600	B	8	Manston
	610	S	14	Gravesend
North Weald	25	B	6	Martlesham
	56	H	16	North Weald
	85	H	15	Martlesham
	151	H	14	North Weald
Kenley	64	S	10	Kenley
	111	H	12	Croydon
	501	H	10	Croydon
	615	H	12	Kenley
Northolt	1	H	10	Northolt
	257	H	12	Hendon
	604	B	10	Northolt
	609	S	15	Northolt
Hornchurch	54	S	12	Rochford
	65	S	11	Hornchurch
	74	S	10	Hornchurch
Tangmere	43	H	13	Tangmere
	145	H	11	Tangmere
	601	H	15	Tangmere
	FIU*	B	4	Tangmere
Filton	92	S	11	Pembrey
	213	H	14	Exeter
	234	S	9	St Eval
Middle Wallop	236	B	11	Middle Wallop
	238	H	10	Middle Wallop
Debden	17	H	14	Debden
Total			348	

*Night fighter interception unit

H: Hurricanes, S: Spitfires, B: Blenheims, D: Defiants

Sector	Squadron	Aircraft	Combat ready	Base airfield
No 12 Group HQ Watnall Nottingham				
Duxford	19	S	8	Fowlmere
	264	D	11	Duxford
Coltishall	66	S	12	Coltishall
	242	H	10	Coltishall
Kirton-in-Lindsey	222	S	12	Kirton-in-Lindsey
Digby	29	B	10	Digby
	46	H	15	Digby
	611	S	3	Digby
Wittering	23	B	10	Colly Weston
	229	H	14	Wittering
	266	S	8	Wittering
Total			113	

Sector	Squadron	Aircraft	Combat ready	Base airfield
No 13 Group HQ Newcastle Northumberland				
Church Fenton	73	H	8	Church Fenton
	87	H	14	Church Fenton
	249	H	10	Leconfield
	616	S	11	Church Fenton
Catterick	41	S	11	Catterick
	219	B	10	Catterick
Usworth	72	S	12	Acklington
	152	S	8	Acklington
	607	H	10	Usworth
Turnhouse	141	D	14	Turnhouse
	253	H	13	Turnhouse
	602	S	12	Drem
	603	S	10	Turnhouse
	605	H	8	Drem
Dyce	263	H	3	Grangemouth
Wick	3	H	12	Wick
	504	H	12	Castletown
Total			178	

92

The men

Both the RAF and the Luftwaffe had sent the cream of their pilots between the wars to their bomber squadrons. Fighter Command in 1940 depended heavily on reservists and part-timers to man its fighters – a quarter of Dowding's squadrons in the Battle of Britain were Auxiliaries, who were often under-trained, and some years past their peak although, paradoxically, some of the greatest British aces would be men past thirty.

Contrary to popular myth, barely 200 of the 3,000 Fighter Command pilots who fought in the Battle of Britain were public-school educated: the best-represented single school was Eton, which provided 22 men. But the élitist affectations of some of the AAF squadrons, with their officers' silk-lined flying jackets and smart sports cars won them a lot of public attention and some resentment from pilots of humbler background who felt excluded.

NCO pilots were still rigidly segregated from their commissioned colleagues on the ground, and by a further touch of service snobbery, 'Direct Entry' or reservist NCOs were cold-shouldered by the 'old sweats' who had come up the hard way, through Halton Apprentices' school or the ranks.

When the Battle began, Fighter Command's pilots were compelled to rely on their very high morale and *esprit de corps* to compensate for major shortcomings of organization and training. As heavy losses developed, the AAF squadrons with their close-knit comradeships took them very hard. Replacements quickly destroyed these units' local peacetime character for ever.

By July 1940, Goering's élite Luftwaffe was not only superbly trained, but many aircrew had battle experience of Spain, Poland or the West. The German training machine had for years been producing 800 pilots a month, against the 200 a month reaching the RAF in 1939. Morale was high, and observers noted that relations between officers and other ranks were much closer than in the RAF.

'We are 3,000 young idealists', wrote a euphoric Luftwaffe cadet, among a huge gathering of his kind addressed by Hitler in the Berlin Sportpalast before their graduation one day in 1940. 'We listen to the spell-binding words and accept them with all our hearts. We have never before experienced such a deep sense of patriotic devotion towards our German fatherland ... I shall never forget the expressions of rapture which I saw on the faces around me today.'
The Cambridge University Air Squadron, founded in 1925

George Barclay went to Stowe public school and Trinity College, Cambridge. He flew a Spitfire for the first time in June 1940. At the age of nineteen he was posted to 249 Hurricane squadron in Yorkshire. He was killed in 1942.

Sandy Johnstone was a civilian navigation instructor, and part-time pilot with 602 (City of Glasgow) Auxiliary Squadron. By 1940 he was twenty-four, a newly married F/Lt flying Spitfires. He became squadron commanding officer on 13 July.

Richard Hillary, who would become a symbol of Fighter Command's romantic sacrifice and write a fine autobiography before his death in 1943, came from Oxford University Air Squadron to the RAFVR in September 1939, and joined 603 Squadron in July 1940.

Ian Gleed was a keen sportsman with his own sailing boat. On 5 July 1940, he moved to Exeter with his squadron with more than 800 hours flying time behind him. He was killed in action.

David Crook had joined 609 (West Riding) Squadron of the AAF shortly before the war: 'To most of us flying was the dominating interest of our lives', he wrote. On 30 June he joined 609 at Northolt near London, and shot down his first German aircraft a few days later. He was killed in action.

Johnny Kent, a Canadian, proved an outstanding flier. He was sent to OTU, where he test-fired a half-second burst before his guns jammed. He was told that this was the only firing practice shortage of ammunition allowed. He joined 303 (Polish) Squadron and later became its commanding officer.

Heinz Bär transferred to fighters from a bomber unit in 1938 and scored his first victory of the war over Poland on 25 September 1939. By July 1940 he had achieved three 'kills' and by May 1945 he had achieved a fantastic 220 victories.

Hans-Karl Mayer served in Spain flying with some of the early Bf 109 combat units. In the Battle of France, he claimed five victories during the RAF's disastrous attack on the German bridgehead at Sedan. In July 1940, he was a *Staffelkapitän* in I/JG53. He was killed over England in October.

'Joschko' Fözö joined the Austrian air force in 1930, and the Luftwaffe after the Anschluss. He went to Spain with *Jagdgruppe* 88 in the Condor Legion. By 1940 he was *Staffelkapitän* in II/JG51, flying Bf 109s.

Max-Hellmuth Ostermann trained as a *Zerstörer* pilot on the Luftwaffe's Bf 110s but had difficulties flying the aircraft because he was so small. In the spring of 1940 he transferred to Bf 109s. His unit, 7/JG54, joined the Battle of Britain early in August. He was killed in 1942.

Johannes 'Macki' Steinhoff, in 1939, was *Staffelkapitän* of 10/JG26, the Luftwaffe's experimental night fighter unit. He led his squadron into action for the first time during the RAF's suicidal daylight 'sweep' against Wilhelmshaven. In February 1940 he took over 4/JG52, and led this unit through the Battle of Britain.

Wilhelm Balthasar flew more sorties than any other German pilot in Spain. Short-sighted, he wore tinted 'sunglasses' to conceal his disability. In the Battle of France he scored twenty-three victories. He was appointed *Gruppenkommandeur* of 111/JG3 but scored only once before being badly wounded. He was killed in July 1941.

How the airforces were organised

Despite the totalitarian powers that Goering and Milch wielded ruthlessly, the Luftwaffe was ill-prepared for a prolonged struggle. It was organized and equipped for short-term, short-range operations in support of the armies. The emphasis was upon the bomber and reconnaissance units, and it was assumed that an enemy air force could be destroyed by heavy bomber attack on its airfields. There were no stockpiles of vital imports such as rubber, aluminium and magnesium. There was a shortage of bombs because Hitler would authorize only sufficient production to meet immediate needs.

The Luftwaffe was organized in self-contained Air Fleets (*Luftflotten*), each equipped with a full range of aircraft types and its own command, support and signals organization. Each was allotted a specific area of operations. Since the occupation of Europe, Air Fleets 2 and 3 had been moved from their bases in Germany to airfields in France and Belgium; 1 and 4 remained in Germany and Poland. A new Air Fleet 5 had been created in Scandinavia.

For the Battle of Britain, a boundary was drawn down the centre of England, and Air Fleets 2 and 3 were allotted operational areas east and west of it, while 5 was committed to north eastern Britain. Air Fleet 5's short-range Bf 109s could not, however, operate across the North Sea and thus played no part in the struggle.

Throughout June, the Luftwaffe's support teams had been working intensively at the new airfields on the Channel Front to create the network of telephone and telex teams, repair facilities and supply dumps essential for a huge air force. Air Fleet 2 established its headquarters in Brussels, 3 in Paris.

The Air Fleet system has been criticized for its inflexibility, but it was probably the best organization for the Luftwaffe at the time. It simply demanded perfect co-operation between the three Air Fleets to make the best use of their forces, and this was not always forthcoming.

It was Britain's good fortune that her air force was incomparably better organized and equipped for the 'worst case' situation of July 1940, in which disaster had befallen her strategy on every front, than for any other possible set of circumstances. The organization of Fighter Command enabled the British readily to commit every available aircraft to their own defence. Dowding had quartered the country into Fighter Group areas: 10, 11, 12, 13. Each possessed its own commander, squadrons, and Operations Room, in which girls of the WAAF using croupiers' rakes moved coloured counters to show the progress of the battle on the map board. Fighter Command and the Group HQs made the strategic decisions about what forces to commit to action. Tactical control of the squadrons 'scrambled' then passed to the vital sector Airfield Control Rooms, which 'vectored' their pilots to meet German formations by simply-coded radio-telephone instructions. All the 'ops' rooms were constantly fed updated information on the attackers' course from the radar stations and Observer Corps centre, via the Filter Room at Bentley Priory.

Because the fighters carried barely an hour's fuel, it was essential to commit them in such a way that there were always relays of reserves to meet new attacks when the first defenders had to 'pancake' and refuel. If squadrons scrambled to meet what proved to be a feint, the entire pattern of defence could be broken. On the other hand, over-caution in committing fighters gave them too little time to gain height for interception. Defending Britain from the Luftwaffe called for superb judgement and timing from Dowding and his Group commanders, and unstinting co-operation between them.

As the Battle progressed, German operations were increasingly influenced by the equally short endurance of their single-engined fighters. At combat power, the Bf 109s could not even reach the limit shown on the map and get home again.

Air Fleet 2

Each of the five Air Fleet commanders took his orders direct from Goering and Milch, and throughout the war no German airman outside the Air Ministry was able to achieve the sort of personal power gained, for example, by the Allied 'bomber barons' later in the war. But lower down the scale, the Luftwaffe's middle-ranking officers had far more latitude than their Allied counterparts.

The Air Fleets' internal organization was clumsy and poorly co-ordinated. Each of the specialized elements except the fighters was controlled by a *Fliegerkorps* HQ. A new post of *Jagdfliegerführer* (fighter leader) had been created, supposedly to centralize command of the fighters under one man answerable directly to the Air Fleet commander. In reality, however, the bomber *Fliegerkorps* HQs, responsible for vastly greater numbers of men, almost always outgunned the *Jafü* in policy arguments, and he was allowed to be little more than a liaison officer, informing the fighter units what the bombers wanted from them. This would have a fatal effect on tactics in the Battle of Britain.

At operational level, the Air Fleets were organized in *Geschwader* of around a hundred aircraft, give or take twenty according to circumstances. These in turn were divided into three *Gruppen*, designated by Roman numerals, and again into three *Staffeln* of about twelve aircraft, designated by Arabic numerals. A *Gruppe* was normally kept together on one airfield. Thus III/JG 26 indicates the third *Gruppe* of fighter *Geschwader* 26.

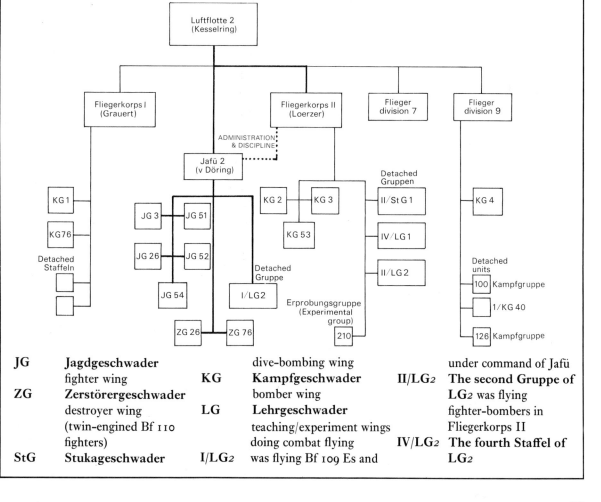

JG	**Jagdgeschwader** fighter wing		dive-bombing wing		under command of Jafü
ZG	**Zerstörergeschwader** destroyer wing (twin-engined Bf 110 fighters)	**KG**	**Kampfgeschwader** bomber wing	**II/LG2**	**The second Gruppe of** LG2 was flying fighter-bombers in Fliegerkorps II
		LG	**Lehrgeschwader** teaching/experiment wings doing combat flying		
StG	**Stukageschwader**	**I/LG2**	was flying Bf 109 Es and	**IV/LG2**	**The fourth Staffel of** LG2

Stavanger
*Luftflotte **5** HQ*

and **X** Fliegerkorps HQ

N ←⊕

British and German air forces late July and August 1940

Genraloberst
Hans-Jürgen Stumpff

Air Vice-Marshal
Trafford Leigh-Mallory

Royal Air Force (RAF):

▲ Fighter Command Group Headquarters (HQ)

━━ Group boundaries

•••• Sector boundaries

✈ Sector Airfields

Luftwaffe (LW):

◆ Luftflotte Headquarters (HQ)

━━ Luftflotte boundary

■ Fliegerkorps and Fliegerdivision HQ

•••• Fliegerkorps boundaries

✈ Luftwaffe Airfields

selected LW units:
⊕ Erpr Gr (Erprobungsgruppe)
⊕ KG (Kampfgeschwader)
⊕ ZG (Zerstörergeschwader)
⊕ JG (Jagdgeschwader)
⊕ St G (Stukageschwader)

Air Vice-Marshal
Richard Saul

Newcastle

Church Fenton

13 HQ ▲   Catterick

✈   ✈
Acklington   Usworth

CHUR
FENTON
sector

13 GROUP

CATTERICK
sector

USWORTH
sector

✈
Turnhouse

DYCE
sector

TURNHOUSE
sector

ACKLINGTON
sector

WICK
sector

13 GROUP
N. Ireland

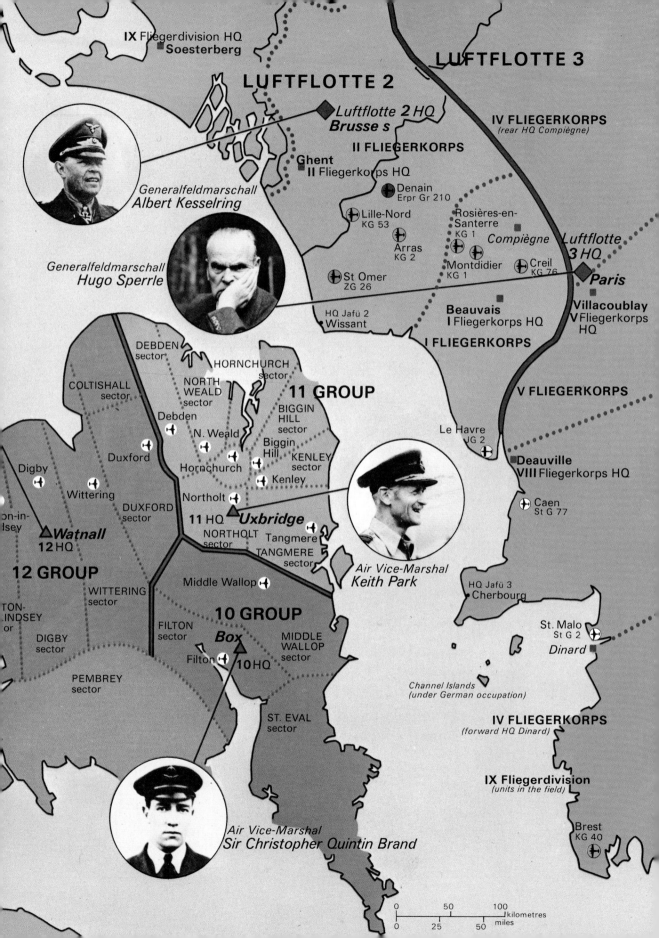

IX Fliegerdivision HQ
■ **Soesterberg**

LUFTFLOTTE 2

LUFTFLOTTE 3

◆ *Luftflotte 2 HQ*
Brusse s

IV FLIEGERKORPS
(rear HQ Compiègne)

II FLIEGERKORPS

Generalfeldmarschall
Albert Kesselring

■ **Ghent**
II Fliegerkorps HQ

✈ **Denain**
Erpr Gr 210

✈ Lille-Nord
KG 53

Rosières-en-
Santerre
✈ KG 1

Compiègne

◆ *Luftflotte 3 HQ*

Generalfeldmarschall
Hugo Sperrle

✈ **Arras**
KG 2

✈ KG 2

✈ Montdidier
KG 1

✈ **Creil**
KG 76

◆ **Paris**

✈ **St Omer**
ZG 26

■ **Villacoublay**
V Fliegerkorps
HQ

HQ Jafü 2
● **Wissant**

■ **Beauvais**
I Fliegerkorps HQ

I FLIEGERKORPS

DEBDEN
sector

HORNCHURCH
sector

COLTISHALL
sector

NORTH
WEALD
sector

11 GROUP

V FLIEGERKORPS

✈ Debden

✈ **N. Weald**

BIGGIN
HILL
sector

Le Havre
✈ JG 2

Duxford

Biggin
Hill

KENLEY
sector

■ **Deauville**
VIII Fliegerkorps HQ

Digby
✈

✈ Wittering

✈ Hornchurch

✈ Kenley

✈ Caen
St G 77

DUXFORD
sector

▲ Northolt
✈

11 HQ
Uxbridge

△ **Watnall**
12 HQ

NORTHOLT
sector

Tangmere
✈

Air Vice-Marshal
Keith Park

12 GROUP

TANGMERE
sector

HQ Jafü 3
● **Cherbourg**

WITTERING
sector

Middle Wallop
✈

St. Malo
St G 2 ✈

DIGBY
sector

FILTON
sector

10 GROUP

Box ▲

MIDDLE
WALLOP
sector

Dinard ■

PEMBREY
sector

✈ Filton /**10 HQ**

Channel Islands
(under German occupation)

ST. EVAL
sector

IV FLIEGERKORPS
(forward HQ Dinard)

IX Fliegerdivision
(units in the field)

Air Vice-Marshal
Sir Christopher Quintin Brand

✈ Brest
KG 40

0   50   100
kilometres
0   25   50   miles

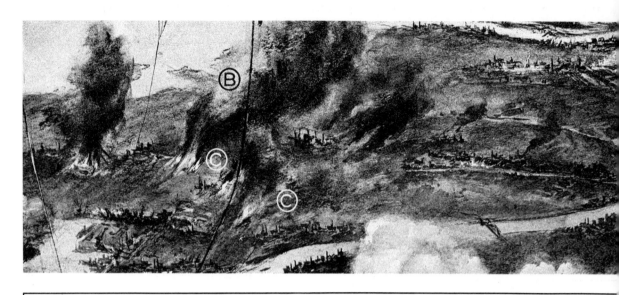

Battle Commanders

'Smiling Albert' Kesselring, commander of Air Fleet 2, was a fifty-five-year-old former army officer who had only reluctantly accepted transfer to the Luftwaffe seven years earlier. He had since become a great air enthusiast, however, and was Goering's Chief of Staff until he found working with Milch intolerable, and was given an Air Fleet to deter him from retiring. When war came, the *Luftflotten* became the key commands, and Milch tried in vain to secure one. He had to content himself with becoming a Field Marshal, alongside Sperrle and Kesselring, in Hitler's July 1940 deluge of senior promotions.

Hans-Jürgen Stumpff commanded the Luftwaffe's third force, *Luftflotte 5* based in Scandinavia. Stumpff was a veteran staff officer who had served under von Seeckt, the architect of German rearmament, in the *Reichswehr Ministerium* in the 1920s. *Luftflotte 5* was much the smallest of the Air Fleets, and

its Bf 109s lacked the range to operate against Britain across the North Sea. After suffering some heavy losses in the early stages of the Battle, Stumpff's forces played no significant rôle after mid-August, and many of his aircraft and pilots were sent to reinforce Air Fleets 2 and 3.

The forbidding, scowling **Hugo Sperrle,** commander of Air Fleet 3, was the most experienced air force officer in Germany. A pilot in the First World War, he had commanded the Condor Legion in Spain. He was fifty in 1940, a huge slow moving, bearlike figure with a passion for luxury to match that of Goering: he took over the fabulous Palais du Luxembourg in Paris as his headquarters. Milch thought him lazy, but retained Sperrle until he was retired in 1944.

Air Vice-Marshal **Keith Park** was Dowding's personal choice for command of 11 Group, his front line in SE England. A forty-four-year-old New Zealander, Park had served as an infantry officer in the First World War before transferring to become a pilot. An austere, mild-mannered man who was perhaps the RAF's greatest expert on all aspects of fighter direction, he logged a hundred hours in his personal Hurricane during the Dunkirk battles, watching his pilots in action. He was now to prove himself a brilliant tactician.

Trafford Leigh-Mallory was irked that he had been left in command of 12 Group since 1937 rather than promoted to the vital 11 Group area. Soon to become one of Dowding's toughest critics, Leigh-Mallory earned a reputation as an ambitious intriguer. Aged forty-eight in 1940, he was an able man but a difficult subordinate to control. Thick-set with heavy jowls and a small, carefully trimmed moustache, he read history at Cambridge before

The aerial battle over the Channel as seen by the German magazine Signal *10 September 1940*

becoming a soldier. He transferred to the RFC in 1916.

Air Vice-Marshal **Sir Quintin Brand** took over the newly-formed 10 Group covering the west of England on 17 July. In keeping with the lesser importance of his area, Brand was given only an initial seven single-engined squadrons. A South African who had shot down a Gotha bomber as a Camel pilot in 1917 during the attacks on London, Brand gave Dowding and Park the dedicated support that Leigh-Mallory was later accused of withholding during the Battle of Britain.

Air Vice-Marshal **Richard 'Birdy' Saul** commanded 13 Group in northern England and Scotland. Squadrons still working up or resting were posted to this quieter area whenever Dowding could afford to release them. Saul was also familiar with the air defence organization in the South-East – he had been Senior Air Staff Officer at 11 Group until he was posted north in 1939.

At the beginning of July 1940 many units of Air Fleets 2 and 3 were still redeploying after the campaign on the continent, and it would be weeks before the Germans approached their full strength. But on 20 July the Luftwaffe could call on the following forces (serviceable aircraft are listed in italics).

	Bf 109 sing. eng. fighter	809	*656*
	Bf 110 twin eng. fighter	246	*168*
	Ju 87 dive bomber	316	*248*
	Ju 88 twin eng. bomber		
	He 111 twin eng. bomber	1131	*769*
	Do 17 twin eng. bomber		
	Long-range reconnaissance	67	*48*
	Short-range reconnaissance	82	*46*

A further 84 Bf 109s based in Scandinavia with *Luftflotte* 5 lacked the range to take part in the battle, but *Luftflotte* 5 was also deployed:

	Bf 110 twin eng. fighter	34	*32*
	He 111 twin eng. bomber		
	Ju 88 twin eng. bomber	129	*95*
	Do 17 twin eng. bomber		
	Long-range reconnaissance	67	*48*
	Short-range reconnaissance	28	*15*

On 1 July 1940, Fighter Command possessed 591 serviceable aircraft and 1,200 pilots. Including aircraft in certain squadrons resting or deploying, the order of battle was made up as follows:

	Hurricanes sing. eng. fighter	463	*347*
	Spitfires sing. eng. fighter	286	*160*
	Defiants sing. eng. fighter	37	*25*
	Blenheims twin eng. fighter	114	*59*

'. . . The Battle of France is over. I expect that the battle of Britain is about to begin. . . . The whole fury and might of the enemy must very soon be turned on us. Hitler knows that he will have to break us in this island or lose the war. If we can stand up to him, all Europe may be free and the life of the world may move forward into broad sunlit uplands. But if we fail, then the whole world, including the United States, including all that we have known and cared for, will sink into the abyss of a new Dark Age made more sinister, and perhaps more protracted, by the lights of perverted science. Let us therefore brace ourselves to our duties, and so bear ourselves that, if the British Empire and its Commonwealth last for a thousand years, men will still say "This was their finest hour".'
Winston Churchill, 18 June 1940

Kanalkampf

In the next six weeks of broken, treacherous weather, each side skirmished warily. Spasmodic night bomber raids were launched against towns all over Britain. There was intensive sea mining of the approaches to British ports. Very effective Bf 109 'sweeps' were directed against southern England, in search of Dowding's fighters. Heavily escorted bomber raids struck convoys and coastal targets the breadth of the English Channel coast. Despite great pressure from politicians and the navy, Dowding sought always to commit his fighters sparingly, to husband them for the battles to come.

Kanalkampf battle diary

The 'diary' below gives an impression of the way the battle developed on some typical July and August days of 1940.

From July to mid-August 1940, the Luftwaffe launched an increasingly powerful succession of probing attacks against British shipping in the Channel and coastal targets. This was the *Kanalkampf*, the first phase of the Battle of Britain. *Oberst* Fink, *Geschwaderkommodore* of KG 2, was named *Kanalkampfführer*, to direct the operation, with two *Stukagruppen* and a fighter *Geschwader* to reinforce his own aircraft. While the Luftwaffe waited for Hitler to give his personal order for the all-out air attack, they sought to weaken Fighter Command in a battle of attrition. It was a 'heads-we-win, tails-you-lose' plan: if the British fighters rose to defend their shipping, they must suffer losses they could ill afford. If they stayed on the ground, British shipping would suffer intolerable losses.

air battle over the Channel

Above: Luftwaffe armourers loading machine-gun belts into the drums for the Bf 110's formidable nose armament: by the end of July, the German ground crews were almost as exhausted as their British counterparts; their aircraft were being called upon to sortie two or three times a day

Left: Spitfire pilots at ease

7 July

Overnight 62 people were killed in scattered attacks on Godalming, Aldershot, Haslemere and Farnborough. During the morning Fighter Command shot down three reconnaissance Dornier 17s off the south coast. Squadrons were repeatedly scrambled to meet German fighter sweeps over southern England, but the Bf 109s had turned homewards again before the Hurricanes could intercept. 54 Squadron's B Flight was 'bounced' by 109s near Manston, and all three Spitfires force-landed, damaged. At 8.30 in the evening 45 Dornier 17s attacked a convoy off Folkestone, sinking one ship and damaging three. The Bf 109 escort surprised 65 Squadron, and dived out of the sun to shoot down three Spitfires without loss to themselves. Two of the German Do 17 bombers were damaged, but overall it was a poor day for the defence, who lost six fighters for only five enemy aircraft destroyed.

8 July

On a clear day perfect for attacks on shipping, the fighters claimed two reconnaissance Do 17s in the morning, although neither is confirmed by German records. At 2 pm, Blue Section of 610 Squadron broke up an unescorted Dornier 17 attack on a convoy off Dover, losing one Spitfire. An hour later, nine 79 Squadron Hurricanes were scrambled from Hawkinge to meet another bomber attack, only to collide with a Luftwaffe fighter sweep. Two of its aircraft were lost. Soon afterwards 234 Squadron scrambled from their Cornish base to meet a Ju 88 attack on another convoy but made no 'kills'. During the course of the day 11 Group's squadrons shot down four Bf 109s in scattered skirmishes. Fighter Command shot down seven German aircraft in the day, for the loss of four.

10 July

The day officially nominated later as the ▶ *page 108*

CONVOY RUNS GAUNTLET OF

Far right above : A famous German propaganda picture : a Bf 110 over the white cliffs of Dover. Sadly for the Luftwaffe, however, the 110 proved less dangerous to Fighter Command than it looked

Far right below : Spitfires of 303 (Polish) Squadron, who made an immense contribution in the later stages of the Battle. This picture was taken afterwards, when they had been re-equipped. In the summer of 1940 they were flying Hurricanes.

A tabloid view of war : the Daily Sketch *centre spread for 23 August*

A close-up of two shells that fell short and wide. Explosions sent columns of water 100 feet high. No ship was hit.

The view from the ⬤ shelled from the F⬤ R.A.F. plane keeps a⬤ ships ran the gaun⬤ than 100 rounds. ⬤ praised the skipp⬤ merchant ve⬤

Another one burst in the wake of two vessels, with a destroyer just beyond them. The shells travelled 20 miles.

WHY HER ⬤ IS SIRE⬤

This bonnie baby g⬤ to Mrs. R. English, ⬤ Morden, just as th⬤ passed " siren was s⬤ was " all clear " wha⬤ should be. They've ⬤ Siren.

-LL-FIRE

while the British convoy was bein...
sterday. High above the ships a...
nemy aircraft. For 80 minutes th...

SHE SWINGS INTO THE PRIZE LIST

This entry in Class "A" of the DAILY SKETCH £1,000 Photo Contest wins the weekly prize of £5 for John Cole, 8, Coneydale, Welwyn Garden City, Herts. He entitled it, "No School for a Month."

'DAILY SKETCH' ROLL of HONOUR

Major John Whiteley, M.P., received the O.B.E. for distinguished service in the field. He is in the R.A.

Lieut. - Colonel H. F. Rance, awarded O.B.E. for distinguished service in the field. In the Royal Corps of Signals.

Brigadier John L. Weston, who was recently invested with the insignia of a C.B.E. at Buckingham Palace.

Margaret Yarde, as a stalwart Girl Guide leader, endeavours to bring down their presumed high temperatures by application of a potent plaster.

Oliver Gordon, as the unconventionally attired butler, can still smile when the riotous goings on have reduced Miss Yarde to despair.

❛ At that moment I saw dimly a machine moving in cloud on my left and flying parallel to me. I stalked him through the cloud, and when he emerged into a patch of clear sky, I saw that it was a Ju 87. I was in an ideal position to attack, and opened fire and put the remainder of my ammunition – about 2,000 rounds – into him at very close range. Even in the heat of the moment I well remember my amazement at the shattering effect of my fire. Pieces flew off his fuselage and cockpit covering, a stream of smoke appeared from the engine, and a moment later a great sheet of flame licked out from the engine cowling and he dived down vertically. The flames enveloped the whole machine and he went straight down, apparently quite slowly, until he was just a shapeless burning mass of wreckage. Absolutely fascinated by the sight, I followed him down and saw him hit the sea with a great burst of white foam. He disappeared immediately, and apart from a green patch in the water there was no sign that anything had happened . . . I had often wondered what would be my feelings when killing somebody like this, and especially when seeing them go down in flame. . . . I was rather surprised to reflect afterwards that my only feeling had been one of considerable elation, and a sort of bewildered surprise that it had been so easy.
D M CROOK, 609 Squadron, 9 July.

I soon found another target. About 3,000 yards ahead of me, and at the same level, a Hun was just completing a turn preparatory to re-entering the fray. He saw me almost immediately and rolled out of his turn towards me so that a head-on attack became inevitable. Using both hands on the control column to steady the aircraft and thus keep my aim steady, I peered through the reflector sight at the rapidly closing aircraft. We opened fire together, and immediately a hail of lead thudded into my Spitfire.

---

10 July continued

start of the Battle of Britain, although no pilot of the time found it that much different from a dozen others in the month. The big convoy, *Bread*, was sighted leaving the Thames Estuary by a heavily escorted reconnaissance Do 17 at 10 am. The Do 17 got home damaged. One of its pursuing Spitfires was shot down when it encountered a Bf 109 sweep near Dover. At 1.31, radar reported German aircraft forming up over the Pas de Calais, and at 1.35 Hurricanes sighted the German bombers, twenty-six Do 17s escorted by five fighter *Staffeln*. Twenty-four of Dowding's fighters were scrambled to reinforce the six already on the scene. A huge dogfight involving over a hundred aircraft developed. Despite the dramatic German claims mentioned by Werner Kreipe, in reality only one 700 ton sloop was sunk. Meanwhile, sixty-three Ju 88s were attacking Falmouth and the Swansea area without loss, confusing the radar by making their approach from the west. Bombs fell on railways, anchored ships and a muni-

13 July

tions factory, causing eighty-six casualties. In the day Fighter Command lost one aircraft and destroyed eight.

Early in the afternoon fifteen aircraft of 238 and 609 Squadrons were scrambled from Warmwell to patrol a convoy expected off Portland. The convoy was in fact late, but the fighters arrived to find fifty German aircraft closing fast, also in search of the ships. One Do 17 and one Spitfire were destroyed. Forty Bf 110s formed a 'defensive circle' which the Hurricanes were unable to break, though they damaged two 110s. Around 4 pm, eleven Hurricanes of 56 Squadron on a sweep over a convoy off Dover met a big force of Ju 87s escorted by Bf 109s. A fierce dogfight followed, after which the British claimed seven Stukas destroyed although German records later showed that all had returned safely. Two Hurricanes were lost. One Bf 109 was later destroyed by Spitfires. In the day, three Hurricanes were lost for six German aircraft destroyed.

One moment the Messerschmitt was a clearly defined shape, its wingspan nicely enclosed within the circle of my reflector sight, and the next it was on top of me, a terrifying blur which came out of the sky ahead. Then we hit.
AL DEERE, 54 Squadron, 9 July.

It is difficult to describe my feelings during the next few days. We had lost three pilots in thirty-six hours, all of them in fights in which we had been hopelessly out-numbered, and I felt that there was now nothing left to care about, because obviously from the law of probability, one could not expect to survive many more encounters of a similar nature. . .'
D M CROOK, 609 Squadron, 10 July.

The convoy had been sighted between Dover and Dungeness. Our briefing took only a few minutes, and within half an hour of being airborne we had sighted the coast of Kent. The Channel was bathed in brilliant sunshine . . . A light haze hung over the English coast, and there, far below us, was the convoy, like so many toy ships with wispy wakes fanning out behind. As soon as we were observed, the ships of the convoy dispersed, the merchantmen manoeuvring violently and the escorting warships moving out at full speed. Anti-aircraft shells peppered the sky. Our fighters now appeared. We made our first bomb run, and fountains leapt up around the ships . . . By now the fighter squadrons of the Royal Air Force had joined in, and the sky was a twisting, turning mêlée of fighters . . . My wing was in the air for three hours in all. We reported one heavy cruiser and four merchant ships sunk, one merchant ship damaged, and eleven British fighters shot down or damaged. We had lost two bombers, two twin-engined fighters and three single-engined fighters during the course of this engagement.
WERNER KREIPE, III KG 2, 10 July.

19 July

Fighter Command reinforced its forward coastal airfields as the weather improved, and nine convoys were at sea off the coast. Yet another of the hapless reconnaissance Do 17s was spotted and shot down at 7.04 am. An hour later four Do 17s slipped undetected over Glasgow and carried out a destructive precision-raid on the Rolls-Royce works before escaping. Shortly before 1 pm, a formation of nine Defiants patrolling south of Folkestone was 'bounced' by Bf 109s and – the total vulnerability of the turret fighters exposed – six were destroyed in a few minutes. One Bf 109 was shot down by Hurricanes hurrying to the rescue. 32 Squadron scrambled from Hawkinge to meet a Stuka attack on Dover harbour, and became entangled in a fierce dogfight with escorting Bf 109s. 43 Squadron from Tangmere engaged Bf 109s off Selsey Bill. In the day, Fighter Command lost ten fighters, five pilots killed and five wounded, against four Luftwaffe aircraft shot down (although thirteen were claimed).

25 July

The Luftwaffe was now sending up strong fighter sweeps to exhaust the defence before launching its bomber attacks. At 12.20 pm, 65 Squadron's Spitfires met Bf 109s off Dover. A quarter of an hour later, twenty Hurricanes became engaged in a dogfight against forty Bf 109s, but the German fighters withdrew as their fuel ran low without loss to either side. 11 Group was caught on the ground as sixty Stukas fell on a Channel convoy. Nine Spitfires of 54 Squadron, urgently scrambled to the rescue, met a huge Bf 109 escort and lost two aircraft without scoring against the Luftwaffe. At 2.30 pm, eight Spitfires of 64 Squadron sent to patrol the convoy met thirty Ju 88 bombers escorted by more than fifty Bf 109s. Fifteen more fighters scrambled. The successive raids and scrambles continued through the afternoon until the last attack at 6.30 pm. In all, fifteen of Dowding's squadrons were engaged during the day, losing six Spitfires against German losses of sixteen.

Tactics

Very early in the battle, it became apparent that Fighter Command's conventional set-piece tactics, based on the old-fashioned 'fighting area attack', were quite inadequate for modern air war. The RAF had trained its pilots to fly in close formation, which demanded that they spend much too much time avoiding collision and not nearly enough spotting the enemy. Fighter Command's traditional sections of three aircraft either in vic or line astern proved highly vulnerable to attack from above or behind. The old First World War rules about the vital advantage of height and of attacking out of the sun were as valid as ever. When a 'tail-end Charlie' was added to a formation specifically to watch its rear, he proved most vulnerable of all. If he weaved constantly he used up his fuel much more quickly than the rest of the formation.

The traditional Fighter Command attack, with aircraft peeling off in turn to dive on the enemy and loose bursts at him one after the other, proved quite impracticable against an enemy who refused to fly a steady and continuous course when being shot at.

152 Squadron is credited with being the first Fighter Command unit to adopt the German system of flying in pairs and fours, which has been the basis of fighter tactics all over the world ever since. 111 Squadron pioneered one remarkable Fighter Command tactic – breaking up enemy formations by head-on line abreast attack. But the unit's alarming rate of air-to-air collisions dissuaded most of their colleagues from emulating them.

RAF regulations stipulated that a fighter's eight guns must be aligned so that their fire converged at 650 yards. A 54 Squadron pilot said 'All this guarantees is a few hits by the indifferent shot; the good shot on the other hand is penalised'. Pilots were already discovering that a German bomber could take heavy fire from 0.303 machine-guns without coming down. To destroy an enemy aircraft, it was essential to get close. More and more pilots aligned

BRITISH FIGHTER TACTICS

their guns unofficially to converge at two or three hundred yards. Sailor Malan and Al Deere believed that 250 yards 'harmonization' and the De Wilde

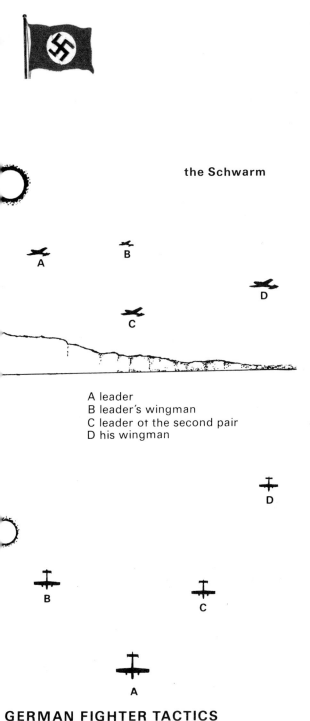

the Schwarm

A leader
B leader's wingman
C leader of the second pair
D his wingman

GERMAN FIGHTER TACTICS

incendiary bullets normally loaded into at least two guns (two carrying armour-piercing rounds and the remaining four normal ammunition) made the dif-ference between damaging and destroying an enemy aircraft. It was the men who flew very close and who had the superb judgement to be able to make a killing deflection shot against a target moving at three or four hundred miles an hour in three dimensions, who would be the aces of the Battle of Britain.

As the fighting intensified, regulations fell away. Pilots flew in shirtsleeves rather than lumber themselves with Irvin suits and gloves. Some liked to fight with their cockpit canopies pushed back, making it easier to bale out in an emergency. The British were discovering the great advantage of the big canopy on the Spitfire, which gave them incomparably better visibility in combat than the very cramped Bf 109. German pilots also envied the sheet of armour plate now fitted behind the seat of all RAF fighters, after a squadron in France early in the war had tried it against official advice that it would 'spoil the balance of the aircraft'.

German fighter tactics were based on the *Schwarm* – what Allied pilots called the 'finger four' – devised by the great German ace Mölders in the Spanish Civil War. A is the leader, B is the wingman who never leaves his side. He flies on the sun side of the leader and low so that the others do not have to look into the glare of the sun to see him.

C is the leader of the second *Rotte* (pair); D is his wingman. In each pair, one man is leader and attacker while the wingman is defender. The two-man unit proved far more psychologically and tactically effective than the traditional three employed by the RAF, who soon adopted the pair system. Fighter Command also learnt from the Luftwaffe to fly in open formations, more difficult to spot in an empty sky than a tight squadron line abreast.

But despite the brilliance of some individual RAF pilots, it would be months before Fighter Command as a whole learnt to match the tactical skill in the air developed by the Germans over the years in Spain, Poland and France. On 17 July, for instance, twelve Spitfires of 64 Squadron flying out of Kenley were 'bounced' off Beachy Head. The Bf 109s destroyed an aircraft and vanished before the RAF formation had even seen them.

No man's sea

Even in mid-summer, the Channel is an unwelcoming refuge. As the July battles intensified, more and more pilots of both sides found themselves compelled to 'ditch' in the sea, either shot down or (often in the case of Bf 109 pilots) out of fuel. It was always preferable to bale out of a fighter rather than land it in the sea, where its huge engine weight caused it to sink like a stone.

Fighter Command had no proper air-sea rescue organization – a mere eighteen motor boats to search for downed aircrew up and down the entire south coast. Again and again, pilots were saved by the merest fluke encounter with passing trawlers or merchantmen, or by a civilian lifeboat putting out from shore. In many cases they simply drowned. British fighter pilots had no dinghies until later in the war, and they were expected to blow up their own 'Mae Wests' in the water, a grotesque burden on an exhausted or wounded man. In any event, without a dinghy few men could survive more than an hour or two in the water.

The Germans were much better equipped. Their pilots wore highly visible yellow skull caps and carried flare pistols, sea-dye, and one-man dinghies. Well-equipped rescue rafts were anchored at intervals the breadth of the Channel. Above all, the Luftwaffe sent out its Heinkel He 59 floatplanes of the *Seenotflugkommando* air-sea rescue unit, capable not only of locating but also of landing to rescue a ditched airman. The Germans claimed to be outraged when Dowding gave the order that such rescue aircraft must be shot down, with or without their red crosses. It was reasoned that a rescued German pilot could be flying in action against Britain again if his rescuers were left unscathed. The Luftwaffe responded by camouflaging and arming the floatplanes.

The crew of a Ju 88 prepare for take-off. Their safety-harness supported them in the water if they had to bale out over the Channel. The British equivalent had to be inflated in the water, which was not always possible

⊙

❝ In a second the cockpit was a mass of flames: instinctively, I reached up to open the hood. It would not move. I tore off my straps and managed to force it back . . . I remember a second of sharp agony, remember thinking "so this is it!" and putting both hands to my eyes. Then I passed out. When I regained consciousness I was free of the machine and falling rapidly.

I pulled the ripcord of my parachute and checked my descent with a jerk. Looking down, I saw that my left trouser leg was burnt off, that I was going to fall into the sea, and that the English coast was deplorably far away. . . . The water was not unwarm and I was pleasantly surprised to find that my life-jacket kept me afloat . . . There can be few more futile pastimes than yelling for help alone in the North Sea, with a solitary seagull for company, yet it gave me a

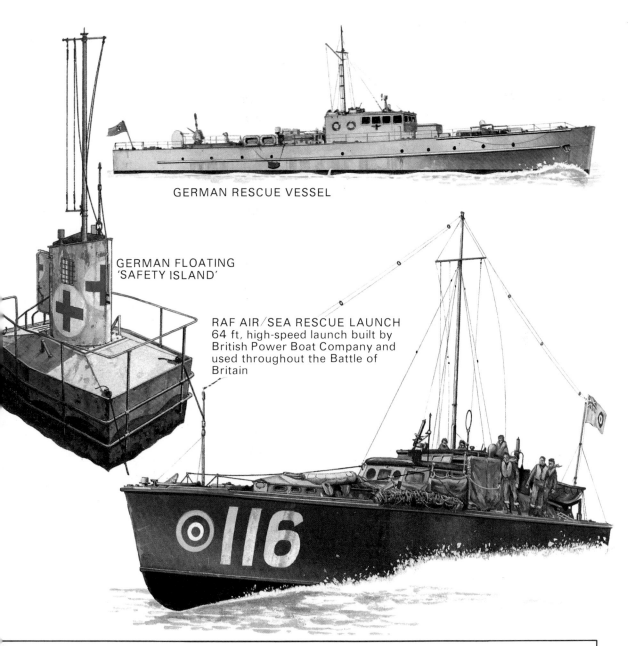

GERMAN RESCUE VESSEL

GERMAN FLOATING
'SAFETY ISLAND'

RAF AIR/SEA RESCUE LAUNCH
64 ft, high-speed launch built by
British Power Boat Company and
used throughout the Battle of
Britain

certain melancholy satisfaction, for I had once written a short story in which the hero (falling from a liner) had done just this. It was rejected.

The water now seemed much colder and I noticed with surprise that the sun had gone in though my face was still burning. . . . I began to feel a terrible loneliness, and sought for some means to take my mind off my plight. . . . I remember as in a dream hearing somebody shout: it seemed so far away and quite unconnected with me. Then willing arms were dragging me over the side; my parachute was taken off (and with such ease!); a brandy flask was pushed between my swollen lips; a voice said, "O.K., Joe, it's one of ours and still kicking" . . . I was safe. I was neither relieved nor angry: I was past caring.

It was to the Margate lifeboat that I owed my rescue.

RICHARD HILLARY, 603 Squadron, 3 September.

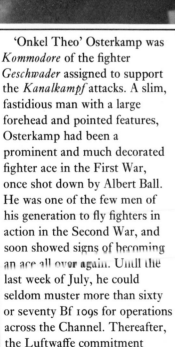

'Onkel Theo' Osterkamp was *Kommodore* of the fighter *Geschwader* assigned to support the *Kanalkampf* attacks. A slim, fastidious man with a large forehead and pointed features, Osterkamp had been a prominent and much decorated fighter ace in the First War, once shot down by Albert Ball. He was one of the few men of his generation to fly fighters in action in the Second War, and soon showed signs of becoming an ace all over again. Until the last week of July, he could seldom muster more than sixty or seventy Bf 109s for operations across the Channel. Thereafter, the Luftwaffe commitment began to build up rapidly.

Bf 110s bombed Dover harbour at first light, but Park refused to allow his fighters to be drawn, waiting for the bombers to come. But as the morning went on, more and more squadrons were scrambled to meet German fighter sweeps, and a succession of desultory engagements took place. At 9.45 Ventnor radar reported a big raid building up off Cherbourg and after a hasty discussion between Park and Brand, twenty-one fighters were scrambled and a further six squadrons ordered to 'readiness'. At 10.07, as 165 German bombers escorted by Bf 109s

Left: Legendary images: Goering and his staff on the Channel discussing their battle plan within sight of the white cliffs of England

and 110s reached mid-Channel, eight of Dowding's squadrons were sent to meet them. They were soon engaged in heavy and costly dogfighting with the fighters, while the German bombers were able to attack Portland and Weymouth almost unscathed. In the afternoon there were several encounters over the scene of the fight, as each side sought to rescue its downed pilots from the sea. There was also a series of separate attacks over convoy *Booty* off the Harwich–Clacton coast, which 'Sailor' Malan's 74 Squadron played a principal part in repelling. In the day's very heavy fighting, thirty British aircraft were lost and thirty-five German.

Aircraft destroyed

The losses of each side in the Battle of Britain are still a matter of fierce controversy. These are the best available figures, compiled from British and German records. I have not included the hundreds of damaged aircraft on each side, many of which needed major repairs before being fit for action again. Losses given here are only those rated by the British 'Category 3 Lost, Missing, or Destroyed', and by the Luftwaffe '100% loss'. Figures show those destroyed in action and those lost in accidents – N-C or Non-Combat.

Battle losses	RAF		Luftwaffe	
	C	N-C	C	N-C
1 July	1	—	10	1
2 July	—	—	3	1
3 July	—	1	4	1
4 July	1	2	3	2
5 July	1	3	2	1
6 July	—	2	3	2
7 July	6	—	5	1
8 July	4	—	7	2
9 July	6	—	11	2
10 July	1	—	8	1
11 July	6	1	15	2
12 July	3	5	8	—
13 July	3	2	6	—
Sub totals	32	16	85	16

	RAF		Luftwaffe	
	C	N-C	C	N-C
14 July	—	—	3	—
15 July	1	2	4	—
16 July	—	—	2	1
17 July	1	—	2	2
18 July	5	1	5	1
19 July	10	—	4	1
20 July	6	2	14	1
21 July	1	1	7	3
22 July	—	2	2	—
23 July	—	4	3	3
24 July	2	2	10	2
25 July	6	1	16	—
26 July	2	2	2	—
27 July	1	2	4	—
28 July	4	1	9	1
29 July	3	1	12	—
30 July	—	1	4	3
31 July	2	3	2	1
1 August	1	1	12	4
2 August	—	2	3	2
3 August	—	—	3	1
4 August	—	2	1	5
5 August	2	—	1	2
6 August	—	5	1	2
7 August	—	5	4	1
8 August	15	2	21	1
9 August	—	2	3	1
10 August	—	—	—	1
11 August	30	2	35	1
Totals	124 +62		274 +56	

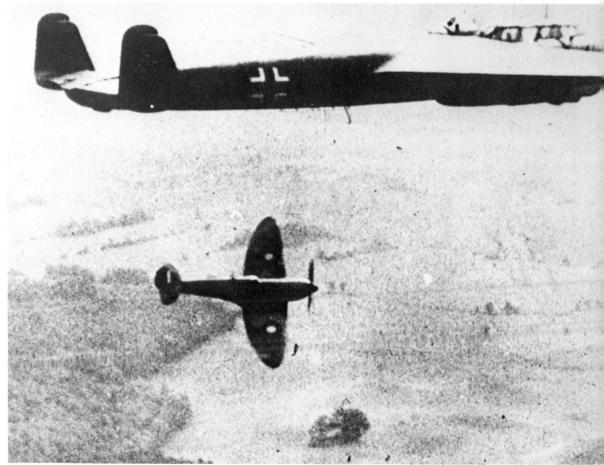

Far left: Armourers work on the nose guns of a Bf 110, so formidable when the Zerstörer pilots could bring them to bear
Middle: A German pilot adds to his victory tally; fighter pilots have always shared the conceit of marking up 'kills' on their aircraft
Left: The coastal convoys were equipped with balloons to impede German low-level attacks. Here they are being transferred from a depot barge to waiting ships
Below left: A Spitfire turns below a Do 17 over south-east England.
Below: A British Channel convoy passing the white cliffs: the photo shows clearly the transmitting and receiving aerials of a Chain Home radar station

❛ I was eight at the time and lived near Bromley, and was daily a spectator of all that went overhead. One Sunday morning early in August I was standing at the top of our garden by the dug-out shelter which my father had sweated to excavate in time. We were watching a dogfight between two fighters high over the Bickley area. They twisted and plummeted, rose and writhed, until finally one dropped in the familiar falling-leaf fashion. I jumped up and down with excitement and shouted "We've got one! We've got one!". My father was surprisingly quiet. Then as no parachute came out and the plane went into a vertical dive, he said softly: "It's one of ours". For an eight-year-old, besotted by Buck Jones who always shot the Injun, or the guy in the black hat, I was stunned. Goodies could get killed as well as baddies. . . .
MICHAEL SALVARD

In comparison with my combats in France, I was very calm. I didn't fire, but tried again and again to get into a good position. But every time I got there the Tommy would break away. . . . Finally my chance came. Below, I saw a 109, and 200 metres behind him, a Spitfire. I peeled off and dived, turning in behind him. Now it was I who sat 200 metres behind the Tommy. Be calm; don't fire yet! I applied full power and slowly closed the gap, as the Tommy did with his own target. Now, at 100 metres, the wingspan filled the Revi gunsight. Suddenly the Tommy opened fire, and the Messerschmitt in front broke away. I had pressed the gun button at the same instant, aiming dispassionately as we went into a slight left-hand turn. My first

Pilots of 19 Squadron, one of Leigh-Mallory's Spitfire units in 12 Group, meet between sorties

shots hit. The Spit streamed a long grey smoke trail and dived steeply into the sea, just off the coast. A great column of water marked the impact. At once I called my victory over the radio, and had enough witnesses to confirm the crash. My first Tommy was down.

MAX-HELLMUT OSTERMANN, 7/JG54, 12 August.

Three Englishmen with radial engines appear, in very tight formation, and I pull the stick into my stomach and zoom up behind these. A quick glance left and right. All clear. I dive and get the leader in my Revi gunsight. I press the button and he goes down, his companions covering him as he disappears. I climb again, searching the sky. To the right there is nothing, but I cannot believe my eyes when I look the other way.

The sky is full of Spitfires, and just a few 109s. I go straight into the dogfight, but at once get a Spitfire on my back. At full speed I try to lose him. Now I have one Spitfire in front and another behind me. Damn it! I dive vertically away to lose him, then climb again. Suddenly I see white trails shooting past. I look back. Yet another is behind me, sending his tracers past my ears like the "fingers of the dead". I will thank God if my mother's son can get out of this dogfight! I manage to outclimb the Spitfires, and try again to help my outnumbered comrades, but each time the Tommies come down behind me. Suddenly a 109 comes past very fast with a Spitfire behind it. This is my chance. I get behind the Spitfire and centre it in my Revi. After a few shots it goes down . . . I watch it crash into the sea with a huge splash.

HELMUT WICK, 3/JG2, 11 August.

The battle scarcely begun

On the eve of the Luftwaffe's major attack on Britain, the lessons of the past six weeks' fighting were disturbing for Fighter Command. Again and again, when its outnumbered fighters met German Bf 109s in force, the British suffered the worst losses. Many British 'victories' had been achieved against lone Do 17s and He 111s. Already, the fighter pilots were terribly tired, after repeated scrambles day after day. British radar had proved of limited value when the Luftwaffe was raiding at short range against the British coast. The WAAF radar operators had learned that it was vital for them to risk everything on reporting their 'educated guesses' about what they could see on their screens, at the first possible moment. It took only five minutes for a German aircraft to cross the Channel, but fifteen for a British fighter to reach altitude to intercept it.

By 19 July, Dowding's losses were rising at such a rate that Fighter Command seemed statistically destined to extinction within six weeks. By the end of the month, he had lost 118 aircraft. Production from the factories had vastly improved, and he was able to restore each squadron to an establishment of twenty fighters plus two reserves. But eighty of his squadron and flight commanders, his most experienced leaders, had gone already. And the battle had scarcely begun.

RDF (RADAR) SCREEN

CH TRANSMITTERS 350 FT HIGH

CHAIN HOME (CH)

CH RECEIVERS 240 FT HIGH

FILTER ROOM BENTLEY PRIORY

OPERATIONS ROOM FIGHTER COMMAND H
BENTLEY PRIOR

TRANSMITTING 135 FT HIGH

RECEIVING 20 FT HIGH

CHAIN HOME LOW (CHL)

LONDON

RAF FIGHTER STATION BIGGIN HILL
SECTOR AIRFIELD

R
H

RAF STATION LYMPNE, KENT
SATELLITE AIRFIELD

RAF STA
HAWKING
SATELLITE

(CH) RADAR (HIGH-LEVEL) RYE, SUSSEX

ENGLISH CHANNEL

DUNGENESS

HEINK

The RAF's daytime response
to a Luftwaffe attack on south-east England

FRANCE

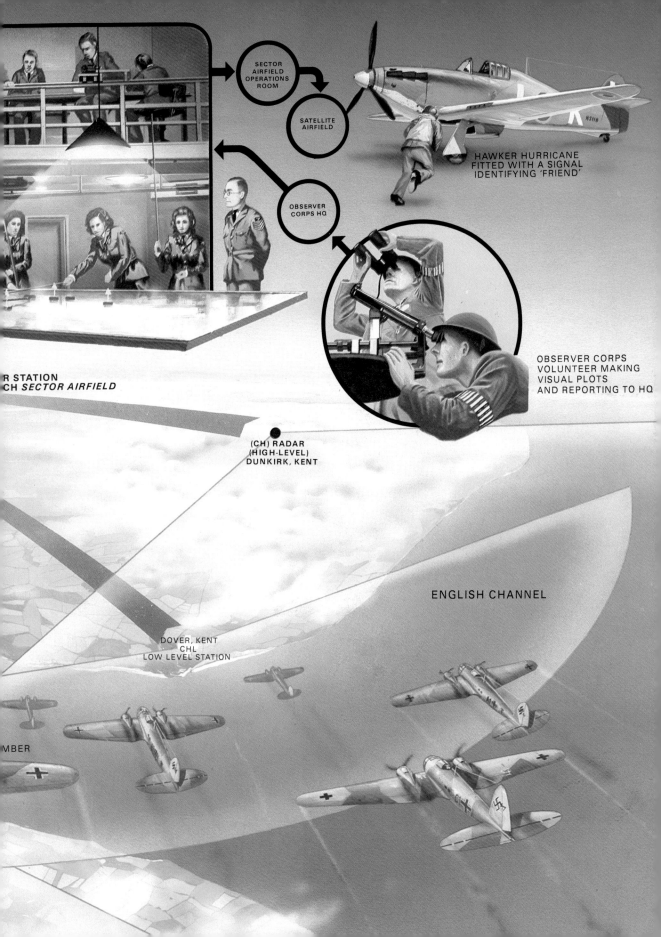

SECTOR
AIRFIELD
OPERATIONS
ROOM

SATELLITE
AIRFIELD

OBSERVER
CORPS HQ

HAWKER HURRICANE
FITTED WITH A SIGNAL
IDENTIFYING 'FRIEND'

OBSERVER CORPS
VOLUNTEER MAKING
VISUAL PLOTS
AND REPORTING TO HQ

R STATION
CH SECTOR AIRFIELD

(CH) RADAR
(HIGH-LEVEL)
DUNKIRK, KENT

ENGLISH CHANNEL

DOVER, KENT
CHL
LOW LEVEL STATION

MBER

An airfield 'somewhere in England'

'I woke as the airman orderly tapped my shoulder and repeated, "Come along, Sir, come along Sir, 4.30" in my ear. It was very cold in the hut and dark, so I wrestled with myself for a few minutes and then jumped out of bed and put on my flying kit quickly, Irvin trousers over my pyjamas, sweater, flying boots, scarf, Irvin jacket. . . . I left the hut to look at my aeroplane. I climbed into the cockpit out of which the fitter had just stepped. "Morning Parish, morning Barnes, put my 'chute on the tail please." I checked the instruments one by one: petrol tanks full; tail trimming wheels neutral; air-screw fine pitch; directional gyro set; helmet on reflector sight with oxygen and R/T leads connected – in fact everything as I liked it for a quick getaway when we scrambled.

Returning to the hut I found Kapan, the orderly, lighting the fire by the light of a hurricane lamp, while Ginger lay fast asleep in a deckchair, his head lolling on his yellow Mae West. I lay down and immediately became unconscious as if doped . . . What seemed the next moment I woke with a terrific start to see everyone pouring out of the hut. . . . I could hear the telephone orderly repeating: "Dover 26 000; fifty-plus bandits approaching from south-east."

Percy shouted, "Scramble George, lazy bastard," and automatically I ran out. Parachute on, pulled into cockpit by crew who had already started the engine. Straps, helmet, gloves, check the knobs, taxi out, got into right position in my section and take off. I put the R/T on, and only then do I wake up and realise I am in the air flying No 2 in Yellow Section. . . .'
GEORGE BARCLAY, 249 Squadron.

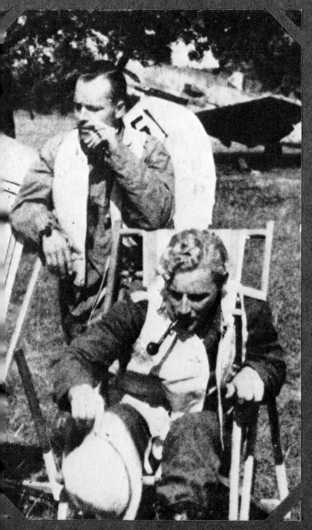

‘ Two or three sorties daily was the rule, and the briefing read: "Free chase over south-east England". The physical as well as the mental strain on the pilots was considerable. The ground personnel and the planes themselves were taxed to the limit . . . Failure to achieve any noticeable success, constantly changing orders betraying lack of purpose and obvious misjudgement of the situation by the Command, and unjustified accusations had a most demoralizing effect on us fighter pilots. . . . We complained of the leadership, the bombers, the Stukas and were dissatisfied with ourselves. We saw one comrade after the other, old and tested brothers in combat, vanish from our ranks. Not a day passed without a place remaining empty at the mess table. The reproaches from higher quarters became unbearable. We had the impression that whatever we did we were bound to be in the wrong. . . . In those days, all the loudspeakers of the "Greater German Reich" from Aachen to Tilsit, from Flensburg to Innsbruck, and from the army stations of most of the occupied countries, blared out the song *Bomben auf En-ge-land*. We pilots could not stand this song from the very start. . . .

ADOLF GALLAND, III/JG26   ♪

The attempt to blind Britain

Like a great deal else about the Battle of Britain, the Luftwaffe's attack on the radar stations was poorly planned, and lacked the weight to be decisive. German Intelligence had failed both to identify all the British stations, and to grasp the significance of the radio-telephone traffic they had been intercepting for weeks, between British controllers and pilots. 'As the British fighters are controlled from the ground by radio-telephone', ran the Luftwaffe's 7 August secret report to operational commands, 'their forces are tied to their respective ground stations and are thereby restricted in mobility, even taking into consideration the probability that the ground stations are partly mobile. Consequently the assembly of strong fighter forces at determined points and at short notice is not to be expected.'

One senior Luftwaffe staff officer opposed attacks on radar stations on the grounds that even if they did provide the British with warning, since the Luftwaffe's purpose was to engage and destroy the greatest possible number of British fighters, the more that could be induced into the air the better.

He was overruled. At 8.40 am on 12 August, sixteen Bf 110s of the élite *Erprobungsgruppe* 210 took off from Calais, detailed for a precision bombing attack on four radar stations. A Bf 109 sweep had already been dispatched to Kent, to draw the defences. When Fighter Command's Filter Room received Rye radar's report of aircraft closing, they nettled the radar operators by giving the plot an 'X' code, meaning that it was of doubtful origin. A few minutes later, Bentley Priory was urgently asking Rye receiver hut what was happening: 'Your X Plot is bombing us', the WAAF telephonist explained primly as a cascade of explosives poured down.

The first section of four Bf 110s attacked Dover, rocking the radar pylons and wrecking some huts. The second strike shook the huts at Dunkirk, Kent. At Rye, every building except the transmitting and receiving block was hit. Eight 500 kg bombs hit the station at Pevensey, cutting off the electricity and putting it off the air.

Now the *Stukagruppen* attacked through the hundred-mile gap torn in the radar screen. They struck the forward fighter airfields at Hawkinge and Lympne without loss. Shortly before noon almost a hundred Ju 88s of KG51, supported by Bf 110s and Bf 109s, launched a fierce attack on Portsmouth docks and shipping in the harbour. Fifteen Ju 88s peeled off to attack Ventnor radar on the Isle of Wight from the landward side. The radar flickered and died.

Far left: A Fighter Command 'Ops room', with the symbols gathering on the plotting table as a raid develops
Left top: A WAAF operator at her radar screen
Left centre: The Receiver Room at a Chain Home low station
Left Bottom: WAAF operators in a Sector Operations Room

The huge dogfight over Portsmouth was still in progress when *Erprobungsgruppe* 210's precision specialists, on their second sortie of the day, hit Manston: 150 bombs hit workshops, hangars and aircraft, enveloping the coastal airfield in smoke. Henceforth, Manston was under almost continual strafing, and was of limited value to Fighter Command. Some officers believed that it should have been evacuated, but Dowding declined to give the order for propaganda reasons. Manston's handful of exceptionally courageous Blenheim night fighter pilots of 600 Squadron worked day after day helping to refuel and rearm fighters that landed there. Most of the ground crews who should have been doing the job were hopelessly shaken by the events of 12 August and after. They went into the shelters and stayed there, defying all pleas to come out.

At the end of this heavy day's fighting, in which the Luftwaffe also launched a succession of lesser raids on coastal towns, Fighter Command had lost twenty-one aircraft against the Luftwaffe's twenty-seven. The original concept of the German attacks had been sound, but the detailed planning and execution lamentable. Of the radar stations, only Ventnor remained off the air, for the next three days. This important opening battle had failed to accomplish any decisive objective for the Luftwaffe.

In the course of the July battles, the Luftwaffe had slowly grasped the importance of Britain's radar network, although they disastrously misunderstood the flexibility of the fighter direction system to which it was linked. They now believed that by hitting the radar chain and some of the British forward airfields at key points, they could punch holes in the defences, opening the way for the major attack to follow.

On 1 August, Hitler's *Führerdirectiv* No 17 authorized Goering to launch a major attack on Britain at his convenience after 5 August. After two postponements, the Luftwaffe's weather forecasters promised that 13 August would give the Air Fleets clear skies for *Adlertag*. On 12 August, élite units of Goering's air force were launched in an attempt to blind Britain on the eve of Eagle Day.

Adlerangriff-

Goering's heralded 'Eagle Attack' was launched in confusion on 13 August, renewed in massive strength by a staff officer's unauthorized decision on 15 August, and thereafter continued in fierce fighting into September. Luftwaffe Intelligence reported absurdly inflated RAF losses and damage to airfields and vital installations, but they could not delude themselves about the alarming losses to Goering's Air Fleets.

Contrary to German belief, Fighter Command could just about tolerate its losses of aircraft by replacement from the factories, but exhaustion and death were taking a critical toll of its experienced pilots. The British commanders'

13 August

On the morning of 13 August, amid a weather forecast of cloud, mist and drizzle Goering personally issued an order postponing *Adlertag*. But this failed to reach *Oberst* Fink's KG 2 headquarters at Arras. Just after 5 am the 50-year-old Fink climbed into his aircraft, and personally led the seventy-four Do 17s of his *Geschwader* onto course for England. The postponement order had also missed his Bf 110 escort which joined the formation over the Channel. When their commander, the one-legged First World War veteran *Oberst* Huth, began to 'jink' his aircraft across the path of the Dorniers, Fink put it down to 'high spirits'. In reality, Huth was trying to convey to Fink that he had received a radio recall. This was not picked up in the Dorniers, because the Signals organization had fitted their radios with the wrong crystals. The formation drove on.

At 7.05 am, they broke cloud at 1,500 feet and bombed the coastal bases at Sheerness and Eastchurch with great accuracy, doing extensive damage. But lacking a Bf 110 escort, they suffered severely at the hands of Fighter Command. Fink returned to Arras in a rage, having lost five Dorniers destroyed and five more badly damaged. Kesselring came from his underground HQ, 'The Holy Mountain', to apologize personally.

But the muddles continued through the morning.

eagle attack

greatest fear was that the Germans would smash the delicate defensive network by their attacks on the Sector Operations Rooms, radar stations and communications links. Some British pilots were becoming increasingly angry that they were again and again in squadron strength against huge forces of enemy aircraft. From now until the end, Dowding and Park had to resist fierce pressure to throw everything they had into the sky against the big attacks. But the essence of their brilliant handling of the struggle was that they saw so clearly that in a battle of attrition, they must be defeated. Fighter Command must achieve its victory simply by continuing to exist.

Left: Luftwaffe bomber crews being briefed. They were lamentably ill-informed about the British defences. Their Intelligence staff entirely misunderstood Dowding's fighter direction system. As the battle developed, the cynicism of German aircrew increased about the dictates of the High Command. There was a sour standing joke of the period about a Luftwaffe pilot closing the English coast and reporting on the intercom: 'Here they come again, the last fifty British fighters.'

Galland wrote: 'In battle we had to rely on our own eyes. The British fighter pilots could depend on the radar eye, which was far more reliable and had a longer range. When we made contact with the enemy our briefings were already three hours old, the British only as many seconds old – the time it took to assess the latest position by means of radar to the transmission of orders to the force in the air.'
Above: Heinkels take off from an airfield in France

13 August continued

A Ju 88 strike turned back on encountering bad weather after crossing the English coast, but one flight engineer baled out at the sight of Spitfires, and was captured wandering through the countryside near Tangmere. Another *Gruppe* of KG 54 was briefed for a feint attack on Portland, then grounded. But no one passed the word to their Bf 110 fighter escort who flew into the arms of two British squadrons and lost an aircraft before they could escape.

As the weather improved, in mid-afternoon new orders were suddenly passed to the Air Fleets. *Adlerangriff* was 'on' after all. There were to be massive attacks on Fighter Command's airfields throughout southern England, spearheaded by the Stuka squadrons.

A few minutes after 5 pm, while a Bf 109 escort engaged the British fighters, *Hauptmann* Brauchitsch, son of the German Army's C-in-C, led his dive-bombers of IV/LG 1 against Detling airfield in Kent. Sixty-seven British airmen were killed in the mess halls, twenty-two aircraft destroyed on the ground and the Operations Block was wrecked. But Luftwaffe Intelligence had blundered again. Detling was not a Fighter Command airfield. Like so many other attacks in the battle, this was a wasted effort against an irrelevant objective.

Meanwhile, other engagements were being fought out all over southern England. Six of nine Stukas on their way to attack Middle Wallop were shot down by Spitfires of 609 Squadron after their Bf 109 escort had turned back, short of fuel. Dowding's controllers were getting the measure of the German Bf 109 'free sweeps', and refusing to be drawn. Whereas on many July days Fighter Command had mounted 600 or more sorties merely in defence of the convoys, on 13 August only 700 sorties were flown against 1,485 by the Luftwaffe.   ▶ *page 135*

Left: Summer 1940. Kent hop-pickers take shelter against the bombers
Far left: The balloons go up
Far left top: A familiar sight that summer: a Heinkel formation photographed from one of the German aircraft

'We had just settled down to the inevitable game of cards in our dispersal hut at Manston (pontoon was the normal relaxation between operations) when the telephone shrilled warningly. How we hated the dispersal telephone; its very note was abnormal and the unexpectedness with which it rang had the immediate effect of producing an awful sick feeling in the pit of one's tummy. A pin could have been heard to drop as, with cards poised and eyes turned expectantly towards the orderly as he reached for the receiver, we strained to hear the message from the now faintly urgent voice which came over the wire.

"Hornet squadron scramble".

. . . Table, cards and money shot into the air as the pilots dived headlong for the door.'
AL DEERE, 54 Squadron, 12 August.

At about 4 pm we were ordered to patrol Weymouth at 15 000 feet. We took off, thirteen machines in all, with the CO leading. After a few minutes I began to hear a German voice talking on the R/T, faintly at first and then growing in volume . . . the German commander talking to his formation as they approached us across the Channel. About a quarter of an hour later we saw a large German formation approaching below us. There were a number of Junkers 87 divebombers escorted by Me 109s above, and also some Me 110s about two miles behind, some sixty machines in all. A Hurricane squadron attacked the Me 110s as soon as they crossed the coast and they never got through to where we were. Meanwhile the bombers with their fighter escort still circling above them passed beneath us. We were up at almost 20,000 feet in the sun and I don't think they ever saw us until the very last moment. The CO gave a terrific "Tally Ho" and led us round in a big semi-circle so that we were now behind them. . . .

At this moment I saw about five Me 109s pass just underneath us. I immediately broke away from the formation, dived on the last Me 109, and gave him a terrific blast of fire at very close range. He burst into flames and spun down many thousands of feet into the clouds below . . . I climbed up through the clouds again to rejoin the fight, but there was nothing to be seen, and so I returned to the aerodrome. All the machines were now coming in to land and everybody's eyes were fixed on the wings. Yes — they were all covered with black streaks from the smoke of the guns — everybody had fired. There was the usual anxious counting: only ten back. Where are the others? they should be back by now. I hope to God everybody's OK. Good enough, here they come! Thank God, everybody's OK! We all stood around in small groups talking excitedly, and exchanging experiences. It is very amusing to observe the exhilaration and excitement which everybody betrays after a successful action like this!
D M CROOK, 609 Squadron, 13 August.

It's a miracle — the miracle of the Marne over again. The pilots were wonderful, but it's a miracle.
SIR HUGH DOWDING to General Pile, 14 August.

The Staffel took off from our new base at Marquise at 15.30. We were flying at 21,000 feet between Ashford and Tonbridge when a single aircraft appeared below, flying at 12,000 feet from east to west. I came very easily down behind him — I think it was a Hurricane on a test flight, because he was quite alone. I still feel very sorry for him, because when I opened fire from about 70 yards range, the aircraft simply exploded into a mass of fragments, with no hope of survival for the pilot.
JOSEF FÖZÖ, II/JG51, 15 August.

Combat with seven Spitfires against five of us in the *Stabschwarm*. I hang at 7,000 metres behind our commander and Eckhardt Roch, and behind us Leibing and März. We were attacked from above and to the left by seven Spitfires.

Dogfight. A 109 reacts by breaking swiftly away. It was Waldi März. I could not warn him by radio because the equipment was not functioning. März landed with 20 hits in his aircraft and a badly overheated engine. I can confirm a victory by Eckhardt Roch . . . From this flight our commander, Hauptmann Ebbighausen, did not return.
Combat report, KARL BORIS, II/JG26, 16 August.

We were surprised to be given the order to scramble from a state of "released", but the reason was all too apparent as we rushed helter-skelter from the Mess to see 30 Ju 87 dive-bombers screaming vertically down on Tangmere. The noise was terrifying as the explosions of the bombs mingled with the din of ack-ack guns which were firing from positions all around us. We could hear the rattle of spent bullets as they fell on the metal-covered nissens where we hurriedly donned our flying kit. Chunks of spent lead fell about us as we jinked out to our aircraft. Our crews, wearing steel helmets, had already started the engines and sped us on our way . . . It was a complete panic take-off with Spitfires darting together from all corners of the field and it was a miracle that no one collided. . . . The air was a kaleidoscope of aeroplanes swooping and diving around us, and for a moment I felt like pulling the blankets over my head and pretending that I wasn't

'The pilots were wonderful, but it's a miracle.'

there! Out of the corner of my eye I caught sight of a Spitfire having a go at another 110 and blowing the canopy clean off it. A Hurricane on fire flashed by and I was momentarily taken aback when the pilot of the aircraft in front of me baled out, until I realised he had come from the 110 I had been firing at. Then it was all over. No one else was about. . .
SANDY JOHNSTONE, 602 Squadron, 16 August.

How much did 'Ultra' help Dowding?

The revelations of the past few years that in World War II Britain was breaking high grade German ciphers have led some people to imagine that Dowding had foreknowledge of all the Luftwaffe's plans. In reality, 'Ultra' decrypts were only of limited value to Fighter Command in 1940. They revealed Goering's full order of battle, for instance, but not the daily strength or serviceability of his squadrons. Thus, between August and October Britain claimed 1,112 German aircraft confirmed destroyed, plus a further 400 'probables', when the real score was only 635. But since Air Intelligence heavily overestimated the Germans' operational serviceability rates, the two errors more or less cancelled each other out.

Early in August, 'Ultra' began to mention a forthcoming 'Eagle Day'. It was clear to Fighter Command that some new development was impending, but they had no hint of what it was to be. Much of the German traffic that would have been most useful to the British went by landline that could not be intercepted. The RAF's 'Y' Service at Cheadle in Cheshire intercepted low-grade W/T signals, and the station at Kingsdown in Kent monitored Luftwaffe R/T (radio-telephone) exchanges. But the RAF's Air Intelligence service was poorly organized in 1940 to make good (and above all, quick) use of what they picked up. In any event, when the situation was moving as rapidly as in the Battle of Britain, with Luftwaffe orders being issued overnight for a battle that was fought and finished by the following lunchtime, it was very difficult to analyse tactical intelligence fast enough for it to be of value to Dowding.

In short, Intelligence gave Fighter Command important clues to the Germans' likely level of activity, but only on isolated occasions: for the 25 August airfield attacks and the 13 September raid on London, for instance, there was direct warning of the Germans' intentions. Radar, the Observer Corps and Dowding's judgment remained the key elements in organizing the defence of Britain.

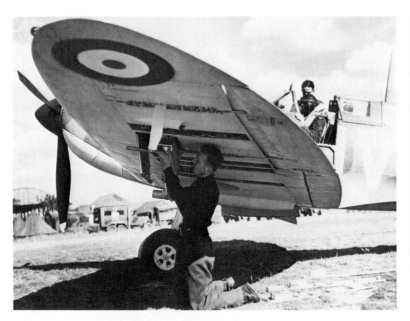

Picture Post, April 2-

13 August continued

The RAF claimed sixty-four victories, and the Luftwaffe eighty-four. In reality, Dowding's men had destroyed thirty-four German aircraft and lost thirteen fighters in the air. Forty-seven aircraft had been destroyed on the ground, but only one was a fighter. By any measure, the day had been an impressive victory for the defenders.

15 August

14 August was a day of slight skirmishes. Dowding seized the opportunity to withdraw his three most battered squadrons to quieter areas. At dawn on the 15th, with another pessimistic weather forecast, Goering decided that there could be no major attack that day, and retreated to Karinhall, where he ordered all his senior officers to join him for a post-mortem on *Adlertag*.

But by mid-morning the weather had cleared. Bruno Lörzer, Goering's World War I crony who now commanded II Fliegerkorps which was scheduled to spearhead the great attack, was away at Karinhall. But all the operational orders had long since been issued. Lörzer's Chief of Staff, *Oberst* Paul Diechmann, looked out at the blue sky and decided to launch the assult on his own initiative.

Having given the order, Diechmann drove to Kesselring's 'Holy Mountain' to watch its progress. Kesselring was away meeting Goering, of course, but his Operations Officer Major Reickoff was appalled when he heard what Diechmann had done. He phoned Karinhall to report to his commander, only to learn that Goering had left orders that his conference was not to be disturbed. Soon after 11 am, the Luftwaffe attack began.

Seventy-two He 111s of the KG 26 – the celebrated Lion *Geschwader* of Air Fleet 5 – opened the assault escorted by twenty-one Bf 110s of ZG 76.

Left: Briefing at a Bf 110 Staffel
Left above: A formation of He 111s
Far left top: An armourer completes checks on a Spitfire's Brownings
Centre top and far left below: Fighter Command Flight Huts: the readiness-room where pilots 'stood by'

Above: A Hurricane as viewed by a He 111
Right: A Spitfire whirls under a He 111's wing.
(There has been discussion as to whether this shot was faked but on balance it would seem to be genuine.)
Left: A London rescue team removes a woman from the ruins of her home

15 August continued

They approached the Scottish coast, hoping to find 13 Group's fighters drawn off to meet a feint from the north by a formation of He 115C floatplanes. But by careless navigation, the raiders' track almost overlapped that of the feint as they closed the British coast. Radar reported a large formation. Lacking 11 Group's experience, the operators estimated 30 'bandits'. 72 Squadron scrambled from Acklington in Northumberland to meet them. The fighters passed 3,000 feet above the huge formation over the North Sea. Their leader flew on eastwards, in order to turn and attack out of the sun. 'Haven't you seen them?', asked one of his pilots over the radio-telephone. The reply was to become famous throughout Fighter Command:

'Of course I've seen the b b b bastards. I'm trying to w w w work out what to do.'

As 72 Squadron peeled off to attack, 13 Group's controller decided to risk everything on a guess that

this was the Luftwaffe's only thrust in the north. He scrambled every squadron from Catterick in Yorkshire to Drem east of Edinburgh to meet the Lion *Geschwader*. He was correct. The hapless Bf 110s, who had left their gunners at home to save weight, formed a defensive circle to protect themselves, but were decimated along with the Heinkels. Fifteen German aircraft were shot down for the loss of one RAF fighter.

Air Fleet 5's other contribution of the day was a raid on Yorkshire by fifty Ju 88s from Aalborg in Denmark. This was met by eighteen fighters from Leigh-Mallory's 12 Group. The commander who would later become the principal exponent of the 'big wing' showed no enthusiasm for mass tactics on this occasion. But his cautious response proved sufficient to destroy seven Ju 88s and fatally damage three more. The raiders destroyed ten Bomber Command Whitleys on the ground at Driffield, but this was a poor return for their severe losses.

While 12 and 13 Groups were fighting off Air Fleet 5, heavily-escorted Stukas fell on Park's Hawkinge airfield, inflicting considerable damage. Most serious, bombs severed power to Dover, Rye and Foreness radar stations, blinding them for most of the day. 54 and 501 Squadrons fought a fierce battle with the Bf 109 escorts.

Throughout the afternoon and evening, the Luftwaffe now mounted a succession of formidable attacks on airfields throughout south and south-east England. The defenders suffered repeated losses from the huge Bf 109 escorts. The damage to the radar network impeded interceptions. The most severe German setback of the afternoon took place when a formation of Bf 110s, attacking Croydon airfield in mistake for Kenley, mislaid their Bf 109 escort. Hurricanes shot down six of the attackers.

It was a disastrous day for the Luftwaffe. They lost seventy-one aircraft destroyed against Fighter Command's twenty-nine. Significantly, only eight Bf 109s were shot down – the fighters continued to outmatch Dowding's men. But the British policy of concentrating on the German bombers (little though this appealed to the more adventurous British pilots) was decisively vindicated. Henceforth in the battle, the Luftwaffe could commit only the proportion of its bomber strength for which fighter cover was available. Air Fleet 5, whose bases were beyond Bf 109 range of Britain, would never again launch a major thrust, and several of its squadrons were transferred to reinforce Sperrle and Kesselring. South-east England became the undisputed cockpit of the battle.

In return for their punishing losses, the Luftwaffe had pressed home their bomber attacks with courage and determination. But failure to pinpoint and concentrate on vital targets ensured that most of the German effort was wasted. In the day, Goering's pilots had flown 1,786 sorties against Fighter Command's 974.

16 August

At his conference on the 15th, Goering made a huge error: he decreed that no further effort should be 'wasted' on attacking British radar stations, 'in view of the fact that not one of those attacked has so far been put out of action'. But among the Luftwaffe's 1,700 sorties on the 16th, a strike by five Stukas put Ventnor radar off the air for a week. Other Ju 87 attacks inflicted major damage on Tangmere, Manston, Harwell, Farnborough and Lee-on-Solent. For the first time, British pilots reported meeting Bf 109s flying close escort on the German bomber formations rather than free-ranging top cover. This was the Luftwaffe's response to desperate pleas from bomber *Geschwader* for better support, and a fatal tactical error.

In the evening, two Ju 88s staged a brilliantly audacious raid on the training airfield at Brize Norton in Oxfordshire, approaching with their wheels down as if they were Blenheims entering the circuit. Their bombs hit hangars jammed with fuelled-up aircraft: forty-six were destroyed and seven damaged. A further eleven Hurricanes at a maintenance unit on the airfield were also destroyed.

The fierceness of the fighting and the casualties were now being matched by growing bitterness among the British on the ground. In a tragic incident in the afternoon, Royal Artillery and Home Guard began firing on two men descending by parachute. They both proved to be Fighter Command pilots. One was killed, and the other – F/Lt James Nicolson of 249 Squadron – narrowly survived his wounds to become Fighter Command's only VC of the war.

18 August

By 12.30, Park's controllers had brought every serviceable aircraft in 11 Group to readiness, to meet what radar reported as the biggest Luftwaffe build-up of the battle. Early in the afternoon the struggle began again. Kenley was badly damaged, and its Sector Operations Room compelled to transfer to a local shop, assisted by herculean efforts from

Post Office engineers relaying vital cable links. 615 Hurricane Squadron lost four aircraft in as many minutes in the air, and six more on the ground during the defence of Kenley. Biggin Hill was slightly damaged, and Poling radar driven off the air for a week. Manston was strafed again.

Dowding's concern was that he had now lost eighty-eight pilots killed and another forty badly wounded in nine days. But the Luftwaffe had their own troubles: in a day of punishing losses, sixteen Stukas had been shot down. It was a crippling demonstration of the dive bomber's vulnerability.

19 August

Each sides' commanders held important meetings. Park told an 11 Group staff conference that henceforward, defence of the Sector Airfields would be the vital priority, and pilots must continue to avoid fighter-to-fighter combat. This was an assertion of priorities which confirms Park's superb judgment, but which increased pressure upon him from those who wanted to see massed forces of British fighters assembled for a showdown with the Luftwaffe – the 'big wing' theorists.

Meanwhile across the Channel, far from demanding more concentration of effort on vital objectives, Goering was telling his Air Fleet commanders to choose their own targets, and urging more attacks on Bomber Command airfields, to inhibit British counter-attacks. The Ju 87 was to be phased out of the battle. Incredibly, there was talk of providing the Bf 110s with Bf 109 escorts – fighters to protect fighters! Goering emphasized that the Bf 109s must fly close escort – further restricting their scope in battle, and exposing his terrible ignorance of the realities of modern air war. Goering believed that Dowding was now reduced to 300 fighters – in reality he had 700.

It was now recognized that the range of the Bf 109 was the key element in the German assault. Air Fleet 3's fighters were ordered to move to fields in the Pas de Calais to extend their range to the utmost limits. Three days of desultory skirmishes followed, while each side regrouped and redeployed.

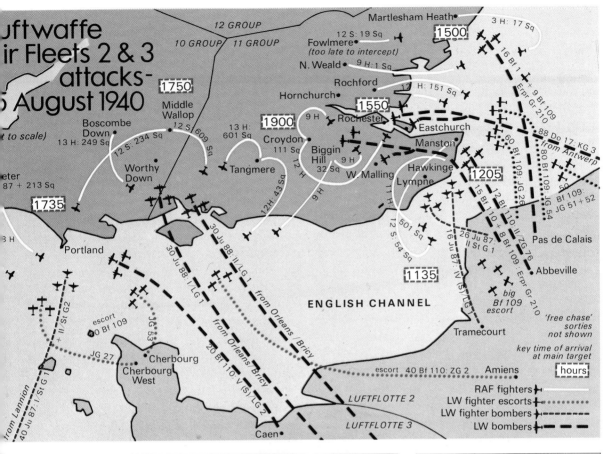

Luftwaffe Air Fleets 2 & 3 attacks— August 1940

(not to scale)

12 GROUP

10 GROUP 11 GROUP

Martlesham Heath•

3 H: 17 Sq

1500

16 Bf 1 + 9 Bf 109. Epr Gr 210

Fowlmere (too late to intercept)

12 S: 19 Sq

N. Weald • 9 H: 1 Sq

Rochford •

1750

Middle Wallop

Hornchurch •

12 H: 151 Sq

1550

88 Do 17. KG 3 from Antwerp

Boscombe Down

13 H: 249 Sq

9 H Rochester

1900

60 Bf 109. JG 26

Exeter

13 H: 87 + 213 Sq

12 S: 234 Sq

609 Sq

Croydon

111 Sq

Eastchurch

Manston

80 Bf 109. JG 54

1735

Worthy Down

Tangmere

12 H

Biggin Hill

32 Sq

9 H

W. Malling

Hawkinge

Lympne

15 Bf 109. JG 26

12 Bf 110 + 8 Bf 109. II/ZG 76

1205

Bf 109. JG 51 + 52

43 Sq

501 Sq

11 H

12 S: 54 Sq

16 Bf 109. Epr Gr 210

Pas de Calais

Portland

26 Ju 87. II St G 1

big Bf 109 escort

Abbeville

1135

16 Ju 87. IV (S)/LG

30 Ju 88. II/LG 1

30 Ju 88. I/LG 1

from Orleans/Bricy

ENGLISH CHANNEL

'free chase' sorties not shown

key time of arrival at main target

escort 40 Bf 109 + II /St G 2

JG 53

JG 27

Cherbourg

Cherbourg West

from Orleans/Bricy

20 Bf 110. V (S) LG 2

Tramecourt

hours

from Lannion

40 Ju 87. I/ V/St G 1

Caen •

escort 40 Bf 110: ZG 2 Amiens

LUFTFLOTTE 2

LUFTFLOTTE 3

RAF fighters

LW fighter escorts

LW fighter bombers

LW bombers

Above: Enigma machine
Left: Hurricane photographed from a He III. August 1940

' I drove over to Tangmere in the evening and found the place in an utter shambles, with wisps of smoke still rising from shattered buildings. Little knots of people were wandering about with dazed looks on their faces, obviously deeply affected by the events of the day. I eventually tracked down the Station Commander standing on the lawn in front of the Officers' Mess with a parrot sitting on his shoulder. Jack was covered with grime and the wretched bird was screeching its imitation of a Stuka at the height of the attack! The once immaculate grass was littered with personal belongings which had been blasted from the wing which had received a direct hit. Shirts, towels, socks, a portable gramophone — a little private world exposed for all to see. . . . Rubble was everywhere and all three hangars had been wrecked. . . .
SANDY JOHNSTONE, 16 August 1940.

I learned within a few seconds the truth of the old warning, "Beware of the Hun in the Sun". I was making pleasant little sweeps from side to side, and peering earnestly into my mirror when, from out of the sun and dead astern, bullets started appearing along my port wing. There is an appalling tendency to sit and watch this happen without taking any action, as though mesmerized by a snake; but I managed to pull myself together and go into a spin, at the same time attempting to call up the Hurricanes and warn them, but I found that my radio had been shot away . . . black smoke began pouring out of the engine and there was an unpleasant smell of escaping glycol. I thought I had better get home while I could; but as the windscreen was soon covered with oil I realized that I couldn't make it . . . I decided that I had better put down in the nearest field before I stalled and spun in. I chose a cornfield and put the machine down on its belly. Fortunately nothing caught fire. . . .   RICHARD HILLARY,
603 Squadron, 17 August 1940.

My Staffel made a curve west of Portland, and crossed the coast between there and Weymouth, in the opposite direction to the bombers. We reached our operational area at 18.25. The bombers passed below us, and we turned to cover them. When we reached the first Ju 88s, a Hurricane squadron appeared, flying in two "vics" with more pairs behind. At once I gave orders to attack, and broke my Staffel into pairs. Immediately after the first attack I saw two Hurricanes go down in flames. We had fought off the first attack. In the meantime some more Hurricanes and Spitfires tried to reach the last Ju 88s. Most of my Staffel were engaged in combat with the Hurricanes. Suddenly I saw a Hurricane diving on the last Ju 88 of the formation. I followed him together with my wingman. The Hurricane opened fire at long range. Simultaneously I fired, also at long range, and the enemy aircraft broke away downwards. While I was attacking my wingman warned me that I was in danger from above and behind. Some seconds later he called that he had been hit. I followed the Hurricane in the dive, and closed to 50 metres. I fired, and the Hurricane went up in flames, the pilot baling out at 500 metres.
HANS KARL MAYER, 1/JG53, 25 August 1940.

This was a photograph that delighted the Ministry of Information — the very image of cockney dauntlessness in the face of Nazi atrocity. Beyond the hugely-inflated British claims, the civilian population were a good deal more upset by German bombing than the newspapers or politicians revealed. Morale held, but by a narrower margin than was generally admitted.

Bomber Command

It is often forgotten that, while Fighter Command was struggling to maintain the defence of Britain in the summer of 1940, the RAF's Bomber Command was attempting to carry out a counter-attack against the Wehrmacht on the continent. In the three months of the Battle of Britain, Bomber Command lost far more aircrew than Fighter Command, and 208 aircraft missing, in addition to many others that crashed inside England.

The RAF had always been deeply wedded to the idea of a bombing offensive along the lines proposed by Douhet and Trenchard. But when the opportunity came, it became clear that senior British airmen had given pathetically little thought to how this was to be carried out. Bomber Command's Whitleys and Hampdens and Wellingtons were bitterly cold and uncomfortable for men asked to fly them for hours across Europe by night. They lacked the kind of sophisticated navigation equipment devised by the Luftwaffe to enable its pilots to bomb in darkness. Crews had never been trained to face the problems of navigating by dead reckoning in a blackout. Given all these handicaps, it is remarkable that during 1940, Bomber Command was able at least to remind the Germans that Britain was still in business.

Thousands of sorties were launched against the German invasion barge concentrations along 'Blackpool front', as pilots called the heavily defended Channel ports. In the summer and autumn of 1940, some twelve per cent of the barges were sunk by British bombing.

The fighter between sorties

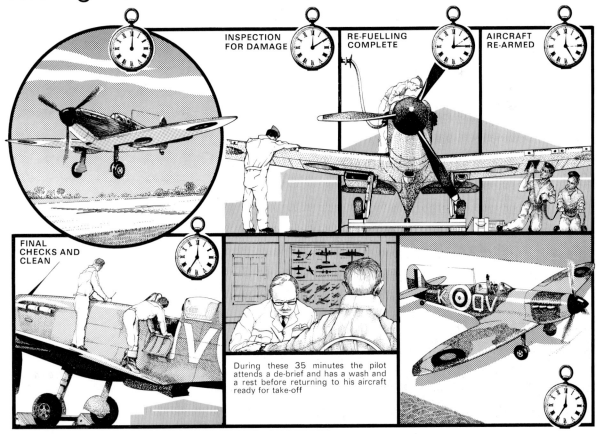

INSPECTION FOR DAMAGE

RE-FUELLING COMPLETE

AIRCRAFT RE-ARMED

FINAL CHECKS AND CLEAN

During these 35 minutes the pilot attends a de-brief and has a wash and a rest before returning to his aircraft ready for take-off

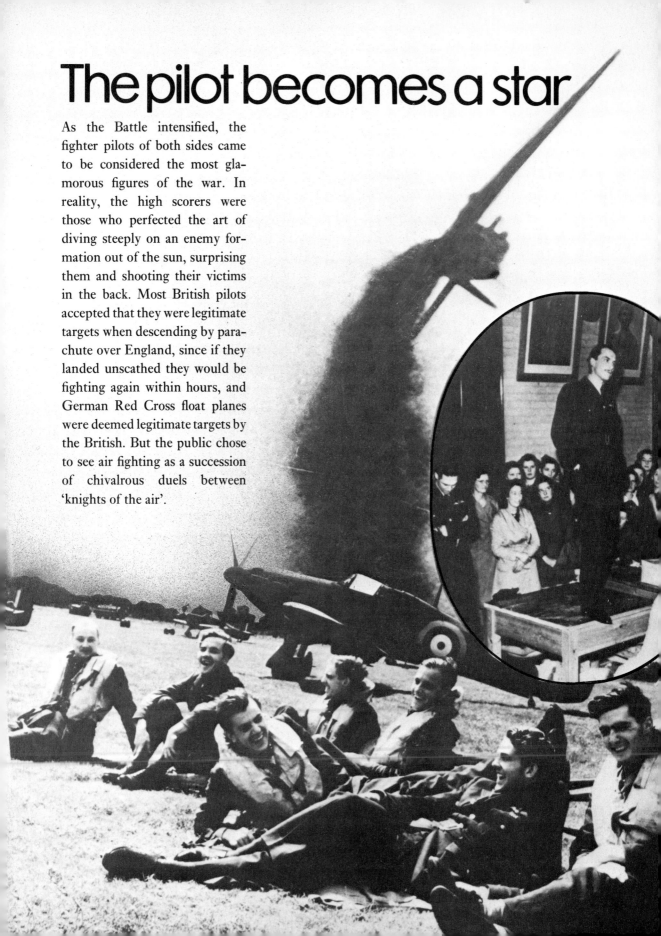

The pilot becomes a star

As the Battle intensified, the fighter pilots of both sides came to be considered the most glamorous figures of the war. In reality, the high scorers were those who perfected the art of diving steeply on an enemy formation out of the sun, surprising them and shooting their victims in the back. Most British pilots accepted that they were legitimate targets when descending by parachute over England, since if they landed unscathed they would be fighting again within hours, and German Red Cross float planes were deemed legitimate targets by the British. But the public chose to see air fighting as a succession of chivalrous duels between 'knights of the air'.

The public image: (far left above) a spiralling Spitfire; (far left below) a cheerful group of unworried British fighter pilots at Hawkinge in the summer of 1940. (Centre) An RAF fighter pilot tells workers at a parachute factory how one of their chutes saved his life after his plane was shot down. Such visits were arranged by the Air Ministry and proved very successful. (Left below) The German aces were also made much of. Aces, such as Galland were frequently photographed being congratulated by Hitler

WE PROPOSE A VOTE OF
OF THE R.A.F. AND OU

BRAIN BEHIND
THE FIGHTERS
Air Chief Marshal Sir Hugh

'YOUNG ADVENTURERS CARD, Aug

R.A.F. WILL DECIDE OUR FATE
Says Captain Liddell Hart

Britannia's R.A.F. Rules the A

88 GERMANS DOW
ALL-BRITAIN RAI

R.A.F.
PATROL—
THE NAZI
DREAD

THEY'LL SOON BE UP AGAIN
Injured R.A.F. Pilots Getting Fit

Daily Sketch

NAZI BOMBER
SHOT DOWN

GOERING'S HEADACHE

'ARE THE HEROES OF HISTORY'

HERO!

Pilot Officer T. C.
Murray, D.F.C.

Flgt.-Lt. J. S. O.
D.F.C.

Sqd. - Leader J.
D.F.C.

Wing-Comdr. J. W.
Gillan, D.F.C.

'HORATIUS OF THE SKIES'
Never was so much owed by so many to so few.
—The Prime Minister

These Are The
Boys Who 'Downed' 15
Raiders In
30 Minutes

"THE VOICE OF THE PEOPLE"
Sunday Pictorial

Sqd.-Leader J. R. A. Peel,
D.F.C. — outstanding
quality as a leader.

Wing - Comdr. J. C.
MacDonald, D.F.C.
for gallantry displayed.

Wing-Comdr. F. V.
Beamish, Distinguished
Service Order.

Flgt.-Lt. J. F. Newman
D.F.C.—gallantry and
devotion to duty.

63 DOWN !

At midnight came the official Air Ministry news
that sixty-three German planes had been shot down
during the day. Twenty-two British machines
were lost, but the pilots of seventeen are safe.
Another great day !

FIGHTERS IN FINE FETTLE

Resting after the scrap and ready to take off again.

ANOTHER victorious day for the R.A.F.

144

The romance of air warfare : the German propaganda magazines made stars of a generation of Luftwaffe fliers as did the popular press in Britain of RAF fliers

RAF airfields under attack

From 24 August to 6 September, the battle entered a new phase, with the Luftwaffe directly seeking to destroy Fighter Command. By dispatching huge forces of aircraft to attack both airfields and important industrial targets, they hoped to force Dowding to commit all his remaining aircraft to a 'meatgrinder' battle which the Germans must win. Meanwhile, by night Luftwaffe bombers attacked a wide range of provincial towns, partly in a further bid to exhaust the defences, and partly in the hope of inflicting crippling damage on British aircraft production. With hindsight, it is apparent that this was the critical phase of the Battle of Britain, because it was now that Fighter Command came closest to destruction.

Above: A hangar destroyed during one of the airfield attacks
Right: The victory board of I/JG 27, a Bf 109 unit *based at Etaples, in Kesselring's* Luftflotte 2. 'Ja' *against an entry indicates a confirmed kill, 'unbest.' a 'probable'*

Abschuß  Tafel
der I. J.G. 27

Lfd.Nr.	Name	Dat.	Flgz-Typ	Abschußort	Anerk.
1.	Uffz. Becher	10.5.40	1 Gl.-Gladiator	Tirlemont	ja
2.	Lt. Axthelm	" " "	1 "	"	"
3.	Oblt. Redlich	11.5.40	1 Fairy-Battle	Tongern	"
4.	" Homuth	" " "	1 Blenheim	Diest	"
5.	Lt. Borchert	12.5.40	1 "	Maastrich	"
6.	Oblt. Homuth	" " "	1 "	Lüttich	"
7.	Lt. v. Weiher	" " "	1 Hurricane	Maastrich	"
8.	Fw. Schröder	" " "	1 Glone	"	"
9.	Oblt. Framm	" " "	1 Blenheim	Maastrich	"
10.	" Framm	" " "	1 "	"	"
11.	Gefr. Kaiser	" " "	1 Hurricane	Tongern	"
12.	Oblt. Framm	" " "	1 "	Maastrich	"
13.	Fw. Sawallisch	" " "	1 Fairy-Battle	"	"
14.	Lt. Zirkenbach	16.5.40	1 Hurricane	Brüssel	unbest.
15.	Lt. Krafftschick	" " "	1 "	"	ja
16.	Fw. Bothfeld	" " "	1 Lysander	"	"
17.	1. Staffel	" " "	1 Hurricane	"	"
18.	2.	" " "	"	"	"
19.	Fw. Kothmann	19.5.40	1 Lysander	La Chapelle	"
20.	Lt. Zirkenbach	" " "	1 Morane	Bayonne	"
21.	Oblt. Homuth	" " "	1 Hurricane	Albert	"
22.	Hptm. Riegel	20.5.40	1 Morane	Laon	unbest.
23.	Lt. Mardaas	23.5.40	1 Spitfire	Calais	"
24.	Oblt. Framm	" " "	1 "	Dünkirchen	ja
25.	Ofw. Ahrens	" " "	1 "	"	"
26.	Lt. Scherer	" " "	1 unbekannt	Boulogne	"
27.	Fw. Kraus	" " "	1 "	"	"
28.	Oblt. Homuth	25.5.40	1 Blenheim	Calais	"
29.	" Axthelm	" " "	1 Wellington	"	"
30.	Lt. Zirkenbach	29.5.40	1 Blenheim	"	"
31.	Oblt. Redlich	" " "	1 Hurricane	Dünkirchen	"
32.	Fw. Kothmann	" " "	1 "	"	"
33.	Oblt. Framm	1.6.40	1 Wellington	"	"
34.	Fw. Sawallisch	" " "	1 "	"	"
35.	Uffz. Sippel	2.6.40	1 Spitfire	"	"
36.	Oblt. Redlich	" " "	1 "	"	unbest.
37.	" Homuth	" " "	1 "	"	ja
38.	" Homuth	" " "	1 "	"	unbest.
39.	" Redlich	5.6.40	1 Morane	Compiègne	ja
40.	Lt. Krafftschick	" " "	1 "	"	"
41.	Lt. Zirkenbach	" " "	1 "	"	"
42.	Lt. Keller	" " "	1 "	Clermont	"
43.	Uffz. Kaiser	" " "	1 "	"	"
44.	Oblt. Homuth	" " "	1 "	Beaurais	"
45.	" Homuth	" " "	1 "	"	"
46.	Lt. Krafftschick	6.6.40	1 "	Clermont	"
47.	Uffz. Kaiser	" " "	1 "	Baye	"
48.	Oblt. Framm	" " "	1 Potez 63	"	unbest.
49.	Lt. Bode	9.6.40	1 Morane	Le Fere-Thier	"
50.	Lt. Krafftschick	" " "	1 Breguet	Soissons	ja

Lfd.Nr.	Name	Dat.	Flgz-Typ	Abschußort	Anerk.
51.	Lt. Zirkenbach	9.6.40	1 Breguet	Soissons	ja
52.	Hptm. Riegel	" " "	1 "		unbest.
53.	" Riegel				"
54.	Oblt. Framm	13.6.40	1 Curtiss	Montmirail	ja
55.	Uffz. Kaiser	" " "	1 "		"
56.	Oblt. Redlich	" " "	1 Battle	Provins	"
57.	Uffz. Neef	" " "	1 "		"
58.	Oblt. Redlich	" " "	1 "	Montmirail	"
59.	Fw. Mitsdörffer	" " "	1 "		"
60.	" Kothmann	" " "	1 "		"
61.	Oblt. Homuth	" " "	1 Bloch 131		"
62.	Fw. Arnold	" " "	1 Fairy-Battle		"
63.	Oblt. Framm	" " "	1 Curtiss	Chateauron	"
64.	" Nebenführ	18.6.40	1 "		"
65.	Lt. Zirkenbach	20.7.40	1 Spitfire	Kanal	"
66.	Oblt. Homuth	" " "	1 "		"
67.	" Homuth	" " "	1 "		"
68.	" Framm	27.7.40	1 "		"
69.	Uffz. Sippel	8.8.40	1 Hurricane	Wight	"
70.	Lt. Zirkenbach	" " "	1 Spitfire		"
71.	Oblt. Krafftschick	" " "	1 Hurricane	Needles	"
72.	Hptm. Neumann	" " "	1 Spitfire		"
73.	Lt. Keller	11.8.40	1 "	Portland	"
74.	Oblt. Homuth	12.8.40	1 "	Wight	"
75.	Fw. Kothmann	1.9.40	1 Curtiss	London	"
76.	Oblt. Homuth	3.9.40	1 Hurricane		"
77.	Uffz. Fuchs	" " "	1 "		"
78.	Lt. Genske	6.9.40	1 Spitfire		unbest.
79.	Oblt. Redlich	7.9.40	1 "		ja
80.	Oblt. Ahrens	9.9.40	1 Hurricane		"
81.	Oblt. Redlich	" " "	1 "		"
82.	Hptm. Neumann	11.9.40	1 "	Dungeness	"
83.	Oblt. Homuth	" " "	1 "	Cherbourg	"
84.	Hptm. Neumann	17.9.40	1 "	Ealrich	"
85.	" Neumann	17.9.40	1 "		"
86.	Uffz. Neef	18.9.40	1 "	London	unbest.
87.	Hptm. Neumann	27.9.40	1 "		ja
88.	Oblt. Redlich	" " "	1 "		"
89.	Fw. Kaiser	" " "	1 Spitfire		"
90.	Lt. Kothmann	" " "	1 "		"
91.	Lt. Kothmann	" " "	1 "		unbest.
92.	Gefr. Wessely	" " "	1 Hurricane		ja
93.	" Wessely	" " "	1 "		unbest.
94.	Oblt. Homuth	30.9.40	1 Spitfire		ja
95.	Lt. Schmidt	" " "	1 "		"
96.	Uffz. Neef	" " "	1 "		"
97.	Lt. Kothmann	5.3.41	1 Hurricane	Malta	"
98.	Uffz. Sippel	19.4.41	1 "	Gazala	"
99.	Oblt. Redlich	" " "	1 "	Tobruk	"
100.	Oblt. Redlich	" " "	1 "		"

24 August

At 8.30 am this Saturday morning, radar reported a major enemy formation. Fighter Command knew that the priceless three day lull was over. Forty Do 17s and Ju 88s with a close escort of sixty-six Bf 109s approached the coast. Only two of the twelve squadrons scrambled to meet them broke through to attack before the Germans turned for home. This had been a feint. Soon after midday, 264 Squadron's Defiants scrambled from Manston to meet a new attack. It was criminal folly to commit them, after the decimation of 141 Squadron a month earlier.

The Defiant crews went to their inevitable fate with great courage: five were shot down.

After renewed bombing, Manston had ceased to function except as a forward refuelling airfield. Hornchurch and North Weald airfields were heavily bombed despite the efforts of the fighter squadrons which broke up the attacking formations. Help requested by Park from 12 Group failed to materialize: Leigh-Mallory's squadrons delayed while they attempted to form up a 'big wing'. Meanwhile further west, Portsmouth naval base was heavily attacked. That night more than a hundred bombers attacked targets around London, causing scattered damage over a wide area.

25 August

Park and Brand refused to be drawn during the morning by German formations cruising over the Channel to provoke the defences. But late in the afternoon, a huge force of more than 300 aircraft approached the South coast, and divided to attack Portland, Weymouth and Warmwell airfield (where a few days earlier the station commander had ordered the cookhouse not to serve meals to fighter pilots at 'unsocial hours'). 17 Squadron's Hurricanes saved Warmwell from worse than minor damage, but all communications cables were severed. F/O Count Manfred Czernin of 17 Squadron shot down three attackers in a head-on attack. Soon after 6 pm, another huge German raid approached Dover, and was with difficulty repulsed by 11 Group's tired pilots. 32 Squadron, now reduced to eight pilots, had to be withdrawn from the battle forty-eight hours later. All of Park's squadrons were now suffering very seriously from exhaustion.

26 August

At first light, German reconnaissance aircraft studied Dowding's airfields closely. From 11 am onwards, 11 Group was fighting a bitter running battle between Canterbury and Maidstone against fifty Ger-

Above: Park's airfields under attack. A German bomb explodes close to the Operations Block.

Left: Another effective German 'action' photograph: a Spitfire going down, smoke streaming from its wing-root; good publicity material for the Luftwaffe

Aircraft destroyed

C Combat	RAF		Luftwaffe	
N–C Non-combat	C	N–C	C	N–C
12 August	20	*1*	27	—
13 August	13	*1*	34	*1*
14 August	4	*3*	19	*2*
15 August	28	*17*	71	—
16 August	22	*6*	44	*2*
17 August	—	*2*	1	—
18 August	35	*8*	60	—
19 August	4	*1*	4	*4*
20 August	2	—	6	*2*
21 August	1	*3*	13	—
22 August	4	*1*	2	*2*
23 August	—	*1*	2	*3*
Totals	133 + *44*		283 + *16*	

man bombers and their eighty-strong escort. 616 Squadron lost five out of twelve aircraft in this action. 264 Defiant Squadron lost a further three, and No. 1 Canadian Squadron, three Hurricanes. But the raiders were turned away from Biggin Hill.

The next raid – forty Do 17s from KG2 and KG3 escorted by 120 Bf 109s and 110s – approached Debden and Hornchurch airfields up the Thames Estuary, causing Park to believe that London was their target. He hastily committed all his available squadrons to stop them. Only three Dorniers finally attacked Debden, inflicting some damage. The remainder turned for home, and suffered heavy casualties now that their Bf 109 escort had been compelled to withdraw by lack of fuel.

A third major attack, on Portsmouth, developed around 4 pm, by fifty He 111s escorted by 107 Bf 109s and 110s. Three fighter squadrons intercepted them, destroying eight German aircraft for the loss of four British. This was Air Fleet 3's last major daylight raid for three weeks.

28 August

Two heavily escorted bomber formations crossed the Kent coast soon after 9 am. Four more of 264 Squadron's unhappy Defiants were lost in this engagement – the last before the aircraft was withdrawn from the daylight battle. Eastchurch airfield was heavily bombed but only slightly damaged. A second raid on Rochford by thirty Dorniers did some damage, and Al Deere, in one of the intercepting Spitfires, was forced to bale out for the third time in the Battle. When Park's fighters scrambled to meet the third raid of the day, it proved to be composed entirely of Bf 109s and 110s – a fighter to fighter battle of exactly the kind the British commanders were anxious to avoid. Fighter Command lost five aircraft for six Bf 109s destroyed. Park sharply reminded his Controllers that they must not be drawn into action against German fighter sweeps.

30 August

After probing attacks in the early morning, the Luftwaffe opened its assault at 10.30 am, with a sweep across Kent by 60 Bf 109s, to which Park did not respond. Soon after 11 am, a huge force of 150 bombers and Bf 110s crossed the Kentish coast.

❝ I saw an Me 110 below me and dived down on him going very fast indeed. Unfortunately I was going too fast and in the heat of the moment I forgot to throttle back, with the result that I came up behind him at terrific speed and overshot him badly. I had a good burst of fire at practically point blank range as he flashed by and then I had to turn away very violently or I should have collided with him. His rear gunner took advantage of my mistake and fired a short burst at me, and put several bullets through my wing, very close to the fuselage and only a few inches from my leg. When I turned round to look for the Hun he had disappeared. Though there was a lot of fighting in progress and machines were turning and diving all over the sky, I had dived down below them all and couldn't do much about it. I returned to base absolutely furious with myself for having missed that Me 110. He was right in front of me, and if only I had not gone at him so wildly I should have had him easily.

Anyway, it taught me to be a little more cool in future. One lives and one learns — if lucky.
D M CROOK, 609 Squadron, 25 August.

Everywhere the strain is beginning to show. I notice people are becoming edgy and short tempered, and one wonders for how long the lads can go on taking it. Yes, things are tough . . . There is little doubt that Hitler is preparing to launch an invasion. . . . Everyone is also keeping a surreptitious eye on the wind direction, for many of us believe it would not be unreasonable to expect poisonous gases to be let off as a prelude to the main strike. . .
SANDY JOHNSTONE, 602 Squadron, 24 August. ❞

30 August continued
They were broken up by 151 and 85 Hurricane Squadrons. Scattered air battles then developed all over south-east England between elements of this raid and Park's squadrons, of whom all were now airborne. S/Ldr Tom Gleave of 253 Squadron achieved the remarkable feat of shooting down four Bf 109s in a matter of seconds. Biggin Hill was slightly damaged by Ju 88s which escaped unnoticed by the 12 Group aircraft supposed to be covering the airfield.

Kesselring now gave Fighter Command no respite. From 1 pm onwards, successive waves of bombers, Bf 109s and 110s crossed the coast at twenty-minute intervals. A lucky hit on the electricity grid knocked out seven key radar stations. 222 Squadron lost eight Spitfires in four combats. Biggin Hill was heavily damaged, thirty-nine personnel killed, and control of its Sector was transferred to Hornchurch. Another group of raiders broke through as far as Luton and attacked the Vauxhall works, killing fifty-three people. 130 aircraft attacked Liverpool during the night.

In the day, Fighter Command flew an unprecedented 1,054 sorties. Some squadrons flew four times, almost all at least twice.

31 August

The Bf 109s had now returned to flying high cover at 25 000 ft, where their performance was far better than that of the Spitfire, slipping and skidding in the thin air, the pilots peering through perspex misted by condensation. A British pilot who lost his formation as he struggled to reach altitude became instantly vulnerable, and this was how many stragglers died.

When Park learnt that the first wave of the day's raiders consisted solely of Bf 109s, he tried to turn back the two squadrons of Hurricanes his Controllers had scrambled to intercept. One unit received the order, but the other – 1 Canadian Squadron – met the 109s and lost three aircraft. Meanwhile, a further thirteen squadrons of fighters had been scrambled to meet 200 raiders approaching up the Thames Estuary. They successfully fought off an attack on Duxford, and intercepted another on Debden in time to prevent critical damage. Croydon was hit, and all the telephone lines at Biggin Hill were

The 'Big Wing' controversy

On 26 August, Park as usual asked 12 Group further north to send squadrons to cover 11 Group's airfields while his own fighters engaged the German raiders. But Debden in Essex was unprotected when the Luftwaffe arrived, and was devastated. Park asked why. Leigh-Mallory replied that he was asked too late.

Prolonged disagreement between the two men now came into the open. Leigh-Mallory, with the formidable support of one of his most celebrated squadron commanders, Douglas Bader, launched a direct attack on Dowding's and Park's handling of the Battle, which reached Churchill's ears through Bader's adjutant, who happened to be an MP. Leigh-Mallory and his pilots shared a resentment that they should be required to play a subordinate role in the struggle, while 11 Group held the front line. In particular, they argued that it was absurd to send penny-packet forces of fighters against the massed formations of the Luftwaffe. Bader had won Leigh-Mallory's support for the concept of scrambling 'big wings', forces of at least three squadrons of fighters, which could meet the attackers on something like equal terms. But these 'big wings' took time to form up in the air, and were often unable to intercept until after the Germans had bombed. This did not matter, argued 12 Group. It was far better to shoot down Germans in substantial numbers on their way home, rather than to snap at their flanks as they approached. Bader also resented tight direction by the ground controllers. The man in the air should make his own tactical decision, he argued.

The rear-gunner of a Heinkel peers out over the barrel of his MG15

All this, of course, was the antithesis of Dowding and Park's tactics in fighting the Battle. They were convinced that they must lose a struggle of attrition, in which each side merely sought to shoot down the maximum number of the other's aircraft. Their central purpose was to break up the German attacks, and prevent the bombers from inflicting decisive damage on their targets.

Henceforth, Leigh-Mallory devoted himself energetically to bringing about the downfall of Dowding and Park. His ideas won increasing support at the Air Ministry and in Downing Street. For the remainder of the Battle, 12 Group's co-operation with and support for 11 Group was unsatisfactory, and contributed materially to the serious damage the Luftwaffe was able to inflict on 11 Group's airfields.

wrecked again. Several radar stations were slightly damaged and put off the air for a few hours. Hornchurch was hit towards evening, and during the night 160 bombers attacked Liverpool and staged nuisance raids around the country. The surviving Defiants were now withdrawn from the daylight battle to retrain as night fighters.

Once again, this had been a bad day for the Luft- waffe, with sixty aircraft shot down or damaged without inflicting vital injury on the defences.

1 September

The drain on Dowding's pilots was now acute: since 1 July, he had lost eleven of his forty-six squadron commanders and thirty-nine of his ninety-seven flight commanders killed and wounded. ▶ *page 159*

Top: A baled-out German pilot is offered a 'nip' by his captors who include the local warden and 'bobby'
Above: George Barclay is debriefed after a sortie
Centre: A civilian victim of the Luftwaffe's arbitrary policy in August. This is the London suburb of Bexleyheath
Right top: Bf 110 Zerstörer in open formation
Right centre: Fighter direction
Right below: Pilots of 249 Squadron at North Weald in September – a photograph that became one of the legendary images of Fighter Command

The aces

There has been endless controversy about who were the top-scoring pilots of the Battle of Britain. Throughout the Battle, for morale reasons, the British did not subject Fighter Command's enormously inflated claims to close scrutiny, or even attempt to collate accurate figures from local reports of crashed German aircraft. It was not that pilots lied about their successes, but simply that an aircraft often went down having been hit by several attackers, each of whom submitted a claim for a kill. The over-estimates of losses were almost always in direct relation to the total number of aircraft engaged. Thus, Leigh-Mallory's 'big wings' were the worst offenders for making inflated claims, in the light of post-war research.

There will never be a definitive list of the top-scorers because of doubts about some kills – even in the light of detailed checks since 1945 – and dispute over some 'shared' claims. Despite this, the men discussed here were beyond doubt the most successful fighter pilots of the Battle.

Francis Mason, who has done exhaustive research on victory claims, suggests in his book *Battle Over Britain* that the 17 British and Allied pilots who achieved 10 or more victories in the Battle were: Frantisek 17, Lock 16 (+1 shared), Lacey 15 (+1 shared), B J G Carbury 15 (+1 shared), R F T Doe 15, C F Gray 14 (+2 shared), P C Hughes 14 (+3 shared), A A McKellar 14 (+1 shared), W Ubanowicz 14, C R Davis 11 (+1 shared), R F Boyd 11 (+1 shared), A McDowall 11, Tuck 10, G C Unwin 10, H C Upton 10, J W Villa 10 (+4 shared), D A P McMullen 10 (+3 shared).

Competition to lead the list of aces – an idea not even officially recognized at this period by the RAF – was fierce within the Luftwaffe. **Werner 'Vati' Mölders** became a successful fighter pilot with the Condor Legion in Spain, then leapt to stardom in first months of the Second World War, collecting twenty-five 'kills' before he was shot down and captured by the French. Released at the Armistice, he soon became the first Luftwaffe pilot to receive the Oak Leaves to the Knight's Cross, for shooting down forty aircraft. On 27 July 1940, Mölders took command of JG 51, becoming the youngest *Kommodore* in the Luftwaffe. A

Aged twenty-eight in 1940, Galland graduated from gliding as a teenager to becoming an instructor for the secret Luftwaffe in the early 1930s. He served in Spain, flying He 51s, but went home to become a ground support specialist before the Condor Legion received the Bf 109s which enabled Mölders to make his big score. In 1940, the competition between Galland and Mölders to be the Luftwaffe's top scorer became one of the Luftwaffe's legends. Following his conviction that the most successful pilots made the best commanders, Goering promoted Galland to *Kommodore* in August. Both Galland and Mölders became regular visitors to Karinhall, but while Goering lavished honours upon them he continued to criticize them bitterly for their failure to do more to protect his bomber squadrons.

Mölders and Galland reached scores of fifty-four and fifty-two 'kills' respective by the end of the Battle of Britain, but they were both overtaken by the brash young prodigy **Helmut Wick**, who achieved fifty-six victories and became *Kommodore* of JG 2 before he was shot down and drowned in the Channel in November. Twenty-five when he died, Wick was a forester's son. A poor scholar as a child, he constantly played truant from school to escape to the woods that he loved. As a teenager, he planned to follow his father as a forester. In 1933, Wick joined the SA, but his father made him leave and finish school. In 1936, he joined the new Luftwaffe, and was taught to fly by Mölders. He scored his first 'kill' in November 1939, and thereafter made meteoric progress through the ranks of the Luftwaffe. He was very popular with his pilots, above all for his indifference to authority. Wick simply loved to fly and to fight.

serious, introverted young man and a practising Catholic, he had to overcome chronic air sickness to fly as a fighter pilot. In Spain, it was Mölders who codified the 'pair' as the vital tactical formation. This idol of the Luftwaffe later became General of Fighters before being killed in an air crash in 1941.

Above: Helmut Wick showing how it should be done
Left: Werner Mölders and Adolf Galland in 1940

Adolf Galland stood second to Mölders in the Luftwaffe's pantheon of fighter pilots, and eventually succeeded him as General of Fighters.

Josef Frantisěk was a Czech regular airman who escaped with an aircraft to Poland after the German occupation of his country, joined the Polish air force and fought the Luftwaffe for three weeks before escaping again to Rumania. There, he broke out of an internment camp and made his way to the Middle East via the Balkans. He persuaded the French to send him to Paris, and fought with the French air force through the battles of May and June 1940, scoring several kills and winning a *Croix de Guerre*. In June he escaped yet again, to England, and after a conversion course to Hurricanes, was posted to 303 (Polish) Squadron of Fighter Command. Frantisěk initially exasperated his colleagues and commanders because he had no interest in air discipline or tactics, but merely pursued Germans with ferocious determination. Then his qualities as a superb fighter pilot were recognized. It was decided to acquiesce in Frantisěk's private war, and let him fly as 'a guest of the squadron'. Before his death in a flying accident a few months later, the Czech pilot achieved seventeen confirmed 'kills', which modern research suggests was the highest Fighter Command score in the Battle of Britain.

James 'Ginger' Lacey was one of the NCO pilots who made up a quarter of Fighter Command's strength in the Battle of Britain. He was a Yorkshire grammar school boy who always wanted to fly, but his parents made him serve a chemist's apprenticeship before he was free to join the part-time RAFVR, and take a civilian job as a flying instructor. In May 1940, he went to France with 501 AAF squadron, and shot down three German aircraft on his first day in action. By the beginning of the Battle of Britain, he was an immensely experienced flyer,

Top: Josef Frantisěk, Above: Bob Stanford-Tuck, Right: 'Ginger' Lacey

although he looked much younger than his twenty-three years. A cool, unemotional man, Lacey survived being shot down several times. He destroyed at least fifteen German aircraft and probably several more during the Battle.

Although **Bob Stanford-Tuck** was not at the very top of the list of Fighter Command aces in the Battle of Britain, he deserves mention as one of the best-known RAF aces of the war. Tuck joined the RAF on a short service commission, and proved such a backward pupil at flying training school that he feared that he would be 'washed out'. But when the war began, he proved to have an outstanding instinct for air fighting, of the kind that marked out all the top aces, much more than mere technical virtuosity. Tuck, aged twenty-four in 1940, fought first with 92 Spitfire Squadron and subsequently with 257 Hurricane Squadron at Debden. He shot down ten aircraft during the battle.

❛ There was only one way to get at the bombers without getting mixed up with the fighter escort. "Stand by for head-on attack and watch out for those little fellows above", I called. Then I brought the squadron round steadily in a wide turn, moving it into echelon as we levelled out about two miles ahead on a collision course. Ease the throttle to reduce the closing speed — which anyway allowed only a few seconds' fire. Get a bead on them right away, hold it, and never mind the streams of tracer darting overhead. Just keep on pressing the button until you think you're going to collide — then stick hard forward. Under the shock of "negative G" your stomach jumps into your mouth, dust and muck fly up from the cockpit floor into your eyes and your head cracks on the roof as you break away below.

PETER TOWNSEND, 85 Squadron, 26 August.

A 109 is just about on my tail; the stick comes back in my tummy, and everything goes away. Now an aileron turn downwards, down. I miss a 110 by inches — down; at 400 mph on the clock. The controls are solid. Nothing seems to be behind me. I wind gently back on the trimming wheel, straighten out and start a steep climb. What seems miles above me the Jerries still whirl. . . . Hell! The Hurricanes have black crosses on them — 109s; coming straight for me, head-on attack. . . . Sights on, I thumb the button. A stream of tracer tears over my head. Blast! missed him. . . . A streak of black comes from his engine, a stream of tracer flashes past my nose. God, I must get out of this. Another aileron turn. . . . Oh God, don't let them get me. I screw round in the cockpit. Nothing is in sight. I scream along just above the water. I glance at the rev counter. I'm so deaf that I'm not at all sure that the motor is going. It looks all right. . . . I'm still alive.

I skim past a tyre, many patches of oil — poor devil! I wonder if all the boys are OK. . . .

IAN GLEED, 87 Squadron, 25 August.

Dearest Ann,

Thank you most awfully for such a grand holiday. It was most refreshing and the ideal 24 hours leave. It did me an immense amount of good to get right into the country and well away from the RAF for a day. I think your little house is delightful and it was very nice to find you all so flourishing. . . . We arrived back at Boscombe Down quite safely, to hear that the next morning (Sunday) we were to move to my present address to defend London. We are having a bit of real "war" now. We have been up four times today and twice had terrific battles with hundreds of Messerschmitts. It is all perfectly amazing, quite unlike anything else, I imagine. One forgets entirely what attitude one's aeroplane is in, in an effort to keep the sights on the enemy. and all this milling around of hundreds of aeroplanes, mostly with black crosses on, goes on at say 20 000 ft with the Thames Estuary and surrounding country as far as Clacton displayed like a map below. We have shot down at least four for certain today and about half a dozen others probably destroyed or damaged. Our casualties — three shot down but all three pilots safe, one being wounded. We are here for a short time, replacing a squadron which needed a rest. I must stop and go to bed, as I am pretty dead beat tonight. I'll come and visit you again when we return to Boscombe Down.

With Love to You all from George.'

GEORGE BARCLAY, 249 Squadron, North Weald, 2 September.

. . . And so August drew to a close with no slackening of pressure in the enemy offensive. Yet the squadron showed no sign of strain, and I personally was content. This was what I had waited for, waited for nearly a year, and I was not disappointed. If I felt anything, it was a sensation of relief. We had little time to think, and each day brought new action. No one thought of the future: sufficient unto the day was the emotion thereof. At night one switched off one's mind like an electric light.

RICHARD HILLARY, 603 Squadron. ❜

New pilots were reaching squadrons with only twenty hours experience of Spitfires and Hurricanes and many were being killed on their first sortie. The authorities were seriously negligent in their failure to use veteran pilots to give combat instruction to the novices before they went into battle. New squadrons, for instance, continued to use the discredited vic formation in action, because no one taught them any better.

The first raid of 1 September developed around 11 am. 120 aircraft attacked Biggin Hill, Eastchurch and Detling. Soon after 1 pm, 120 aircraft crossed the Kent coast. Bf 109s and 110s caught 85 Squadron as they climbed to intercept, and five Spitfires were lost or fatally damaged, four of the pilots being killed or seriously wounded. At 5.30 pm a third big attack, entirely composed of Bf 109s, failed to draw the defences. But under cover of the fighters a handful of Do 17s broke through to Biggin Hill. This time, the bombing caused critical damage, wrecking the Sector Operations Room and all communications. Once again the Post Office engineers began the desperate struggle to repair the cables without which the defences must collapse.

2 September

The Controllers now felt compelled to maintain standing patrols over the Sector Airfields as raids developed, severely reducing the number of fighters available to advance and intercept. Biggin Hill, Kenley and Hornchurch were hit again, and the Brooklands airfield beside the vital Hawker and Vickers factories was hit for the first time. Eastchurch bomb dump blew up wrecking all the airfield's communications' systems.

3 September

The airfield attacks continued, with North Weald very seriously damaged, and the defences hampered by the need to fly standing patrols. Two Blenheims returning to North Weald after a scramble were shot down by Hurricanes who mistook them for Ju 88s. The bombers' Bf 110 escort performed unusually well on this occasion, and shot down several British fighters. It was a poor day for the defenders – sixteen aircraft lost for sixteen German.

Goering held a conference of his Air Fleet commanders at The Hague during the day. Kesselring was as usual most optimistic, accepting the German Intelligence reports that the RAF was down to its last few dozen aircraft. Hugo Sperrle was more sceptical, and in reality accurate: he thought Dowding might have up to a thousand fighters left. It was agreed that as winter approached, it was vital to hasten a decision in the Battle. Hitler had forbidden direct attacks on London, but there was nothing to stop attacks on the London docks, an obvious military target. The British must be attacked at points that they would be compelled to defend at any cost.

4 September

Luftwaffe Operations Staff IA order of 1 September had called for an all-out attack on the British aircraft factories, which Dowding and Park had feared for days. On the 4th, after a morning of attacks on the Kentish airfields, a formation of twenty Bf 110s attempted to slip through the defences and attack the Hawker factory at Brooklands. En route, they were met by nine Hurricanes of 253 Squadron who did terrible damage. In a few minutes, six German aircraft were shot down and one damaged for no British loss. The remaining Bf 110s broke through to Brooklands, but bombed the Vickers works in error. Eighty-eight people were killed and more than six hundred injured, and it was four days before production of Wellingtons could resume. The Short Bros. factory at Rochester, producing Stirling bombers, was slightly damaged by another raid. And once again, the Bf 109s scored heavily against the defenders: nineteen British fighters were shot down for twenty-one German aircraft.

5 September

Twenty-two German formations attacked over a period of eight hours. Fighter Command lost twenty-two aircraft shot down against twenty-one German aircraft destroyed, although ▶ *page 163*

Left : A Heinkel crew prepares for take-off. German bombers were designed to group the crew as close together as possible to give each other practical and psychological support
Top left : A Spitfire goes down. It was vital to bale out as rapidly as possible after being hit, before intolerable G-forces developed in the falling aircraft.
Above : A Dornier 17 and Bf 110s in the air

'31st August was my most successful day. After a long roundabout chase, I was able to shoot down a Hurricane, but noticed soon afterwards that my oil cooler was leaking. I came from far north of London to about 10 km into the Channel from Dover before I pulled the aircraft up to around 250 metres and baled out. My wingman had stayed with me all the time. I had been able to radio my position to base, and within half an hour a Do 18 landed to fish me out of the water. After being taken to the Boulogne Air Sea Rescue Centre where I had a beer glass full of cognac and some pea soup, I was picked up by a vehicle from my Staffel, and got back to the Gruppe about 2 pm. I was flying with them again on the next sortie, and scored two more victories against Hurricanes. . .
HEINZ EBELING, 9/JG26.

We in JG52 were very inexperienced. In two months, our strength fell from thirty-six pilots to four. We really wasted our fighters. We didn't have enough to begin with, and we used them in the wrong way, for direct close escort. We were tied to the bombers, flying slowly — sometimes with flaps down — over England. We couldn't use our altitude advantage nor our superiority in a dive. Of course, the Spitfire had a marvellous rate of turn, and when we were tied to the bombers and had to dogfight them, that turn was very important.'
GUNTHER RALL, 8/JG52.

. . . Two further pilots have come to us straight from a Lysander squadron with no experience whatsoever on fighter aircraft. Apparently demand has now outstripped supply and there are no trained pilots available in the Training Units, which means that we will just have to train them ourselves. However it remains to be seen whether we can spare the hours, as we are already short of aircraft for our own operational needs. It seems a funny way to run a war. . .
SANDY JOHNSTONE, 602 Squadron, 3 Sept

COMBAT REPORT.

Sector Serial No. .... (A)

Serial No. of Order detailing Flight or Squadron to
   Patrol .... (B)

Date .... (C)   31st August 40

Flight, Squadron .... (D) Flight: **A**   Sqdn.: **85**

Number of Enemy Aircraft .... (E)   30 Do 215 100 { ME 109 / 110

Type of Enemy Aircraft .... (F)   2 Do 215 PROBABLE

Time Attack was delivered .... (G)   14. 45

Place Attack was delivered...................... (H)   S.E. edge of LONDON

Height of Enemy .... (J)   16 000'

Enemy Casualties .... (K)   2 Do 215 PROBABLE

Our Casualties .... Aircraft .... (L)   NIL

               Personnel .... (M)   NIL.

GENERAL REPORT .... (R)

E.A. were sighted coming from S.E. As HYDRO Leader
I positioned myself and the Sqdn. between the sun and
the enemy formation of Do's. When in position approx
a thousand feet above the leading formation carried
out a quarter attack from the sun. I opened fire
on one of the leading E.A. formations and saw one
Do. wheel over and go down. I brought my sights
onto another formation on the right of the leading E.A.
and opened fire at approx 200 yards and closed until
I nearly hit him. Piece of metal flew off and one
engine burst into flames. This a/c went down. As I
pulled up a M.E.109 came into my sight and I gave
a quick burst but had to break before I saw the
results. Immediately I broke   Signature   Gaward P/o
away downwards and climbed   O.C. { Section HYDRO LEADER.
                                   Flight 'A
into the sun but found the   Squadron 85 .Squadron No.
the enemy formation had
broken up and turned. From then on, I carried out a
number of attacks on M.E.109s but again could not

stay to see results.

Above: A detail from a painting by Roy Nockolds
Left: A combat report

5 September continued

many more bombers were damaged. Five oil storage tanks at Thames Haven were set on fire.

6 September

The Hawker works at Brooklands was slightly damaged, and Dowding lost twenty-three fighters shot down. He now felt compelled to classify his squadrons into 'A' – all those in 11 Group, plus those in 10 and 12 likely to find themselves in the front line; 'B' – squadrons not in the front line, but fully equipped and manned to fight; and 'C' – all those either too exhausted or too deficient in machines and experience for front-line service. Many of his best squadrons such as Townsend's 85 had now suffered so severely that it was essential for them to be replaced. Having learnt that it was suicidal to intercept from below, many 11 Group units now refused to accept Controllers' orders until they had gained vital height.

Had the Luftwaffe but known it, Fighter Command was close to the end of its tether. But Goering's men, suffering their own terrible losses, were doubly dispirited by disappointment. They were repeatedly assured that victory was imminent, yet the British continued to crowd the sky around them.

⊙

' Our dispersal point, with ground crews' and pilots' rest rooms, was in a row of villas on the airfield's western boundary. Invariably I slept there half-clothed to be on the spot if anything happened. In the small hours of 24 August it did. The shrill scream and the deafening crash of bombs shattered my sleep. In the doorway young Worrall, a new arrival, was yelling something and waving his arms. Normally as frightened as anyone, not even bombs could move me then. I placed my pillow reverently over my head and waited for the rest. Worrall still had the energy to be frightened. I was past caring. It was a bad sign; I was more exhausted than I realized.'

PETER TOWNSEND, 85 Squadron, Croydon.

Aircraft production in Britain

If the senior officers of the Royal Air Force had been left to have their own way before the war, their cherished bomber production plans would have ensured that Fighter Command did not possess the tiny margin of strength by which it survived the Battle of Britain. In the same spirit, if the Air Ministry had been left in charge of aircraft production throughout 1940, it is most unlikely that enough fighters would have been produced to enable Dowding to maintain his defences.

But when Churchill became Prime Minister on 14 May 1940 he established a new Ministry of Aircraft Production. He appointed the newspaper tycoon Lord Beaverbrook to run it. Beaverbrook was a self-willed, ruthless dictator who had been given a peerage in the First World War by Lloyd George, for political services. Over his desk hung a notice: 'Organisation is the enemy of improvisation'. The Air Ministry believed that Beaverbrook's function was to manufacture the aircraft that the air marshals wanted, and they were furious to discover that Beaverbrook's vision was much wider. Scorning the airmen's anxiety to maintain bomber production to pursue their strategic bombing fantasies, he recognized clearly that all that mattered in the summer of 1940 was fighter production for the defence of Britain. With brutal disregard for the Air Ministry's feelings, he set about dramatically increasing fighter production.

Before the war, 'shadow factories' had been created, under the direction of big industrialists such as Lord Nuffield, in readiness to build aircraft when hostilities began. But by the summer of 1940 when Beaverbrook took up his post, the vital Spitfire 'shadow factory' at Castle Bromwich, Birmingham, had yet to produce a single aircraft. Beaverbrook telephoned Vickers-Supermarine, makers of the Spitfire, and told them to take over Castle Bromwich from the Nuffield organization, which had been running it, and to forget about the Air Ministry's orders that Castle Bromwich must also tool-up for Wellington and Halifax bombers.

Beaverbrook also launched the successful Atlantic ferry, flying aircraft from America to Britain to shortcut the lengthy freight delays by sea. During the winter of 1940–41, 160 aircraft flew the Atlantic to enter RAF service, although the Air Ministry had claimed that the scheme was impracticable. Beaverbrook also contracted the American Packard company to build Rolls-Royce Merlin engines under licence, after Henry Ford refused to support the British war effort. Beaverbrook made the Packard deal entirely on his own initiative, and only secured Churchill's approval afterwards.

But Beaverbrook's most vital contribution was in galvanizing the Civilian Repair Organization, created before the war. Sixty-one per cent of all aircraft struck off squadron strength because they could not be repaired on the airfields flew again after being rebuilt by the CRO. These 'new' fighters were a critical reinforcement to the Spitfires and Hurricanes coming from the factories. Beaverbrook also seized control of the Air Ministry's Storage Units, and took direct responsibility for dispatching new aircraft to the Group commanders, as they informed him what replacements were needed.

Like Dowding, Beaverbrook had a son fighting in the Battle of Britain, and each evening he telephoned Park at 11 Group to discover how many new fighters he needed the next day, and Max Aitken at his squadron, to ensure that he had come home safely from the day's fighting. After Park and Dowding, Beaverbrook deserves a large share of the credit for Fighter Command's survival in 1940.

Right: Lord Beaverbrook, the newspaper tycoon, became a brilliant Minister for Aircraft Production Far right: Saucepans to Spitfires: part of the national collection of aluminium utensils being broken up for the smelters and thence to the aircraft factories, Beaverbrook's public relations inspiration

A Planned production under the Harrogate programme of January 1940 (pre-Beaverbrook)
B Actual production of all types of aircraft
C *Planned production of fighters under the Harrogate programme (pre-Beaverbrook)*
D *Actual production of fighters*

	A	B	C	D
February	1,001	719	171	141
March	1,137	860	203	177
April	1,256	1,081	231	256
May	1,244	1,279	261	325
June	1,320	1,591	292	446
July	1,481	1,665	329	496
August	1,310	1,601	282	476

Britain's average monthly fighter production rose from 155 in the first quarter of 1940 to 340, 563 and 420 aircraft in successive quarters. In 1940 as a whole, the German aircraft industry was producing an average of only 156 single-engined fighters a month. Lack of reserves – indeed of any realistic industrial preparation for a long war – would henceforth tell heavily against Germany and her air force.

The attack on London

On Saturday, 7 September, Goering stood on the cliffs at Cap Blanc Nez with Kesselring and Lörzer, watching the great German formations sweep overhead. 'I myself have taken command of the Luftwaffe's battle for Britain', he announced to the German people on the radio. On that day, in response to Bomber Command's attacks on Berlin, the first major air assault on London took place. Although the capital would now suffer months of punishment from the Luftwaffe, Goering had disastrously lost sight of strategic priorities. The diversion of forces against London was one of the greatest blunders of the battle.

Aircraft destroyed

Losses from 24 August to 6 September 1940
inclusive:

	RAF		LUFTWAFFE	
	C	N–C	C	N–C
24 August	24	*I*	30	*4*
25 August	16	*I*	20	*I*
26 August	27	–	34	*3*
27 August	1	*3*	5	–
28 August	17	*I*	26	*3*
29 August	9	–	12	*4*
30 August	20	*5*	24	*2*
31 August	34	–	28	*I*
1 September	15	*I*	5	*3*
2 September	23	*II*	26	*3*
3 September	15	*3*	12	*4*
4 September	18	*2*	21	*I*
5 September	21	*I*	21	*I*
6 September	22	*I*	34	*3*
Totals	262	*30*	298	*33*

⊙

'We got on patrol and drifted up and down the sky. Then suddenly: "Hullo, Ganer leader; Hullo, Ganer leader, bandits on your right, over". And there sure enough was a tiny slanting black line which we knew were bombers. We turned towards them. I turned the gun button to "Fire" and looked to see that the reflector sight was working OK. I opened the hood, and immediately I could see 50 per cent better, although it is 50 per cent colder. I saw that the rapidly closing bombers were surrounded by black dots, which I knew to be Me 109s. So we were in for it this time! Before we knew where we were, we were doing a beam attack on the Dornier 215s. All I remember is trying to avoid hitting anyone else as we attacked, and being conscious of Me 109s coming down to attack us. I had a long burst at one section of Dorniers and as I broke away noticed at least two lagging behind and streaming glycol or white smoke. Those weren't necessarily the ones I had fired at. . . . The odds today have been unbelievable (and we are all really very shaken!). There are bombs and things falling around tonight and a terrific gun barrage. Has a blitz begun? The Wing-Commander's coolness is amazing and he does a lot to keep up our morale — very necessary tonight.
GEORGE BARCLAY 249 Squadron, 7 September 1940.

It was burning all down the river. It was a horrid sight. But I looked down and said: "Thank God for that", because I knew that the Nazis had switched their attack from the fighter stations thinking they were knocked out. They weren't, but they were pretty groggy.
KEITH PARK, AOC 11 Group, 8 September 1940. ♪

Far left: 'Bombing-up' a Stuka Staffel
Left: Ground crew prepare a Heinkel

Aircraft destroyed

Losses from 7 September to 15 September 1940 inclusive:

	RAF		LUFTWAFFE	
	C	N-C	C	N-C
7 September	28	3	38	–
8 September	4	1	13	2
9 September	21	–	25	2
10 September	–	1	4	2
11 September	31	–	22	4
12 September	2	–	3	3
13 September	2	1	6	–
14 September	13	1	7	2
15 September	26	1	56	–
Totals	127	8	174	15

Top: Goering addresses aircrew in France
Below: Map reading from the nose of a Heinkel, showing the aircraft's 'all-round' vision

7 September

Anticipating no special developments this Saturday, Keith Park was away from his own headquarters visiting Bentley Priory. He had just issued a warning to his Controllers about the dangers of adding a few thousand feet of height to their directions to the fighters, to ensure that they intercepted above the raiders. The practice was causing dangerous delay in the time taken by squadrons to reach fighting altitude. Park also re-emphasized the vital importance of avoiding fighter-to-fighter combat.

It was almost 4 pm when the plotters reported a surge of large approaching formations. Almost a thousand German aircraft, one-third of them bombers, closed the English coast as Fighter Command was frantically brought to readiness. To Dowding and Park, it seemed evident that the Luftwaffe was going for the battered Sector Airfields yet again. Eleven squadrons scrambled at 4.17 pm. By 4.30, all twenty-one squadrons around London were in the air or taking off. The sight that they encountered east of Sheppey astounded them: a formation one and a half miles high, covering 800 square miles of sky. It was now apparent that London must be the target. The fighters were vectored urgently towards Thames Haven and Tilbury. The East End and the docks suffered terribly, and bombs fell as far beyond the West End as Kensington. Warehouses crammed with rum, rubber, ammunition, pepper and flour burned, while thousands of firemen from all over southern England – 80 per cent of them unskilled Auxiliaries – struggled to control the huge blazes. From 8.10 pm until 4.30 the following morning, 318 bombers continued the attack in waves along nine miles of Thames waterfront; 448 civilians were killed in London and the suburbs, and many more badly injured. Meanwhile, Fighter Command had lost very heavily in their efforts to counter the huge daylight formations: thirty-one fighters had been destroyed; 249 Squadron lost six Hurricanes in one action against some sixty Bf 109s, without shooting down a German aircraft. The Germans lost thirty-nine aircraft destroyed in the day.

9 September

After a day of desultory raids on the London area on the 8th, further heavy night raids on the capital confirmed that the Luftwaffe had now entirely shifted strategy. Another 412 civilians had been killed – fifty in one block of flats; every railway line southwards from London was blocked. Henceforth, Sperrle's Air Fleet 3 would conduct the night war, while Kesselring's *Luftflotte* 2 attacked by day. The bombers attacked in waves throughout the afternoon of the 9th. One attack was broken up by a massed interception by some seventy of Park's fighters. Once again, however, Leigh-Mallory's squadrons disobeyed orders to cover the 11 Group airfields, and flew south to join the battle. Douglas Bader's Duxford Wing claimed nineteen German aircraft destroyed, although none was subsequently confirmed by German records, for the loss of four Hurricanes. During the night, the City of London was once again badly hit and a further 370 civilians killed. The Luftwaffe lost twenty-seven aircraft destroyed in the day, against twenty-one of Fighter Command.

11 September

Kesselring and Sperrle launched co-ordinated attacks on London throughout the afternoon. The German bombers suffered heavily once their fighter escort had been forced to withdraw as their fuel ran low. Fighter Command's most serious mishap of the day came when No 1 Canadian Squadron and No 41 Spitfire Squadron, brought in to intercept too low, were jumped by Bf 109s, and lost twelve aircraft, six pilots being killed. But the Germans, constantly assured by their commanders that the British were down to their last reserves of aircraft, were appalled to find each formation met by huge forces of up to sixty or seventy British fighters. Fighter Command lost more severely than the Luftwaffe on the 11th, but the Germans were denied the satisfaction of knowing this.

Far right: Hurricanes. These were early production models with the two-bladed airscrew
London under attack:
Right: A classic image of the blitz. This famous photograph shows St Paul's Cathedral amidst smoke from burning London
Below: Another legendary view of London. The City of London is shown ablaze after the heavy Luftwaffe raids of 7 September 1940

‘ The light was poor so I set off towards the French coast hoping that I might find the damaged bomber when, quite unexpectedly, I saw a twin-engined aircraft that, at first, looked like a Hampden. As I got closer it began to look less familiar and then its rear gunner opened fire, so even though it was not the Ju 88 I was looking for, I immediately attacked. It was quite fascinating and made a pretty sight in the gloom watching my tracer sail gracefully towards the German while at the same time his came streaming back at me like a string of gleaming red beads. After my third burst the enemy made a sharp turn to port and the silhouette it presented was that of a 110. I can remember the picture it made so terribly clearly, it was like a picture out of a book on air firing — "at this angle place your sights there and FIRE" — which is precisely what I did and his starboard engine flew to bits . . .
JOHNNY KENT, 303 Squadron, 7 September 1940

. . . All we could see was row upon row of German raiders, all heading for London. I have never seen so many aircraft in the air all at the same time. . . . The escorting fighters saw us at once and came down like a ton of bricks, when the squadron split up and the sky became a seething cauldron of aeroplanes, swooping and swerving in and out of the vapour trails and tracer smoke. A Hurricane on fire spun out of control ahead of me while, above to my right, a 110 flashed across my vision and disappeared into the fog of battle before I could draw a bead on it. Everyone was shouting at once and the earphones became filled with a meaningless cacophony of jumbled noises. Everything became a maelstrom of jumbled impression — a Dornier spinning wildly with part of its port mainplane missing; black streaks of tracer ahead, when I instinctively put my arm up to shield my face; taking a breather when the haze absorbed me for a moment . . .
SANDY JOHNSTONE, 602 Squadron, 7 Sept. 1940.

Luftwaffe's Order of Battle 7 September 1940

Unit	Aircraft	Qty	Airfield
LUFTFLOTTE 2 BRUSSELS			
Field Marshal Kesselring			
Long-range Bombers			
Stab KG 1	He 111	5	Rosières-en-Santerre
I/KG 1	He 111	22	Montdidier
II/KG 1	He 111	23	Montdidier
Stab KG 2	Do 17	6	Saint-Léger
I/KG 2	Do 17	12	Cambrai
II/KG 2	Do 17	20	Saint-Léger
III/KG 2	Do 17	20	Cambrai
Stab KG 3	Do 17	5	Le Culot
I/KG 3	Do 17	25	Le Culot
II/KG 3	Do 17	23	Antwerp/Deurne
III/KG 3	Do 17	19	Saint-Trond
Stab KG 4	He 111	5	Soesterberg
I/KG 4	He 111	16	Soesterberg
II/KG 4	He 111	30	Eindhoven
III/KG 4	Ju 88	14	Amsterdam/Schiphol
Stab KG 26	He 111	3	Gilze-Rijen
I/KG 26	He 111	7	Moerbeke
II/KG 26	He 111	7	Gilze-Rijen
Stab KG 30	Ju 88	1	Brussels
I/KG 30	Ju 88	1	Brussels
II/KG 30	Ju 88	24	Gilze-Rijen
Stab KG 40	Ju 88	1	Bordeaux
Stab KG 53	He 111	3	Lille
I/KG 53	He 111	19	Lille
II/KG 53	He 111	7	Lille
III/KG 53	He 111	4	Lille
Stab KG 76	Do 17	3	Cormeilles-en-Vexin
I/KG 76	Do 17	19	Beauvais/Tille
II/KG 76	Ju 88	21	Creil
III/KG 76	Do 17	17	Cormeilles-en-Vexin
Stab KG 77	Ju 88	1	Laon
I/KG 77	Ju 88	31	Laon
II/KG 77	Ju 88	25	Asch
III/KG 77	Ju 88	19	Laon
KGr 126	He 111	26	
Dive-bombers and Ground-attack Aircraft			
Stab St G 1	Ju 87 and Do 17	5	Saint-Pol
II/St G 1	Ju 87	29	Pas de Calais
Stab St G 2	Ju 87	9	Tramecourt
II/St G 2	Ju 87	22	Saint-Omer
IV/St LG 1	Ju 87	28	Tramecourt
II(Schlacht)	Bf 109	27	Saint-Omer
Single-engined fighters			
Stab JG 1	Bf 109	3	Pas de Calais
Stab JG 3	Bf 109	3	Pas de Calais
I/JG 3	Bf 109	14	Pas de Calais
II/JG 3	Bf 109	21	Pas de Calais
III/JG 3	Bf 109	23	Pas de Calais
Stab JG 26	Bf 109	3	Pas de Calais
I/JG 26	Bf 109	20	Pas de Calais
II/JG 26	Bf 109	28	Northern France
III/JG 26	Bf 109	26	Northern France
Stab JG 27	Bf 109	4	Etaples
I/JG 27	Bf 109	27	Etaples
II/JG 27	Bf 109	33	Montreuil
III/JG 27	Bf 109	27	Sempy
Stab JG 51	Bf 109	4	Saint-Omer
I/JG 51	Bf 109	33	Saint-Omer
II/JG 51	Bf 109	13	Saint-Omer
III/JG 51	Bf 109	31	Pas de Calais
Stab JG 52	Bf 109	1	Laon/Couvron
I/JG 52	Bf 109	17	Laon/Couvron
II/JG 52	Bf 109	23	Pas de Calais
III/JG 52	Bf 109	16	Pas de Calais
Stab JG 54	Bf 109	2	Northern France
I/JG 54	Bf 109	23	South Holland
II/JG 54	Bf 109	27	South Holland
III/JG 54	Bf 109	23	South Holland
I/JG 77	Bf 109	40	Northern France
Twin-engined Fighters			
Stab ZG 2	Bf 110		
I/ZG 2	Bf 110	10	Amiens and Caen
II/ZG 2	Bf 110	10	Guyancourt/Caudran
Stab ZG 26	Bf 110	3	
I/ZG 26	Bf 110	14	Abbeville
II/ZG 26	Bf 110	17	Crécy-en-Ponthieu
III/ZG 26	Bf 110	17	Barley and Arques
V (Z) LG 1	Bf 110	19	Ligescourt
Gruppe 210	Bf 110/109	17	Denain

Long-range Reconnaissance Aircraft

1(F)/22	Do 17 and Bf 110	9	Lille
1(F)/122	Ju 88	3	Holland
2(F)/122	Ju 88 and He 111	9	Brussels/Melsbroek
3(F)/122	Ju 88 and He 111	10	Eindhoven
4(F)/122	Ju 88, He 111 and Bf 110	9	Brussels
5(F)/122	Ju 88 and He 111	11	Haute-Fontaine

Coastal (Reconnaissance and Minelaying)

1/106	He 115	4	Brittany
2/106	Do 18	6	Brittany
3/106	He 115	6	Borkum

LUFTFLOTTE 3, SAINT-CLOUD
Field Marshal Sperrle

Long-range Bombers

Stab LG 1	Ju 88	3	Orléans/Bricy
I/LG 1	Ju 88	13	Orléans/Bricy
II/LG 1	Ju 88	19	Orléans/Bricy
III/LG 1	Ju 88	19	Châteaudun
Stab KG 27	He 111	4	Tours
I/KG 27	He 111	13	Tours
II/KG 27	He 111	15	Dinard and Bourges
III/KG 27	He 111	13	Rennes
I/KG 40	Fw 200	4	Bordeaux
Stab KG/51	Ju 88		Orly
I/KG 51	Ju 88	13	Melun
II/KG 51	Ju 88	17	Orly
III/KG 51	Ju 88	27	Etampes
Stab KG 54	Ju 88		Evreux
I/KG 54	Ju 88	18	Evreux
II/KG 54	Ju 88	14	St André-de-l'Eure
Stab KG 55	He 111	6	Villacoublay
I/KG 55	He 111	20	Dreux
II/KG 55	He 111	22	Chartres
III/KG 55	He 111	20	Villacoublay
KGr 100	He 111	7	Vannes
KGr 606	Do 17	29	Brest and Cherbourg
KGr 806	Ju 88	18	Nantes and Caen

Dive-bombers

Stab St G 3	Do 17 and He 111	6	Brittany
I/St G 3	Ju 87	34	Brittany

Single-engined Fighters

I/JG 53	Bf 109	27	Brittany
Stab JG 2	Bf 109	2	Beaumont-le-Roger
I/JG 2	Bf 109	24	Beaumont-le-Roger
I/JG 2	Bf 109	18	Beaumont-le-Roger
III/JG 2	Bf 109	19	Le Havre

Twin-engined Fighters

Stab ZG 76	Bf 110	2	
II/ZG 76	Bf 110	12	Le Mans
III/ZG 76	Bf 110	8	Laval

Long-range Reconnaissance Aircraft

7(F)/LG	Bf 110	9	
4(F)/14	Bf 110 and Do 17	9	Normandy
3(F)/31	Bf 110 and Do 17	5	St Brieuc
3(F)/121	Ju 88 and He 111	6	North-West France
4(F)/121	Ju 88 and Do 17	5	Normandy
1(F)/123	Ju 88 and Do 17	7	near Paris
2(F)/123	Ju 88 and Do 17	8	near Paris
3(F)/123	Ju 88 and Do 17	9	Buc

LUFTFLOTTE 5, KRISTIANSUND
General Stumpff

Single-engined Fighters

II/JG 77	Bf 109	35	South Norway

Long-range Reconnaissance Aircraft

2(F)/22	Do 17	5	Stavanger
3(F)/22	Do 17	5	Stavanger
1(F)/120	He 111 and Ju 88	2	Stavanger
1(F)/121	He 111	2	Stavanger

Coastal Aircraft

1/506	He 115	6	Stavanger
2/506	He 115	5	Trondheim
3/506	He 115	6	List

15 September

This was the climax of the Battle of Britain, for never again did the Luftwaffe come against Fighter Command in such strength. In the previous week, Dowding's men had been strengthened enormously by the ending of the airfield attacks and a sharp decrease in the number of sorties they were called upon to fly. Kesselring's first big assault of the day was met by a mass of Park's fighters, reinforced by 12 Group's Duxford Wing, as it approached London just before noon. The hundred Dornier Do 17s of the main formation broke up without reaching the capital, and bombed at random across southern England. Two bombs fell on Buckingham Palace.

Goering on the Channel coast: the Reichsmarschall pays a morale-boosting visit

They failed to explode, but were a godsend for the British propaganda machine.

Soon after 2 pm, a second huge formation closed on London. 170 Hurricanes and Spitfires, refuelled and rearmed after the morning battle, intercepted the Luftwaffe. At last, Fighter Command was meeting the raiders in sufficient strength to inflict decisive losses. The German fighter escorts totally failed to protect the bomber formations from destruction. Minor German raids attacked targets in 10 Group's area, south-west England, without doing decisive damage.

Winston Churchill was visiting 11 Group's Operations Room at Uxbridge during the day, and met Park's famous answer to his question about reserves: 'There are none'. In reality, however, the day's fighting beyond doubt went decisively in favour of Fighter Command. Dowding had lost twenty-seven fighters, but had destroyed fifty-six German aircraft.

Goering initially attempted to brush aside the scale of his losses, claiming that the RAF would be eliminated in a matter of days. But time had run out on him. The autumn weather was deteriorating;

Hitler and the army's High Command clearly perceived that the Luftwaffe had failed to destroy Fighter Command in time to carry out an invasion before the weather became impossible. On 17 September, the British intercepted a secret German signal ordering the dismantling of German invasion air transport facilities in Holland. 'Sealion' was indefinitely postponed. While fierce air fighting continued by day until October, and night bombing throughout the winter, Dowding's Fighter Command had essentially achieved its victory, merely by continuing to exist.

' This is the date after which I believe Hitler's chances will rapidly dwindle. The weather holds good in a miraculous manner but there are faint premonitory puffs of wind from the South-West and a chill in the air. Dispatches received through Switzerland say that there are the beginnings of a press campaign in Germany breaking the news to the people that England is to be subdued by blockade and bombing. If this is true, Hitler is on the downgrade. I can't for the life of me puzzle out what the Germans are up to. They have great air power and yet are dissipating it in fruitless and aimless attacks all over England. They must have an exaggerated idea of the damage they are doing and the effects of their raids on public morale. . . . Just as I finish writing this, the heavy guns commence giving tongue and the little Irish maid comes in to turn down the bed. She went over to Victoria to see the plane which crashed there and is very pleased because she saw the dead German crew extracted from the wreckage.

RAYMOND LEE, United States Military Attaché in London, 15 September 1940

Over London my *Schwarm* met a formation of Englishmen, around sixty fighters . . . I made a head-on attack on a Spitfire. The enemy tracer flew past my canopy, but the Englishman went spinning down in flames. Perhaps he had lost his nerve. Now a wild dogfight began. It was

best to break away. Now I had four Spitfires on my tail. I was 18 000 metres, and I pushed the stick forward and dived away at full speed, pulling out at ground level with my wings fluttering. No British fighter could have followed my wild dive. I looked behind me. Damn! There were two Spits on my tail again. There was no time to draw breath. My only chance of escape lay in my flying ability at low level, hedgehopping to the Channel over houses and around trees. It was no use, one of them was always there and I couldn't shake him off. He hung a hundred metres behind me. Then we were over Dover. I thought: "He can't keep this up" as I fled out over the wavetops — but the Spitfire stayed behind. I jinked to right and left as the pilot opened fire and the bullets splashed into the water in front of me. I blinked the sweat out of my eyes. The French coast was now in sight. My fuel was getting low. I kept squinting behind so as not to miss the moment when he broke away. "Wait, my friend", I thought. "You must return soon, and then I will be the hunter". Cap Gris Nez loomed up in front, and I skimmed over it one metre above. Suddenly the Tommy climbed steeply and slowed down. . . . At once I turned my Me 109 and zoomed up in a tight bank, engine howling, straight at him. I fired one burst from close range — I nearly rammed him — and the Spitfire went straight into the sea. He flew fantastically.

WILHELM BALTHASAR, III/JG 3, 23 September 1940

'Sailor' Malan's 'Ten Commandments' for the successful fighter pilot, which later in the war became part of RAF official doctrine:

1 Wait till you see the whites of their eyes before opening fire. Fire short bursts of about one to two seconds and only when your sights are definitely 'on'.

2 When shooting think of nothing else. Brace the whole body with feet firmly on the rudder pedals having **both** hands on the stick. Concentrate on your right sight (*Note rule 3*).

3 Always keep a sharp look-out even when manoeuvring for, and executing an attack, and in particular immediately after a breakaway. Many pilots are shot down during these three phases as a result of becoming too absorbed in their attack. Don't watch your 'flamer' go down except out of the corner of your eye; in fact, 'keep your finger out'.

4 If you have the advantage of height you automatically possess the initiative.

5 Always turn and face the attack. If attacked from a superior height wait until your opponent is well committed to his dive and within about 1,500 yards of you. Then turn suddenly towards him.

6 Make your decision promptly and smartly. It is usually better to act quickly and decisively when attacked or evading, even though your action is not necessarily the best possible.

7 Never fly straight and level for more than 30 seconds at any time whilst in the combat area or at any time when enemy aircraft are likely to be encountered.

8 When diving to attack always leave a proportion of your formation above to act as top guard.

9 Initiative; aggression; air discipline; teamwork; are words that mean something in air fighting.

10 Get in quickly, punch hard, get out smartly.

Top right: The Prime Minister walks among the rubble of Battersea
Top left: The enemy in the sky
Below right: Terror comes to Buckingham Gate, Victoria
Below left: Pilots of 249 Squadron

A Polish pilot gives his after action report to a squadron Intelligence Officer

On the British side, 3,080 aircrew are officially listed as having taken part in the Battle of Britain and 520 of them were killed. More than eighty per cent were British-born. The remainder included Poles, Czechs, Frenchmen, Americans and others as listed below. But the bare figures conceal the full extent of the Allied contribution to Fighter Command. These volunteers, almost all men who had come to Britain at their own expense or after extraordinary escapes and adventures, brought a fierce, sometimes savage determination to the struggle.

The Poles were the most numerous, and also made the greatest contribution. They deeply resented the *canard* that their air force had been wiped out in the first hours of the German invasion in September 1939, for some of them had flown and fought until the bitter end. They were much more highly-trained than most British pilots of the period, although they had no experience of high-performance monoplanes, and they were also remarkable marksmen. In a Fighter Command gunnery contest

early in 1941, three Polish squadrons took the first three places with scores of 808, 432 and 193. The best British squadron came fourth, with 150. This helps to explain how the Poles achieved such remarkable results in the Battle of Britain. Most Polish pilots spoke no fluent English, and were given British squadron and flight commanders to lead them, alongside their own officers. They were not allowed to become fully operational until late August 1940. But thereafter, their scores were phenomenal. In September, 303 Polish Squadron achieved the highest 'kill' rate in Fighter Command. In the Battle as a whole, these wild men of 303 and one other Polish squadron, 302, contributed seven and a half per cent of Fighter Command's entire total of enemy aircraft detroyed. Their squadrons 'swung into the fight with a dash and enthusiasm which is beyond praise', wrote Dowding. 'They were inspired by a burning hatred of the Germans, which made them deadly opponents.' It must be significant that six of the twelve top-scoring Fighter Command 'aces' were non-British.

The following is a breakdown by nationality of the participants in the Battle of Britain:		
		killed
United Kingdom	2,543	418
Polish	147	30
New Zealand	101	14
Canadian	94	20
Czech	87	8
Belgian	29	6
South African	22	9
Australian	22	14
Free French	14	Nil
Irish	10	Nil
United States	7	1
Southern Rhodesian	2	Nil
Jamaican	1	Nil
Palestinian	1	Nil
Totals	3,080	520

Ground defences

Breakfast at an AA gun site in central London

It is often forgotten that in addition to Fighter Command, Britain was defended against the Luftwaffe in 1940 by a huge army of gunners and search-light-operators and barrage-balloon crews who laboured day and night amidst intense discomfort (and often boredom) for very little recognition.

In the first year of the war, the gunners claimed to have shot down 444 German aircraft over Britain. In reality, of course, their score was only a fraction of this total – Dowding's pilots became accustomed to hearing their own claims disallowed and credited to the ground defences 'because we must encourage

the guns'. But, despite the terrible inadequacy of their equipment, the gunners made a very real contribution to the defence of the airfields in August and throughout the battle by forcing the German bombers to fly high and thus bomb less accurately.

Anti-Aircraft Command was a branch of the British Army that was placed loosely under the direction of Dowding at Fighter Command, and given a headquarters in the grounds of Bentley

Priory. This arrangement might have worked very badly but for the fact that General Sir Frederick Pile, the wartime C-in-C of AA Command, was not only an outstanding soldier but a great admirer and friend of Dowding. The two men met every day throughout the battle to co-ordinate the defences, and worked in total harmony until Dowding's sacking.

Pile commanded seven AA divisions – 1,200 heavy and 587 light guns supported by 3,932 searchlights deployed regionally around Britain. They were lamentably equipped. The pre-war designers of British anti-aircraft batteries and sighting gear assumed that enemy aircraft would fly a constant course and speed, and made no provision to deal with the twisting, diving attack of a Luftwaffe bomber under fire.

Sir Frederick Pile

There was an acute shortage of the vital Kerrison predictors that enabled the gunners to aim their shells (which might take forty or fifty seconds to reach an aircraft's altitude) accurately in the enemy's path. There were no proximity fuses to explode shells around a bomber. The Royal Navy – which before the war had told AA Command that its ships would be providing supporting fire for the ground defences – suddenly insisted, in September 1939, that the lion's share of available guns must be sent to cover fleet anchorages. At the beginning of the Battle of Britain, Dowding's headquarters were protected by four guns; the vital Rolls-Royce works at Derby by twenty-two; the Bristol aircraft works by eight; and the Royal Navy's base at Rosyth in Scotland by ninety-six.

Gun crews were sent to man sites for months on end in the most primitive and demoralizing isolation – living in tents that blew down under the blast when their guns fired, without comfort or even basic amenities. Some batteries were posted on forts in the river estuaries, others aboard coastal steamers. In the face of their difficulties, it is remarkable that

throughout the battle Pile's men fought with such devotion.

Most of the heavy 4.5 inch and 3.7 inch guns were deployed around key towns and factories in batteries of four, which were linked to a local Gun Operations Room. The Army's pre-war Director of Artillery had decreed that more than 300 guns should be set in concrete emplacements which made it impossible to move them – to Pile's fury, for throughout the battle, as the Luftwaffe changed tactics, so the guns needed to be moved to cover the latest key targets.

It was during the night blitz that the guns became vital, in the winter of 1940 when the night fighters were almost impotent. 'The defences at night . . . were technically unfit for dealing with any but the bombers of twenty years earlier', wrote Pile. In the early summer, searchlights, operating in groups of three and linked to the local Sector Airfield Operations Room, searched the sky nightly, guided by the primitive (and all but useless) sound locators, and by the early GL2 gun-laying radar sets which were still suffering acute teething troubles as well as being in short supply.

By autumn, however, Pile decided that the searchlights were far more helpful in guiding Luftwaffe crews to vital areas than in spotting bombers for the guns and fighters. Britain was abruptly blacked out. The searchlights were only switched on when a specific enemy aircraft was being tracked. Overnight, the Luftwaffe's navigation difficulties became much more acute – although morale among the searchlight crews slumped.

But the gunners were achieving little more. On 10 September, faced with the desperate pounding of London and the urgent need to show the civil population that the defences could hit back, Pile called all his brigade and battery commanders in the London area to a conference at the TA Drill Hall in

Brompton Road. That night, he told them, every gun around the capital would shoot blind into the night at its maximum rate of fire as soon as the raiders arrived overhead. He said afterwards that he himself had not dignified the policy by calling it a barrage (as did the newspapers next morning), for it was too crude to be any such thing. But it drove the Luftwaffe higher. More important, it did much for the morale of Londoners, at some cost in casualties from shells that failed to explode in the air, and ploughed back to earth to detonate in private homes and gardens. It was 'a policy of despair', said Pile, but it continued for much of the rest of the blitz. In September 1940 alone, the gunners fired 260 000 rounds of heavy AA ammunition, which appalled Churchill when he knew how few German aircraft had suffered from this hail of fire.

The third element in the ground defence system was the network of barrage balloons tethered around vital targets to discourage low-flying bombers. On 31 July 1940, there were 1,466 balloons deployed around Britain, under the command of the RAF, and each manned by twelve men responsible for raising and lowering their huge gasbags as the weather changed – they were particularly vulnerable to thunderstorms. The balloons were a useful deterrent to enemy pilots nervous of hitting their cables, especially at night. Aggressive Bf 109 pilots on their daylight sweeps over Britain often found themselves reduced to shooting down balloons to justify their attacks, when British fighters refused to be drawn to engage them.

From the spring of 1941 onwards, more and more of the work of the ground defences was taken over by women of the ATS and WAAF – there were 312 000 men in AA Command alone, and many of them were urgently needed elsewhere. There was initially intense resistance to women being sent to gun and searchlight sites. One of Pile's senior female officers suggested that 'women might smash valuable equipment in a fit of boredom'. In reality, by the end of the war they were doing much of the vital work on the sites.

It is easy to argue that, in terms of enemy aircraft shot down, the ground defences did not justify the immense resources committed to them. But any pilot who had attacked a target in the face of heavy flak, or approached a Gun-Defended Area at night and watched the searchlights probing the sky for aircraft, would testify to their impact on the determination and accuracy of bombing.

Repairing one of the gasbags: WAAFS at work on a barrage balloon

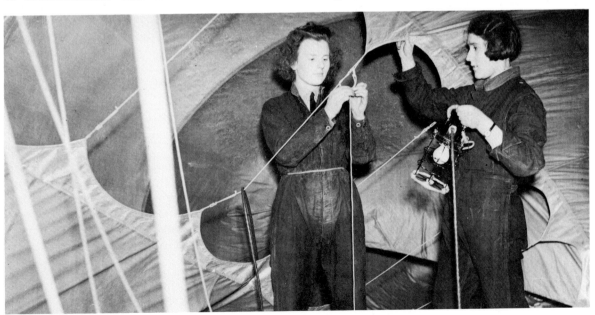

They also served

Fire Watchers

In September 1940, the authorities found that the civil defences were being swamped by the deluge of Luftwaffe incendiary bombs, which represented no critical threat if they were found and doused quickly, but could ignite entire factories and warehouses if they fell unseen. The first Fire Watchers' order merely demanded that all major factories and businesses detail workers to patrol their premises outside working hours for incendiaries. In December, new regulations were introduced, calling on every man working less than sixty hours a week and every woman working less than forty-five hours for forty-eight hours' fire-watching a month. The only equipment provided was a bucket or sand or a stirrup pump. By 1943 the Fire Guard had a paper strength of six million.

Auxiliary Fire Service

Before the blitz began, there was constant friction between Britain's 6,000 professional firemen and the 60 000 volunteers who had signed up for the Auxiliary Fire Service in the last years before war. In the winter of 1939–40, AFS numbers dwindled as its men were called up for the services. But when the bombing of Britain began in earnest, the critical importance of the fire service was recognized. With poor equipment and very little training, the Auxiliaries worked long hours under appalling conditions through the autumn and winter of 1940. When they began to live down an unfortunate early reputation for looting wrecked buildings, they won the respect of even the sceptical professional firemen.

Air Raid Wardens

The Air Raid Warden service was created in 1937, to provide 'leaders and advisers' to supervise air raid shelters, issue gas masks and check black out. By the coming of the blitz, there were ten wardens to every square mile of London, mostly middle-aged or elderly men (although one in six were women). The service was controlled by twelve Regional Commissioners answerable to the Ministry of Home Security, and did much valuable warning and rescue work during the blitz, although the petty tyrannies of wardens who chastised offenders who lit cigarettes in the black outs aroused a lot of public resentment and mockery.

Auxiliary Police Corps

Outside London – which was a complex and special problem – the civil defence organization of local areas usually centred on the police force, and county Chief Constables were often Chief ARP Wardens. The police were trained in anti-gas and ARP measures, and the Women's Auxiliary Police Corps provided full and part-time drivers and telephonists. In country areas, the local bobby often found himself called upon to guard baled-out Luftwaffe men, direct rescues from bombed buildings, or find transport for shot-down British pilots trying to get back to their stations. The police stations of south-east England became clearing houses for all manner of victims and survivors in 1940.

Post Office engineers

Among the unsung heroes of the battle was a handful of Post Office engineers, who worked day and night – often while bombing was still continuing around them – to repair shattered telephone and telex links that were the vital arteries of the air defence system. At Manston on 24 August, the engineers worked for hours beside an unexploded bomb, to reconnect the fighters and Operations Room to Group Headquarters. Elsewhere on Fighter Command's airfields, electricity workers were called on to take the same risks, to restore wrecked power lines.

The WAAF

In 1939, there were only 43 000 women in all three British armed services. But by the summer of 1940, the Women's Auxiliary Air Force was manning radar sets, switchboards, plotting tables and communications throughout Fighter Command, and WAAFs later took over most of the cookhouses, parachute packing, transport driving and even some aircraft maintenance. When the Luftwaffe began its attacks on British airfields late in August 1940, the WAAFs continued to man the vital Operations Rooms, suffering severe casualties during the attacks on the Sector airfields. Perhaps partly because of their rôle in Fighter Command, the WAAF remained the most glamorous and sought-after of the women's services. By the spring of 1941, there were 100 000 girls serving with the RAF.

183

SPITFIRE I OF NO 54 SQUADRON,
PILOT: 'AL' DEERE

MOTOR TRANSPORT
SECTION

PERSONNEL QUARTERS

PARACHUTE-PACKING
HALL

HANGARS

ZIGZAG TRENCHES
FOR PERSONNEL
UNABLE TO REACH
UNDERGROUND
SHELTERS

AIRFIELD DEFENCE
ACK ACK GUN

BF 109E of III/JG 26
'SCHLAGETER' GESCHWADER

SPITFIRE
'SCRAMBLES'

BF 109E

ANTI-BLAST
REVETMENTS

AIRFIELD DEFENCE
ACK ACK GUN

PILOT'S
READY ROOM

'L' INDICATES
3 STAFFEL OF I GRUPPE

'H' STAFFEL INDIVIDUAL
CALL SIGN LETTER

REAR-GUNNER'S FLEXIBLE MOUNTED
7.92 MM MG 17 MACHINE-GUN

STUKAGESCHWADER
CODING T6 – STG2
'IMMELMANN'

PITOT-STATIC
TUBE (MEASURES
AIRCRAFT SPEED)

TRAFFIC
CONTROL
AND RESCUE

DIVE-BRAKE IN
OPEN POSITION

JUNKERS 87B

AUTOMATICALLY
FOLDING BOMB CRUTCH

BOMB CARRIERS EMPTY

WIND-DRIVEN SIREN
ON BOTH
UNDERCARRIAGE LEGS

ANTI-BLAST
REVETMENTS

DIRECT HIT ON
SPITFIRE 'SCRAMBLING'

500 KG (110 LB)
HE BOMB

CAMOUFLAGE
NETTING
IN POSITION

An airfield under German attack

ANTI-BLAST REVETMENTS

The Blitz British cities under attack

It is only with hindsight that it is clear that 15 September was the turning point of the Battle of Britain. German daylight attacks on cities and airfields continued well into October. But Dowding's ability to maintain an effective air defence was never again as seriously threatened. By the end of October, barely a hundred German bombers were still committed to daylight operations, but 1,150 were assigned to night bombing. The British Government was deeply concerned that night bombing could wreck vital factories, especially when it was discovered that the Luftwaffe was bombing 'blind', by radio-guided beam. But it never seemed likely that Britain could be forced to surrender by the collapse of civilian morale – as Trenchard and the other prophets of air power had predicted.

Above: One of Goering's formations on course for Britain
Left: London in the wake of a night attack

18 September

Partly under pressure from the 'Big Wing' enthusiasts at the Air Ministry, and partly because the British tactical position had improved greatly, Park now committed his squadrons at least in pairs whenever possible. Six squadrons including the Biggin Hill and Hornchurch 'pairs' intercepted German Bf 109 high-altitude sweeps during the morning. As usual in fighter to fighter combat, losses were about equal. Later in the day when a handful of Ju 88s under very heavy Bf 109 escort bombed Chatham and Rochester, Park refused to send up his fighters. A later unescorted Ju 88 formation was met by more than a hundred British fighters, and severely mauled. The Duxford Wing claimed thirty bombers destroyed – their real score was four.

24 September

Goering had now issued new orders for his aircraft to concentrate on British aircraft factories. Early in the afternoon, Bf 110s of the crack *Erprobungsgruppe* 210 launched an eight-minute hit-and-run attack on the Woolston Spitfire factory at Southampton. The factory itself escaped serious damage, but ninety-eight senior employees were killed. Park's fighters turned back other small bomber raids before they reached London. Once the Luftwaffe had been deflected, the controllers ordered the British aircraft back to their airfields rather than suffer unnecessary losses in pursuit.

25 September

German reconnaissance had revealed thin defences around Bristol. At 11 am, under cover of diversionary raids on Plymouth, Falmouth, Swanage and Southampton, 58 He 111s hit the Bristol aircraft factory at Filton, causing heavy damage that temporarily halted production, and inflicted more than three hundred civilian casualties. Five bombers were shot down on their way home.

Legendary fighter pilots

Herbert Ihlefeld was one of the Luftwaffe's old stagers, a veteran of Spain where he achieved seven victories. Aged twenty-seven, in August 1940 he took over I/LG2, and on 13 September received the *Ritterkreuz* for his twenty-one victories. Later, in Russia, he became the fifth German fighter pilot to score a hundred. He had flown more than a thousand combat sorties by the end of the war, yet survived to enjoy a peaceful retirement.

Joachim Müncheberg was twenty-one in 1940, a *Leutnant* in III/JG26 who had opened his score within weeks of the beginning of the war by shooting down an RAF reconnaissance Blenheim. In August, he was promoted to *Staffelkapitän* of 7/JG26, and received the *Ritterkreuz* for his twentieth victory on 14 September. He was later transferred to the Mediterranean, where he claimed nineteen British fighters destroyed during the attacks on Malta. He had scored 103 kills by the time of his death in March 1943, when he collided with an American Spitfire in action in North Africa.

Walter 'Gulle' Oesau was one of the old Condor Legion *Experten*, who had scored eight victories in Spain. In 1940 he was *Staffelkapitän* of 7/JG51 on the Channel Front. He gained one of his first successes shooting down a 111 Squadron Hurricane on 10 July, but his victory was somewhat diminished by the falling British fighter hitting a Dornier 17, which fell into the Channel beside it. Oesau got his

Ritterkreuz for the twentieth victory on 20 August and was promoted to *Hauptmann*. He took command of III/JG51, and led it until November 1940. His tally stood at 123 victories when he was killed in action in May 1944.

Hans-Joachim Marseille became a Luftwaffe legend, with 158

credited victories by the time of his death in 1942. Marseille was born in 1920. He joined I/LG2 on the Channel Front as an officer cadet, and quickly established a reputation as a formidable fighter pilot. He achieved his first 'kill' on his third sortie, and thereafter his score mounted rapidly – many of his successes came in North Africa,

gunner; a dead navigator, and the pilot coughing up his lungs as he lands . . . I think if you do that it has a better effect on their morale. . .'.

Douglas Bader began the war as a frustrated civilian ex-pilot. In 1931, a few months after graduating from Cranwell, he had crashed while doing low-level aerobatics. By a miracle, he survived, but had both legs amputated, and was retired from the RAF. In November 1939, after a bitter struggle against service bureaucracy, Bader was allowed to serve in Fighter Command. He rapidly proved that he could fly better with tin legs than most men with real, and in June 1940 took command of 242 Squadron in Leigh-Mallory's 12 Group. Bader possessed the fiercely combative spirit that characterized all the finest fighter pilots. He scored his first 'kill' on 11 July. A forceful exponent of the 'big wing' theories with which Leigh-Mallory belaboured Dowding, Bader took command of the Duxford Wing in August, becoming one of the most celebrated – and controversial – officers in Fighter Command.

Peter Townsend was an army officer's son who went to Cranwell in 1933, on leaving public school. He shot down two German aircraft during the early spring of 1940. On 1 July he took command of 85 Hurricane squadron, which he led with distinction until he was shot down and wounded on 31 August, having survived a ditching in the North Sea on 11 July. The handsome, elegant Townsend symbolized the upper-class glamour of one section of Fighter Command that delighted the press. He was also a superb pilot, being credited with six 'kills' in July and August.

where he was posted in the spring of 1941, and remained until his death, attempting to 'bale out' of his crippled Bf 109 after an air battle.

'Sailor' Malan ended the war as one of the top-scoring Allied aces. A South African, his amiable smile concealed a passionate hatred for the Germans. By May 1940, Malan

was a flight commander in 74 Squadron, and became CO on 8 August. At thirty, he was older than most pilots but he became regarded as one of the greatest fighter leaders and tacticians of the war. Malan claimed to believe it was better to send a German plane home crippled than to shoot it down: '. . . with a dead rear

27 September

As the night attacks continued to batter towns in the south and Midlands, Kesselring launched strong daylight raids that made the 27th one of the most bitterly contested days of the Battle. The Luftwaffe opened its attack with a series of fast Bf 110 strikes south of London, to draw and exhaust the defences. The 110s suffered heavily. Fifty-five Ju 88s followed, meeting with disaster. They were late for their rendezvous with the Bf 109 escort, and met the British fighters without protection. Bf 109s and 110s arrived belatedly to support them and both sides suffered high losses. Sperrle meanwhile rashly attempted to repeat the successful attack on Filton. 10 Group's fighters were waiting, and damaged the raiders severely. *Erprobungsgruppe* 210 lost four aircraft, including that of its brilliant commander, Martin Lutz.

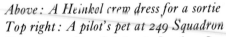

Above: A Heinkel crew dress for a sortie
Top right: A pilot's pet at 249 Squadron
Top centre: Fire-fighting in London, September 1940
Top left: Aircrew of a Ju 88 Staffel addressed by their commander
Below right: Last moments of a Luftwaffe crew over England

' Our two Spitfires hummed easily along the air paths . . . The world of last night seemed a long way off, and I wondered how, by contrast to this ecstatic feeling I had now, I could ever have descended to the general debauchery which characterized last night's behaviour. I wondered what the alternatives were. Were we to sit in our rooms and read a book, or sit in the mess and do a crossword puzzle or read all about the war, or write letters to our loved ones in case we got no further opportunity, or should we go to the cinema? I didn't think any of these activities would really be adequate as a sequel to the day. It would be physically possible to sit down by oneself in one's room and read a book after fighting Germans at a great height and at great speed at intervals during the day — but it would be unnatural. It was no longer a mystery to me why fighter pilots had earned such a reputation for being somewhat eccentric when they were on the ground. I knew why it was, and I knew that if I were alive this evening I should get drunk with the others and go wherever they went.
ROGER HALL, 152 Squadron, September 1940 ♪

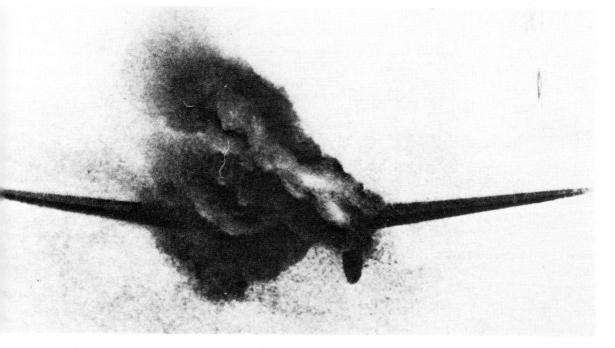

Night fighter

' The night was beautiful. Below us the isolated pieces of cumulus had gathered themselves together into a large bank of cloud which was itself being piled upon by more broken pieces coming in from the sea. The whole of it was lit up with a wonderful iridescence by the moon above us, and when I could afford to take my eyes off the sky in front, I could see the shadow of our machine flit quickly and silently across the backcloth of cloud like some ghostly bird. We had been orbiting for almost half an hour without seeing a thing when quite suddenly I caught sight, from the corner of my eye of a Heinkel III gliding silently and apparently furtively towards the coast beneath us. In a fever of excitement I switched on the intercom and shouted to Fitz "There it is Fitz – below us – see it?" I called up Carmen and gave them the tally-ho and they acknowledged my message and wished us the best of luck. The Heinkel was apparently unaware of our existence as we approached it from above. Our aircraft shud-dered slightly as Fitz opened up on the bomber with the four turret guns pointing directly backwards and firing up at the bomber's cockpit from a range of little more than twenty yards. I could see our bullets hitting the bomber's centre section from underneath, and the shots were like small dancing sparks creeping upwards to the cockpit of the enemy machine. For what seemed an age Fitz continued to pour his shots into the front part of the Heinkel without anything to happen. Then suddenly but quite slowly the huge aircraft started to roll up on its starboard wingtip, like a fighter in slow motion. I was pondering this scene in a detached sort of way when without warning the whole vault of the night sky burst into light. There was a gargantuan explosion and the very firmament seemed to reverberate around us as the bomber disappeared. . . . The stars in their courses became dull red in the heavens and the cumulus beneath became a vivid white. . . . Ours had been the first machine shot down in the squadron's short history. ROGER HALL, 264 Defiant Squadron, 15 August 1940 ◗

Throughout the war, the principal defence against the night bomber was the radar-equipped night fighter. In the summer and autumn of 1940, Fighter Command possessed a handful of Blenheim night fighters with experimental Air Interception radar. But the sets were so unreliable that the crews achieved few successes. By autumn, the first of the Beaufighters – a much more successful development of the Blenheim – were coming into service, but interceptions were still very erratic. In November and December 1940, for instance, in 606 sorties by radar-equipped British fighters, only seventy-one radar contacts were obtained, and only four German aircraft destroyed.

The backbone of the British night fighter effort through the winter of the blitz were six squadrons of Hurricanes and Defiants, whose only real modifi-cation for their task was that they were painted black. In 491 sorties on forty-six nights, they shot down eleven German aircraft, located with general guidance from the ground controllers in the Sector Operations Rooms, and by direct observation in the light of fires or searchlights. In all, up to the end of 1940 the night blitz cost the Luftwaffe only fifty-four aircraft destroyed and twelve more lost in accidents over Britain – a mere one per cent of sorties dispatched, far less than Bomber Command was losing over Germany.

Above far right: A night fighter pilot
Above right: A Hurricane night-fighter pilot signals 'Chocks away'
Below right: Pilots of 600 Squadron (Blenheim night fighters) on stand-by, August 1940

LONDON BURNS

HAWKER HURRICANE
NIGHT-FIGHTER WITHOUT RADAR

LONDON

RAF FIGHTER STATION
BIGGIN HILL *SECTOR AIRFIELD*

RAF FIGHTER STA
HORNCHURCH *SECTOR*

SEARCH LIGHTS

RAF FIGHTER STATION LYMPNE
KENT
SATELLITE AIRFIELD

RAF STATION
HAWKINGE, KEN
SATELLITE AIRFIEL

(CH) RADAR
(HIGH-LEVEL) RYE,
SUSSEX

KNICKEBEIN
RADIO BEAM
(DOTS AND DASHES

FOLKESTO

DUNGENESS

KNICKEBEIN BEAM STATION

HEINKEL HE III
BOMBER

FRANCE

SECTOR AIRFIELD OPERATIONS ROOM

BRISTOL BLENHEIM
NIGHT FIGHTER
WITH RADAR

PATROLLING HAWKER
HURRICANE WITHOUT RADAR

(CH) RADAR
(HIGH-LEVEL)
DUNKIRK, KENT

SECOND BEAM INTERSECTING
KNICKEBEIN AT TARGET TO TELL
BOMB AIMER TO RELEASE BOMBS

DOVER, KENT
CHL
LOW LEVEL STATION

ENGLISH CHANNEL

he RAF's night-time response
o a Luftwaffe attack on south-east England

Bombing Britain 'blind'

In the summer of 1940, a brilliant young British scientist named R V Jones rocked the British defence establishment. Jones, working for the Scientific Intelligence section of MI5, said that after studying German night bomber operations, he had become convinced that the Luftwaffe was using some sort of radio beam guidance to enable them to bomb targets in Britain 'blind'. It was a deeply alarming prospect for the War Cabinet. If the Germans had an effective beam system, they could devastate Britain's vital factories at will, and with the poor state of night defence, there was nothing effective Fighter Command could do to stop them. A specially equipped RAF Anson took off into the night air over England to investigate Jones's inspired guess. The crew found a mysterious beam about 450 yards wide, with all the characteristics of the Lorenz blind-landing system's beam. After close investigation of crashed German aircraft and interrogation of captured aircrew, Jones was able to report to the Prime Minister that the Germans were using a beam codenamed *Knickebein* – literally, 'crooked leg'. A German pilot listened for a continuous signal from the *Knickebein* transmitter in France to tell him that he was on course. If he veered left, the signal broke into morse dots; right, and he heard morse dashes. A second beam intersected at the target, and told the bomb-aimer when to release his load.

Having identified the beams, it became possible to counter them. Hospital electro-diathermy sets and old Lorenz equipment were pressed into service to jam the transmissions, under the control of a specially created new RAF unit, No 80 Wing. By September, *Knickebein* had been thwarted.

A more sophisticated German development was already in service, however. The *X-Gerät* beam system was accurate to 120 yards. The Luftwaffe's *Kampfgruppe* 100 was a crack 'Pathfinder Force' specially trained to use *X-Gerät*. They did so with devastating effect against several British cities – and in a precision attack on the Spitfire factory at Castle Bromwich on Eagle Day. Pilots flew through a series of intersecting beams which alerted them as they closed the target. On passing the third beam, the bomb aimer punched a clockwork timing device, which released the bombs on the target. Fortunately for the British, Scientific Intelligence identified *X-Gerät* and enabled jamming measures to be adopted before British industry suffered catastrophe. But even without beams, the Luftwaffe managed to do an impressive amount of damage. Because so much of Britain is close to coastlines, it was incomparably easier for the Germans to navigate to British targets by dead reckoning than for Bomber Command's crews to find cities far inside Germany.

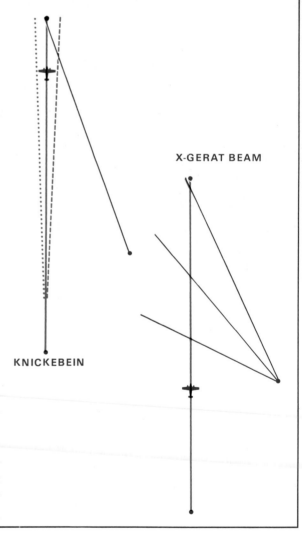

X-GERAT BEAM

KNICKEBEIN

The Old Bailey after a raid

Forty Heinkels escorted by Bf 110s struck towards the Westland aircraft factory at Yeovil, but were driven back by 10 Group's fighters.

7 October

A constant procession of Bf 109 sweeps over Kent were met in strength. P/O MacKenzie of 501 Squadron smashed the tail of one German fighter with his wing, having run out of ammunition. The 109 fell in the sea, and MacKenzie lived to tell the tale. Twenty-five Ju 88s escorted by fifty Bf 110s once again attempted to hit the Westland plant. They lost heavily without inflicting much damage, although a direct hit on one air raid shelter caused 98 casualties.

15 October

The Luftwaffe was at least successful in forcing Fighter Command into the air to meet almost every raid now, for the blitz on London was causing great concern. Many attacks were turned back, but those that got through could scarcely fail to do serious damage. A morning 'strike' by Bf 109s wrecked the approach to Waterloo station and temporarily closed the lines. South Bank factories were badly hit, and in another raid later in the morning, more than fifty civilians died. During the evening, the Luftwaffe launched another huge raid, wrecking parts of the docks, Paddington, Victoria, Waterloo and Liverpool Street stations. The city was yet again badly hit; 512 people were killed in London and the suburbs, 11 000 made homeless. Another German force attacked Birmingham later in the night.

30 September

Two waves of two hundred German aircraft approached London soon after 9 am, to be met by twelve squadrons of British fighters. Most of the raiders were turned back over Kent. An hour later, a Bf 109 sweep at extreme range over Weymouth retreated after a brief engagement. During the afternoon, a hundred bombers escorted by two hundred fighters attempted to reach London. One *Gruppe* of Ju 88s broke through to the southern suburbs with their Bf 109 escort, but lost heavily.

27 October

For anyone who supposes that the Battle of Britain ebbed away in September, giving Dowding's pilots a rest, it is worth noticing that on this not untypical October Sunday, Fighter Command flew 1,007 sorties (more than on 15 August) in efforts to meet the German hit-and-run raids, mostly against airfields in eastern England. The British lost ten aircraft to shoot down 11 Luftwaffe attackers. The squadrons based in south-east England continued to be called upon to fly under intense pressure well into the winter.

' Even if the German figures of enemy aircraft destroyed were perhaps over-estimated, the fact that their fighter strength obviously did not diminish could only be accounted for in this way: England, by a great concentration of energy, was making up her losses in the peaceful nine-tenths of her territory.
ADOLF GALLAND, III/JG 26, 27 September 1940

I may be wrong, but things seem to be easing off a bit these days . . . we only spot 109s cruising around at heights well above 30 000 feet. These occasionally make furtive darts at us before soaring up again to their superior position, where they seem content to sit in a kind of haughty dignity. We gather the boys at Biggin Hill are finding the same things . . . this sense of relaxation even seems to be permeating into the lives of the local civilians . . . Could it be that the Germans have had enough?
    SANDY JOHNSTONE, 602 Squadron, 2 Oct 1940

I suppose it sounds as if we are having a grand time — well I suppose we are really — I'm realizing an ambition, but it's a bit tough to see fellows wiped off one by one. There are only four officers in the squadron, myself included, who have come through September entirely unscathed, and of the five officers, myself again included, who were at Cranwell together, I am the only survivor. But it's remarkable how hardened one gets to people not coming back. Normally this warfare is thrilling, and a successful scrap puts me on top of the world — but I won't deny it has its frightening moments, though having survived the frightening moments is also very exhilarating! About knitting for the winter — I would very much like a pair of thick woollen socks — longer than socks are usually, but shorter than stockings! It's getting infernally cold at 25 000 feet! . . . Must stop and go to bed — we come to readiness at 6.05 am!
    GEORGE BARCLAY, letter to his sister, Oct 1940

Top: Stripping the engine covers off a Heinkel
Below: Kesselring (right) visits one of his Heinkel units
Top right: 'Stand-by' at a Fighter Command Station

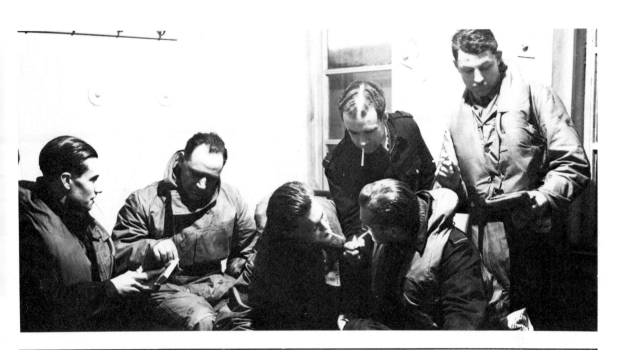

Aircraft destroyed

Losses from 16 September to 31 October 1940

	RAF		LUFTWAFFE	
	C	N–C	C	N–C
16 September	2	2	9	–
17 September	6	2	8	–
18 September	11	–	18	1
19 September	–	–	8	–
20 September	7	1	3	–
21 September	–	–	9	1
22 September	–	–	2	2
23 September	10	–	13	3
24 September	7	4	7	–
25 September	3	2	13	2
26 September	7	–	8	2
27 September	28	–	49	1
28 September	15	2	8	2
29 September	5	1	8	–
30 September	15	3	41	1
1 October	6	–	6	6
2 October	3	–	14	3
3 October	–	1	8	–
4 October	1	–	9	1
5 October	7	–	14	1
6 October	–	3	6	1
7 October	13	2	19	1
8 October	2	3	10	1
9 October	3	2	11	–
10 October	5	3	2	5
11 October	9	2	5	2
12 October	9	3	5	–
13 October	3	–	2	–
14 October	1	–	2	1
15 October	15	4	12	–
16 October	1	1	10	–
17 October	5	2	9	3
18 October	–	6	11	1
19 October	–	1	1	2
20 October	4	–	9	1
21 October	–	3	5	1
22 October	5	–	9	2
23 October	1	–	3	1
24 October	–	4	2	5
25 October	10	9	19	2
26 October	5	4	9	–
27 October	9	1	11	1
28 October	–	1	8	2
29 October	6	4	18	6
30 October	7	–	8	–
31 October	–	1	2	–
Totals	246	77	463	64

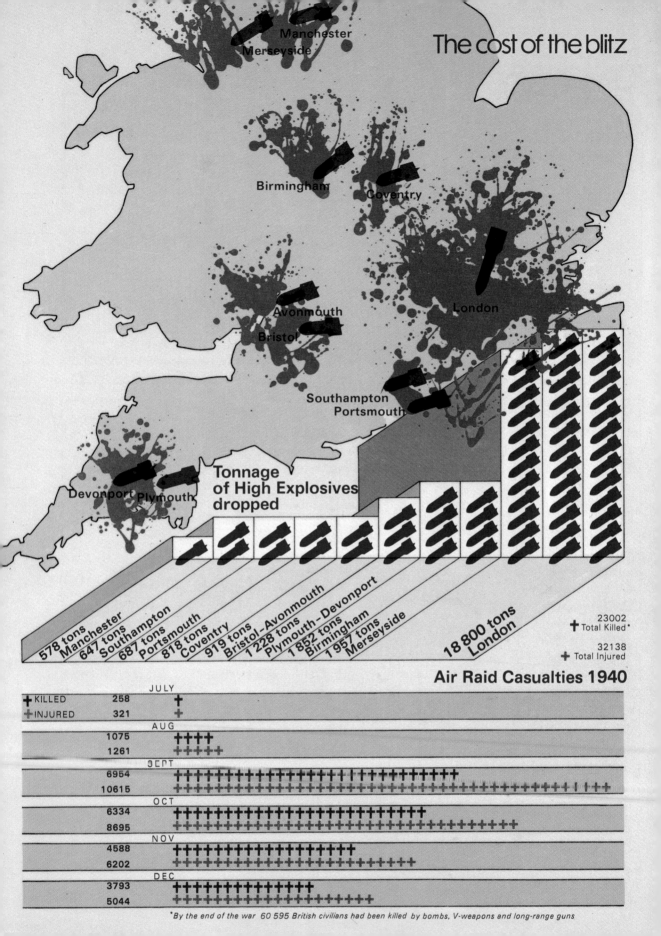

The cost of the blitz

Manchester
Merseyside

Birmingham

Coventry

London

Avonmouth
Bristol

Southampton
Portsmouth

Devonport Plymouth

Tonnage of High Explosives dropped

578 tons Manchester		
647 tons Southampton		
687 tons Portsmouth		
818 tons Coventry		
919 tons Bristol – Avonmouth		
1 228 tons Plymouth – Devonport		
1 852 tons Birmingham		
1 957 tons Merseyside		
18 800 tons London		

✝ 23002 Total Killed*

✝ 32138 Total Injured

Air Raid Casualties 1940

✝ KILLED	258	JULY ✝
✝ INJURED	321	✝
	1075	AUG ✝✝✝✝
	1261	✝✝✝✝✝
	6954	SEPT ✝✝✝✝✝✝✝✝✝✝✝✝✝✝✝✝✝✝✝✝✝✝✝✝✝✝✝✝✝✝✝✝✝✝✝
	10615	✝✝✝
	6334	OCT ✝✝✝✝✝✝✝✝✝✝✝✝✝✝✝✝✝✝✝✝✝✝✝✝✝✝✝✝✝✝✝✝✝✝
	8695	✝✝✝✝✝✝✝✝✝✝✝✝✝✝✝✝✝✝✝✝✝✝✝✝✝✝✝✝✝✝✝✝✝✝✝✝✝✝✝
	4588	NOV ✝✝✝✝✝✝✝✝✝✝✝✝✝✝✝✝✝✝✝✝✝✝
	6202	✝✝✝✝✝✝✝✝✝✝✝✝✝✝✝✝✝✝✝✝✝✝✝✝✝✝✝✝✝
	3793	DEC ✝✝✝✝✝✝✝✝✝✝✝✝✝✝✝✝✝✝
	5044	✝✝✝✝✝✝✝✝✝✝✝✝✝✝✝✝✝✝✝✝✝✝✝✝

*By the end of the war 60 595 British civilians had been killed by bombs, V-weapons and long-range guns

The home front

❛ Didn't know where to start; got my tin hat and gas mask to look OK and show I knew something of what was wanted. Somehow got on to stuffing a corpse (old woman) on a door, very heavy with three other people taking it out of first aid post round to back of hospital towards the garage where nurse (or sister) had said; on the way met "Eddie" young porter who said he was "in charge" of the mortuary. He said fill up the mortuary before the garage, so slowly onward to mortuary. I very tired suggested a rest, gratefully accepted, one of the men said we should dump her anywhere, as she was beyond help, go and help the wounded. Nobody replied tho' I agreed with him mentally but thought it better to go up to mortuary – not to leave old girl in the open. Then Eddie thought of barrow, got it, and we put her on it. Eddie and I took her up the mortuary; fetched out a metal "marble slab" on wheels, rolled her off the door onto it, she being covered by a thick red curtain blood-stained; took her into mortuary where already 4–5 corpses in similar bloody condition. Took back barrow to FA post, dumped it near door and looked for more work.

Voluntary first aid orderly writing to Mass Observation, September 1940 ❜

In recent years, the heroic legend of the resistance of British people to German air attack in 1940 has been closely scrutinized and even debunked. British wartime propaganda exaggerated popular defiance of the Luftwaffe: perhaps 'London can take it', but many individuals living in the capital and in the provincial cities worst hit by the blitz obviously could not. Some local authorities responded disgracefully inadequately to the bombing – Southampton was notorious. There was a serious collapse of morale in some badly blitzed towns, notably Coventry.

But overall, even under heavy bombing, British society held together and continued to function. British workers continued to produce munitions in the factories with limited disruption in the wake of raids. At the end of the Battle of Britain and the blitz, the British people did indeed have something to be proud of. Merely by continuing to go about their daily lives, they confounded all the pre-war prophets of air power, and defeated Goering's objectives in the latter stages of the Battle.

It is difficult to generalize about the behaviour of

A Dornier at the moment of attack 'somewhere over Britain' in the summer of 1940 the British in 1940, because everyone reacted to the threat of invasion and the bombing in different ways: some were terrified, some apathetic, a few genuinely exhilarated even as the bombs exploded around them. By far the most interesting evidence of popular attitudes is contained in the archives of Mass Observation, an organization set up just before the war by Dr Tom Harrisson, which encouraged hundreds of ordinary people to keep diaries of their daily lives and experiences, and report to MO month by month. Today, the MO reports form the most varied – and uncensored – contemporary testimony about British morale in the war.

The British were lucky – and the Luftwaffe foolish – about the manner in which they were allowed to come to terms with bombing during 1940. In the 1930s, the prophets of Armageddon from the air had conditioned the public to expect a devastating attack from the Luftwaffe within days of the outbreak of war. Instead of this, however, in the spring and summer of 1940, occasional Luftwaffe aircraft flew over Britain on reconnaissance or harassing operations, dropping spasmodic bombs to little effect. The British became conditioned to the sirens, and to the idea that air attack was nothing like as bad as they had been led to expect. Through the summer and autumn of 1940, the Luftwaffe's attacks on civilian targets increased in intensity. Yet still most people found that they emerged from their shelters satisfied enough to be themselves alive. There was no mass panic.

When the big raids on London began in September, at first the city was almost brought to a halt. Thousands of people stayed away from work or went home early. Industries and services of all kinds were seriously crippled. But as the raids continued, the life of the capital returned to something like normal. The need to earn a living drove even nervous Londoners to their shops and offices. Later in the blitz, it was noticed that industrial production was restored in most cities attacked long before general morale recovered – again, the need to turn up and collect a pay packet was a powerful spur.

The Luftwaffe's early raids on London, which concentrated on the East End, could have caused something close to a social uprising had they continued: there was bitter local resentment about the terrible damage in Stepney and Shoreditch, the feeling that the authorities were doing precious little for the victims, above all the awareness that the smarter quarters of London were unscathed. But then the German attacks became more diffuse: Chelsea and Westminster were badly hit. Best of all for national unity, Buckingham Palace was bombed. The tide of resentment ebbed, although in some provincial cities there was also anger about the poor showing of local authorities in coping with attacks. It was learned that the most prominent 'trekker' to leave Southampton each afternoon to avoid the night's raids was the Mayor, who abandoned his office at 3 pm and quit the city to sleep elsewhere.

The most agreeable surprise for Britain in 1940 was that far fewer people were killed by bombs than anyone had expected. In April 1939, at the height of gloomy predictions, a million funerary forms were issued by the Government, anticipating air raid casualties. In the event, by the end of 1940, only 23 000 people had been killed, despite a long succession of devastating German attacks against almost impotent British night defences. London suffered worst – 13 596 dead and 18 378 in hospital.

Contrary to popular myth, relatively few Londoners spent the blitz in the tube shelters: 177 000 or four per cent of the city's population even at the height of the blitz. Early in September when the East End was suffering worst, there was often a mass exodus during the afternoon to the apparent safety of the West End, but this stopped when the raids began to straddle the entire city. Nine per cent of Londoners spent the nights in public shelters, twenty-seven per cent in private ones. The remainder – a majority of the capital's population – stayed firmly at home. Another interesting survey showed that forty-two per cent of men and nineteen per cent of women spent their nights in bed, while thirty-nine per cent of men and forty-six per cent of women slept on sofas or mattresses on the floor –

usually downstairs. On 12 September, Mass Observation asked a sample of Londoners how much sleep they had had the night before, during heavy raids. Thirty-one per cent said none at all; thirty-two per cent, less than four hours; only fifteen per cent more than six hours. But as the blitz progressed, people became inured to the noises of night bombardment, and more and more slept longer and longer. In the early days too, people found the raids very time consuming: preparing for the night's alerts, living through the disturbances, clearing up afterwards ate deeply into everyone's time and – still more – into their reserves of emotional energy. But by the spring of 1941, most people in Britain had refashioned their lives to take account of the blitz. It had become a reality like income tax and winter snow, unless the day came when one's own home or family joined the casualty figures.

The fact that British society survived the blitz reasonably sound owed more to the common sense and decency of ordinary people than to the authorities responsible for coping with the problems of bombing. The homeless found that pitifully little was done for them: by the end of September, huge numbers of people – 25 000 in London alone – were living in overcrowded local authority Rest Centres. A string of different departments and Ministries was responsible for different elements of a refugee's life: rations, housing, furniture, education, and so on, and many families which had suffered terribly were treated with great insensitivity. Most of the Government's thinking about the problems of the blitzed centred on material needs – there was no real provision for human advice or assistance.

Before the war, an elaborate Air Raid Precaution organization had been created, with Town Clerks or Chief Constables appointed as local ARP Controllers, 400 000 paid full-time wardens, and hundreds of thousands more part-time volunteers. In the long hiatus of the Phoney War, many of the part-timers dropped out from boredom, and some of the paid wardens found themselves disposed of, as a Government economy measure.

When the blitz began in earnest, some of the Controllers and their organizations were found sorely wanting. Even more serious were the deficiencies of the fire service. The government had assumed that the peacetime fire organization would be adequate to deal with the problems of bombing. Yet the vast scale of the fires started by the Luftwaffe overwhelmed the system – on 20 December 1940, the Liverpool fire service was attempting to deal with 500 major blazes on Merseyside. There were 600 in a single night among the warehouses and business district of Manchester. The professional firemen, supported by a growing body of volunteer Auxiliaries, did their job as well as they could, but much better machinery was needed for reinforcing blitzed areas from all over the region. In August 1941, belatedly, a national fire service was created. Eventually, there were two million people serving as wardens, firewatchers and firemen in the huge organization that grew up to meet the threats of bombing.

As with everything else to do with the Luftwaffe's war on Britain in 1940, the attacks on the cities were eventually ineffectual because they were so poorly planned. Goering made the same mistake that Bomber Command was later to commit against the cities of Germany: he failed to concentrate his forces against vital targets until they were destroyed. The attack on Coventry in November dealt a devastating blow to the city – but industrial production was back to normal in five days. It was months before the Luftwaffe hit Coventry seriously again. Yet many observers who saw the numbed and shattered people of the city in the aftermath of the November raid believed that if the Luftwaffe had come back two or three times in the following week, Coventry could have been brought to a total halt. And the British night defences could have done nothing effective to stop them.

But the Luftwaffe did not go back to Coventry, and continued to attack London and provincial towns to an erratic pattern that defied logic. To some extent, it may be argued that this increased the tension for those in the cities below: just as nerves began to recover from one major raid, a new

attack would suddenly fall upon them. But any benefits in the morale battle gained by sporadic attacks were far outweighed by the ability of the cities and their civil defence forces to withstand occasional battering when they might well have cracked under repeated bombardment. American service observers who studied the blitz on Britain with great care in 1941, to pass on the lessons to their own airmen, concluded that the Luftwaffe might have dealt the British a serious blow if they had planned their operations properly, even long after the turning point of the Battle of Britain in mid-September. But they did not, and British industry survived.

Perhaps the most astonishing feature of the Battle of Britain and the revelation of the British people's

ability to withstand bombing is that from 1940 onwards, the British Government set about investing huge resources in its own Bomber Command. Against all logic, it allowed the Royal Air Force to spend most of its resources and the lives of 56 000 aircrew attempting to break the will of the German people in just the way that Fighter Command and the British people had proved could not be done.

Far left: Remains of a Bf 109 that exploded over Plumstead Road, Woolwich, 20 October 1940
Left above: 'Dear, dear! what on earth was it I had to do – call the fire-brigade, ring up the doctor, or just cross the road?' Punch, 6 May 1940
Left: Training the Home Guard in aircraft recognition
Above: A British pilot after baling out

‘ Ferdie and I seemed to be alone over the western part of Kent . . . London, with its barrage balloons floating unconcernedly, like a flock of grazing sheep ten thousand feet above it, was now feeling the full impact of the enemy bombers. As we approached South London the ground beneath us became obscured by smoke from the bomb explosions which appeared suddenly in the most unlikely sort of places — an open field, a house, a row of houses, a factory, railway sidings, all sorts of things. Suddenly there would be a flash, then a cloud of reddish dust obscuring whatever was there before, and then drifting away horizontally to reveal once more what was left of the target. I saw a whole stick of bombs in a straight line advancing like a creeping barrage such as you would see on the films in pictures like "Journey's End" or "All Quiet On The Western Front", but this time they were not over the muddy desolation of No Man's Land but over Croydon, Surbiton and Earl's Court. I wondered what the people were like who were fighting the Battle of Britain just as surely as we were doing, but in a less spectacular fashion. . . .

ROGER HALL, 152 Squadron, September 1940

Mrs R made us all some tea — just for something to do, I think, because we were all awash with tea already. That's one trouble about the raids, people do nothing but make tea and expect you to drink it. There was a nasty, nervous feeling in the kitchen. Every time there was a thud, Mrs R would say, "Is that a bomb?" — and Mr R would answer "No, s'a gun". I felt all swollen up with irritation, a bloated sort of feeling, but actually it was fear, I knew very well. A horrid, sick sort of fear, it's quite different from worry, much more physical. E says to me, "Let's get out of here, let's get some air", and out we go, into the garden. It is a beautiful summer night, so warm it was incredible, and made more beautiful than ever by the red glow from the East, where the docks were burning.

We stood and stared for a minute, and I tried to fix the scene in my mind, because one day this will be history, and I shall be one of those who actually saw it. I wasn't frightened any more, it was amazing; maybe it's because of being out in the open, you feel more in control when you can see what's happening. The searchlights were beautiful, it's like watching the end of the world as they swoop from one end of the sky to the other. . . .

A London girl writing to Mass Observation, 9 September 1940

I can't bear it, I can't *bear* it! If them sirens go again tonight, I shall die! Kilburn woman, 17 September 1940

When the air raid siren sounded at about 8 30 pm, I was walking on Wimbledon Common with C. . . . We were walking along the centre of the road, although all the time I was eager to walk to one side, under the trees. Four young boys passed us, going in the opposite direction. They seemed quite unperturbed. We could still hear a plane and see the searchlights trying to locate it. Suddenly a swishing noise came creeping along to the left of us, increasing in force and sound as it came. The noise seemed parallel to the ground. C threw me on the ground and covered my head. As I fell, triangular spurts of flame seemed all around; the whole effect was like a gigantic jumping cracker. I seemed quite numb, my mouth was full of grit and dirt. All was quiet, and pieces of earth showered down on us. We both got up. Laughed a little — we were terribly dirty. We walked down the road home. I felt very excited, flushed and warm. Ready to laugh a lot, and probably talking a great deal. . . .

A London girl writing to Mass Observation, 7 September 1940

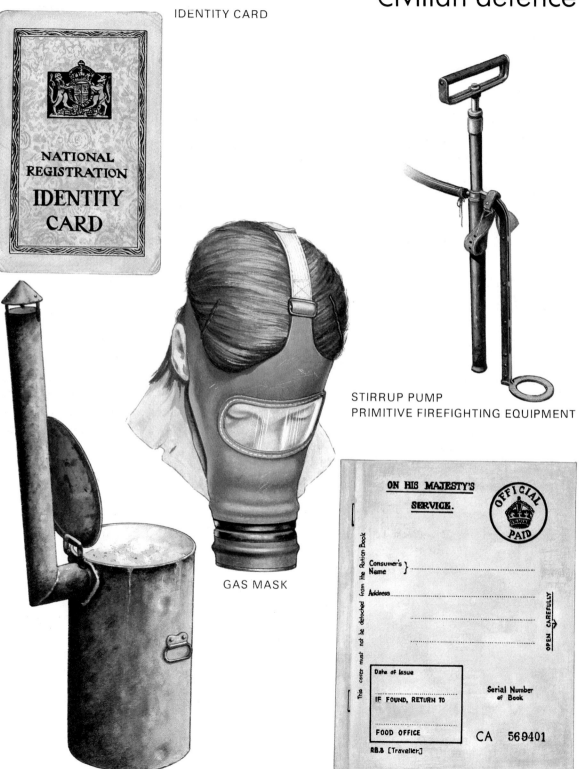

IDENTITY CARD

Civilian defence

NATIONAL REGISTRATION IDENTITY CARD

STIRRUP PUMP
PRIMITIVE FIREFIGHTING EQUIPMENT

GAS MASK

ON HIS MAJESTY'S SERVICE.

OFFICIAL PAID

This cover must not be detached from the Ration Book

Consumer's Name

Address

OPEN CAREFULLY

Date of Issue

IF FOUND, RETURN TO

Serial Number of Book

FOOD OFFICE

CA 569401

R.B.3 [Traveller]

MOBILE FIELD KITCHEN

BRITISH RATION BOOK

Above: A convent provides a bizarre setting for air-raid practice
Right above: Camouflage mania: a suburban public house in the autumn of 1940
Right below: Alien faces: fear of gas dominated pre-war air-raid planning

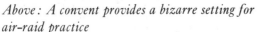

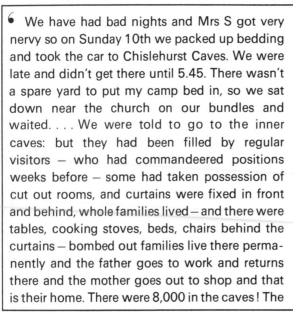

❛ We have had bad nights and Mrs S got very nervy so on Sunday 10th we packed up bedding and took the car to Chislehurst Caves. We were late and didn't get there until 5.45. There wasn't a spare yard to put my camp bed in, so we sat down near the church on our bundles and waited. . . . We were told to go to the inner caves: but they had been filled by regular visitors – who had commandeered positions weeks before – some had taken possession of cut out rooms, and curtains were fixed in front and behind, whole families lived – and there were tables, cooking stoves, beds, chairs behind the curtains – bombed out families live there permanently and the father goes to work and returns there and the mother goes out to shop and that is their home. There were 8,000 in the caves! The sanitary arrangements were good – parts partitioned off and were disinfected – but alas, one was too near us – a man's – and one would have thought that everyone would have finished by bed time, but all night long the sound went on and on and on. I got to sleep at last – soundly – but at 4 am everyone woke up and coughed for half an hour – then went to sleep again – the current of air was changed then I hear – 5 am – the lights were full on and the canteen opened. At 6, we got up and folded our things. . . . We arrived home at 7.30 and I am very glad to have had the experience.

Kent woman writing to Mass Observation, November 1940 ♪

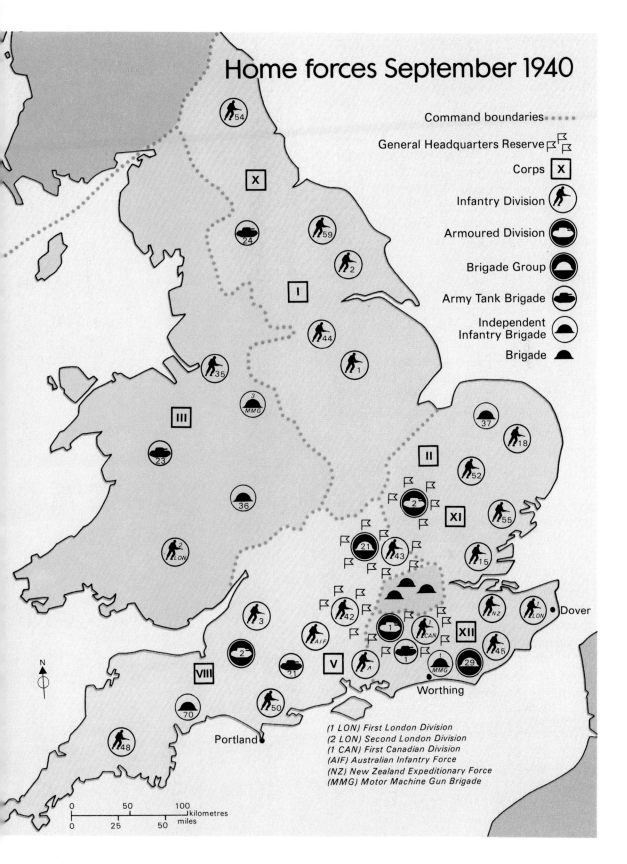

Home forces September 1940

Command boundaries ·····
General Headquarters Reserve
Corps X
Infantry Division
Armoured Division
Brigade Group
Army Tank Brigade
Independent Infantry Brigade
Brigade

Dover

Worthing

Portland

N

0   50   100
kilometres
0   25   50
miles

(1 LON) First London Division
(2 LON) Second London Division
(1 CAN) First Canadian Division
(AIF) Australian Infantry Force
(NZ) New Zealand Expeditionary Force
(MMG) Motor Machine Gun Brigade

' Daylight had overtaken us and I felt a wreck, still having curlers under my turban. Mother was cooking breakfast and everybody had started to shovel away the mud, so I started on our front path. My sister came back and we had breakfast. Then began a hectic day. First we cleaned up outside, swilling down water, dumping debris into the road for the council to remove. Then we began to sweep away plaster inside. There was another big hole on the landing, a smaller one in my sister's bedroom. Then it began to rain, so I put on old clothes and went onto the roof. This was very discouraging. There was a huge hole above the bathroom and quite 20 more small ones; one chimney was off and another had a nasty lean. Everywhere were dripping sounds. I put buckets, tubs, bowls under the worst. I rammed a piece of lino over the landing hole and old mats over the bathroom one. Descended to lunch hungry.

West London Girl writing to Mass Observation, 10 November 1940

In Coventry. . . . There were more open signs of hysteria, terror, neurosis observed than during the whole of the previous two months together in all areas. Women were seen to cry, to scream, to tremble all over, to faint in the street, to attack a fireman, and so on. The overwhelmingly dominant feeling on Friday was the feeling of utter helplessness. The tremendous impact of the previous night had left people practically speechless in many cases. And it made them feel impotent. There was no rôle for the civilian. Ordinary people had no idea what they should do.

Mass Observation report on Coventry after its big attack, November 1940

Above far right · An Anderson shelter
Above, centre and left: Educating Britain · some wardens became obsessive about the dangers of even a lighted cigarette
Far right: Evacuees. Many London children had their first sight of the countryside in 1940
Right: London shopfront, September 1940

you never know who's listening!

CARELESS TALK COSTS LIVES

Left: Piccadilly Circus Underground station in the midst of the blitz
Left below: Esprit de corps *in the suburbs: wardens' variety troupe*
Below: Wardens at Erith, Kent, Civil Defence headquarters rehearse their air-raid drill

The battle won

Between 18 and 30 September 1940, the number of German barges photographed by RAF reconnaissance in the Channel ports between Flushing and Boulogne declined from 1,004 to 691. On 25 October, 'Ultra' decrypts revealed to the British Government that the Luftwaffe had disbanded one of the special administrative units attached to the invasion forces. On 31 October, the Defence Committee chaired by the Prime Minister agreed that the danger of invasion had now become 'relatively remote'. The British forces deployed to defend the nation against 'Sealion' were stood down from 'immediate readiness' for the winter.

The Government did not feel entirely safe from invasion until Hitler attacked Russia in June 1941. But with his brilliant instinct for war, Churchill had sensed the Nazis' hesitation, indecision, and final flinching from invasion the previous autumn and dispatched Britain's pathetic reserves of armour to the Western Desert.

With hindsight, it is possible to see the immense significance of Hitler's lack of personal interest both in the detailed 'Sealion' plan and in the Battle of Britain. In all his other major initiatives – Austria, Czechoslovakia, Poland, Norway, the attack on the West and the invasion of Russia – Hitler was involved in planning down to the finest detail, and pored over maps with his commanders far into the night. But beyond ordering the staff studies to be made for 'Sealion', and authorizing Goering to launch his great attacks, Hitler never took any real part in the *Kanalkampf* operations. He wanted at least a formidable demonstration on his western flank, and perhaps, if the opportunity presented itself, a cheap *coup* against Britain. But when it became apparent that the price of 'Sealion' would be very high, he lost interest. He turned to preparing for the real thrust – against Russia.

But none of this should suggest that the threat to Britain was not real, or that the Battle of Britain was not a decisive encounter. If Goering's air fleets had succeeded in destroying the British defences, Hitler would almost certainly have seized his chance to launch an invasion. At the very least, with Fighter Command ruined, the Luftwaffe would have been able to bomb Britain in daylight with impunity, and inflict appalling damage that might ultimately have forced the British to surrender.

A great lesson of the Second World War was that air power could achieve formidable results if air superiority could be gained, by the fighters, to enable the bombers to operate effectively. This is what the Battle of Britain was about, it was this failure to achieve air superiority that signalled the Luftwaffe's defeat by the winter of 1940, even if the RAF was unable to stop the night blitz.

Goering probably understood in the summer of 1940 that Hitler was not committed to 'Sealion', and that if Britain was to be totally defeated, the burden of achieving this must fall on the Luftwaffe. He saw a unique opportunity to prove the power and enhance the prestige of his air force. But he had only the crudest notions of how an air battle should be fought. In the beginning at least, he seemed to regard the attacks by his bombers merely as a convenient method of drawing the RAF into the sky and shooting down its fighters. His plans assumed that the British would meet the attack with every fighter they could put in the air, and become drawn into a struggle of attrition that they must lose.

If the British had indeed responded in this way, many air marshals and members of the Government would have heartily approved. It required great moral courage as well as strategic judgment for Dowding and Park to fight the Battle of Britain by their brilliant measured strokes. Their refusal to send fighters into the air to meet the great German Bf 109 sweeps over south-east England was a classic display of masterly inactivity. The other inspired move was to order the British fighters to concentrate on shooting down bombers. It did not conform to any of the romantic notions about chivalrous jousts between knights of the air, but it baffled and finally defeated the Luftwaffe.

Tactics in the air proved to have changed little between 1918 and 1940. The most effective formula for shooting down an enemy aircraft was to dive at very high speed out of the sun, and fire from below and behind while pulling up out of the dive. Acceleration counted for more than maximum speed in combat, and in this respect the Hurricane and the Bf 110 were markedly inferior. British squadron tactics and formations were notably less effective than those of the Luftwaffe, not surprisingly when the Germans could draw on all their experience in Spain. In mass fighter-to-fighter combats, the German pilots proved superior to the British, again as a result of much greater training and experience. It is miraculous that the pilots of Fighter Command were able to achieve as much as they did, when their preparation for battle had been inadequate to the point of criminal negligence.

The top aces on both sides were distinguished by very good eyesight, marksmanship, and a willingness to fly very close to the enemy before opening fire. It was characteristic of the British that while their top-scoring pilots earned some publicity and decorations, they were given nothing like the star treatment Goering accorded his top men – Galland, Mölders and Wick. Throughout the war, the RAF's machinery of promotion and command appointments ground onwards, apparently regardless of a man's achievement.

Although the Luftwaffe's bases in France seemed frighteningly near to Britain, they proved to be significantly too far for the German fighters. The Bf 109s never possessed more than thirty minutes' combat endurance over Britain. This drastically reduced the value of the Germans' advantage in numbers. The Germans could only win the Battle of Britain if their Bf 109s could overwhelm the British fighters in the air, and the fact that they were unable to do so was chiefly the result of their poor endurance. It is astonishing that Milch and Udet did not see the need for disposable fuel drop tanks on Bf 109s in the summer of 1940. If they had done so, the shape of the Battle might have been decisively changed. When the American air force introduced the Mustang long-range escort fighters over Europe at the beginning of 1944, after months of disastrous losses and inaccurate bombing, the 8th Air Force gained air superiority over the Luftwaffe in a matter of weeks.

There are still some old Luftwaffe men who claim that there never was a Battle of Britain, or that even if there was, the British did not win it, because the Luftwaffe was still undefeated when its *Geschwader* were transferred eastwards in the spring of 1941 to prepare for the invasion of Russia. It is certainly true that Fighter Command did not win command of the air over Britain in the summer of 1940 – the Luftwaffe was able to launch harassing raids and night attacks almost with impunity. But Fighter Command achieved victory merely by remaining in existence, and preventing the Germans from gaining the air superiority that they needed either for invasion or for a decisive bomber offensive.

Whatever his other failures, Leigh-Mallory deserves some credit for mustering his 'big wings' over London on 15 September, because it was the moral effect on the Germans of seeing huge forces of British fighters meeting their attacks that convinced them that they were getting nowhere at great cost. The British did not destroy Goering's Air Fleets in 1940, or even come within measurable distance of doing so. But they inflicted losses that were quite unacceptable unless some decisive success was being achieved. By the winter of 1940 the leaders of the Luftwaffe had concluded that this was not, and never would be achieved. Thus they progressively disengaged their forces from the battle.

To the British in the early winter of 1940, it was much less clear than it is to us today that they had won the Battle of Britain. Yet one might imagine that Dowding and Park were the heroes of the hour for their handling of Fighter Command through

Aircraft replacement

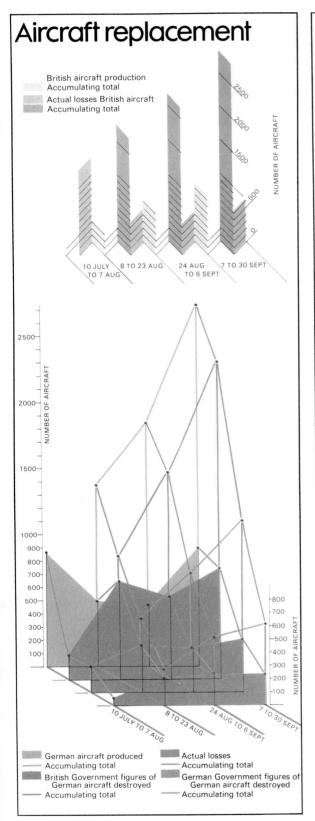

British aircraft production
Accumulating total

Actual losses British aircraft
Accumulating total

NUMBER OF AIRCRAFT

2500
2000
1500
500
0

10 JULY TO 7 AUG   8 TO 23 AUG   24 AUG TO 6 SEPT   7 TO 30 SEPT

NUMBER OF AIRCRAFT

2500
2000
1500
1000
900
800
700
600
500
400
300
200
100

800
700
600
500
400
300
200
100

NUMBER OF AIRCRAFT

10 JULY TO 7 AUG   8 TO 23 AUG   24 AUG TO 6 SEPT   7 TO 30 SEPT

German aircraft produced
Accumulating total
British Government figures of German aircraft destroyed
Accumulating total

Actual losses
Accumulating total
German Government figures of German aircraft destroyed
Accumulating total

'Gerald Maxwell came in . . . Apparently he has been given a kind of roving commission to size up the situation in the Fighter Command. He was not only one of the best British aces in the last war but he has one or two young brothers in a Fighter Squadron and is intensely interested in their success. . . . He showed me a copy of a memorandum he had prepared at the Prime Minister's request and which has been presented to Churchill. It pointed out an extremely dangerous situation in the Fighter Command, in which it would seem that dour, dogmatic, stuffy old Dowding has managed to lose the confidence of all the fighter pilots. The complaint seems to be that he never has any contact with them and fails to appreciate how important it is for him to see and talk with them, especially with some squadron that has suffered severe losses. The whole trend of affairs indicates that there is a strong movement to replace Dowding by someone who is more of a leader. . . . Of course, Maxwell feels very strongly about the matter. One of his young brothers has already had eight of the terrific experiences in all of which he was either shot down or wrecked . . .

RAYMOND LEE, United States Military Attaché in London, 16 October 1940

Reichsmarschall Goering . . . was entranced by the idea of General Douhet. I myself doubt whether he ever grasped the full implications of the Italian's doctrine . . . though the air battles over England were perhaps a triumph of skill and bravery so far as the German air crews were concerned, from the strategic point of view, it was a failure and contributed to our ultimate defeat. The decision to fight it marks a turning point in the history of the Second World War. The German air force, lacking any clear objective laid down by the Supreme Command, was bled almost to death . . .

WERNER KREIPE, Chief Operations Officer, *Luftflotte* 3

the summer and autumn. Instead, they found themselves summoned to a meeting at the Air Ministry, attended by Newall as Chief of Air Staff and Portal as Chief of Air Staff Designate. Sholto Douglas was only an air vice-marshal, but as Deputy Chief of Air Staff, he had authority over Dowding. At the meeting it was immediately clear, in Park's words, that he was to be 'the public prosecutor'. It was the kind of inquest one might have expected after a military disaster. Dowding and Park were under indictment for having reacted too cautiously to the Luftwaffe by committing only small forces of fighters against the massed German formations. Leigh-Mallory was invited to make his case that the 'big wings' were a far more effective method of beating the German raids, and incredibly, he had been allowed to bring Douglas Bader, a Squadron Leader, to spearhead the attack on his Commander-in-Chief. Leigh-Mallory claimed that he could get the five squadrons of the Duxford Wing into the air in six minutes, and that in a further twenty-five they could be as far as Hornchurch. But as the great fighter ace 'Johnnie' Johnson has pointed out, on one occasion shortly before this meeting, the Duxford Wing had taken seventeen minutes to leave the ground and another twenty to form up and set course from base. Bader, according to his biographer, told the meeting 'that the chap in the air, not the Controller, should decide when, where and how to meet the enemy'. It was the characteristic plea of a man of action, who still yearned to fight his wars 'by the seat of his pants'.

It was soon clear that this meeting had been organized merely as a mile-post on the road to getting rid of Dowding and Park. Airmen have always made great claims for the qualities of Sir Charles Portal as Chief of Air Staff, but his reputation seems founded on thin ice when it is remembered that Portal agreed to the sacking of Park and Dowding, the subsequent elevation of Leigh-Mallory, and later the ill-directed bombing campaign against Germany.

Dowding was abruptly telephoned at Stanmore and asked to clear his desk within twenty-four hours.

The Air Council 'have no further work to offer you', said the official letter. The Air Ministry's official booklet 'The Battle of Britain', published a few months later, made no mention of either Dowding or Park. The great Air Officer Commanding (AOC) 11 Group was relegated to Training Command. Leigh-Mallory took over his job, and later Dowding's. 'To my dying day I shall feel bitter at the base intrigue which was used to remove Dowding and myself as soon as we had won the Battle of Britain', said Park many years later.

It must be accepted that Churchill either acquiesced in or even possibly prompted the sacking of Dowding. Fighter Command's Commander-in-Chief lacked the extrovert confidence and assurance that the Prime Minister liked to see in his commanders, and there are hints that Dowding somehow incurred his animosity during the summer of 1940. Churchill could behave with great brutality to those whom he decided were serving the war effort badly. Like Wavell, Dowding was a victim of the Prime Minister at his most callous.

Thus the men who won the Battle of Britain suffered disgrace and ingratitude. Among the losers, on the other hand, it seemed to no one's advantage to conduct a search for scapegoats. Sperrle continued in his command until 1944. Kesselring later achieved great distinction commanding the German forces in Italy in 1944. Milch became one of the most important men in Germany, taking control of Udet's department as well as his own when Udet committed suicide in November 1941.

Goering never again enjoyed the power and prestige that he had achieved at his zenith in June 1940. It was tacitly recognized that the Luftwaffe had failed, and that Goering's disastrous inability to plan or direct the Battle had been largely responsible. 'The Fat Man' had launched his assault with a superb air weapon: the Luftwaffe's bombing techniques were far in advance of anything possessed by any other air force in the world. But by his failure to decide on a systematic strategy for the Battle, to concentrate on vital targets and, above all, by his fatal blunder in falling for the great lure of London

Between sorties

as a target, Goering had stumbled to defeat. The real tragedy for the Luftwaffe was that because the *Reichsmarschall* commanded a powerful political position in addition to leading the Luftwaffe, there was no possibility of calling him to account. For the rest of the war, the Luftwaffe suffered the consequences of being commanded by this indolent sybarite, broken in energy and purpose for anything except retaining his own offices and power. Until the end, the German air force possessed outstandingly brave and determined aircrew, struggling to keep the war going with inadequate aircraft and equipment, not because the technology was lacking to do better, but because political and industrial control was so poor. For the Luftwaffe as well as for its leader, June 1940 had been the summit of glory.

As the struggle widened, and became in the fullest sense a world war, the scale of the fighting dwarfed the encounters of 1940. In the entire Battle of Britain, Fighter Command lost only 530 aircrew, killed. In 1943 and 1944, Bomber Command would lose more than this in a single night of the attack on Germany. In America, Roosevelt was already ordering industry to manufacture 50 000 aircraft a year.

Yet in the summer of 1940, Dowding's 3,000-odd pilots had been enough, just enough, to make Britain's survival possible. Almost as important, they had done an enormous amount to convince America that Britain could survive, and was worth supporting. Roosevelt's close associate 'Wild Bill' Donovan, together with a number of distinguished American correspondents in London headed by Ed Murrow and Drew Middleton, painted a picture of Britain under siege that impressed the President and many of his people more than the bilious defeatism of his Ambassador in London, Joseph Kennedy. After a month of the blitz, Kennedy went home to resign in October 1940. Robert Vansittart, Halifax's Chief Diplomatic Adviser, wrote of him: 'Mr Kennedy is a very foul specimen of double-crosser and defeatist. He thinks of nothing but his own pocket. I hope that this war will at least see the elimination of this type.' By the end of 1940, many influential Americans had come to believe that sooner or later, they must enter the war. Even Kennedy never fulfilled his threat to oppose Roosevelt's re-election in November.

There is one further small postscript to the Battle of Britain: at Fighter Command, it was decided to stage a big war game, recreating the air battles of September, to vindicate the 'big wing' principle. Leigh-Mallory, now in Park's chair at 11 Group, reacted to the German threat in the way that he had always argued was best. The result was a fiasco. The Umpires decreed that Biggin Hill and Kenley had been bombed before Leigh-Mallory's 'big wings' had even got off the ground. But to the air marshals, who would have denied the RAF even the bare minimum of fighters to win the Battle of Britain if pre-war planning had been left in their hands, these things were not important. They were concentrating their energies on planning Bomber Command's massive bomber offensive against Germany, designed to fulfil all their pre-war dreams of strategic warfare. They would spend the rest of the war attempting to do to Germany exactly what the Luftwaffe had signally failed to do to Britain in 1940.

Churchill and the Battle

The name of Winston Churchill will always be indelibly associated with the Battle of Britain. Although he remained Britain's director of war until 1945, Churchill would especially be remembered for his words of defiance in 1940, at the moment when many highly-placed people in Britain secretly feared that the war was lost.

It is a minor irony that the Prime Minister played virtually no part in the conduct of the Battle of Britain itself. His greatest contribution was made before it began, when he appointed Beaverbrook as Minister of Aircraft Production. Thereafter, although he followed every day's fighting with passionate interest and concern, he could do nothing to help Dowding and Park and their pilots. Such interventions as he made were indeed positively mischievous, such as his urging that the training of pilots should be reduced to speed the flow of men to the squadrons. He cannot be absolved of responsibility for the mean treatment of Dowding and Park when the Battle was won. Leigh-Mallory's and Bader's advocacy of a simple policy for shooting down Germans appealed more strongly to his combative nature than Dowding's more cautious tactics and reserved manner.

Yet having said all this, nothing diminishes Churchill's towering stature as the voice and inspiration of Britain's defences in 1940. His oratory and unshakeable determination first persuaded the British people that the war could be continued after the fall of France, then mobilized them in their own defence, then filled them with enthusiasm for their own triumph.

Churchill was delighted by his visits to the fighter airfields and Operations Rooms during the Battle. General Pile, who commanded the AA guns, has vividly described Churchill's glee, watching a heavy battery in action in Richmond Park one night, 'while all around the Germans were dropping bombs and many fires were raging.' The Prime Minister refused to be hurried on to his next engagement. 'This exhilarates me,' he said. 'The sound of the cannon gives me a tremendous feeling.' He contemptuously declined offers of a helmet, and drove home in the early hours of the morning in exultant high spirits. In complete contrast to Hitler, Churchill was exhilarated and inspired by direct contact with the battle, by smelling gunpowder and talking to the men at their guns and dispersals.

Although his tactical judgment was often poor, Churchill understood at once the significance of the Luftwaffe's shift from attacking Fighter Command to bombing London. He scented victory – or all that Britain could hope for, the avoidance of defeat. 'I was glad that, if any of our cities were to be attacked, the brunt should fall on London,' he wrote. 'London was like some huge prehistoric animal, capable of enduring terrible injuries, mangled and bleeding from many wounds, and yet preserving life and movement.'

Churchill's broadcasts and speeches brilliantly flattered the British people. If the spirit of the blitz was a little more hesitant than the Prime Minister suggested, by the end of 1940 he had convinced the British that they had inflicted a great defeat on Hitler by their efforts. In reality, of course, the British were no nearer to defeating Germany than they had been in June. It would be years, if ever, before Britain alone could build an army remotely capable of facing the Wehrmacht on equal terms. Britain had no means of frustrating any major German move on the Continent. Hitler was still unchallenged master of Europe.

Churchill in the uniform of an Air Marshal of the Royal Air Force (painting by C J Orde). Unlike previous wartime Prime Ministers, Churchill saw himself as overall director of the war effort and he underlined his position by wearing the uniform of any of the three services when he felt it to be appropriate

Opposite: Two recent photographs of Biggin Hill showing how some Battle of Britain airfields were developed and expanded in the years after the war and are today busy bases of the Royal Air Force, flying clubs, and various commercial organizations

Left: Interest in the Battle of Britain continues as is shown in this photograph of aircraft excavation

Below: A typical sequence of events showing what happened when a 1940 fighter crashed

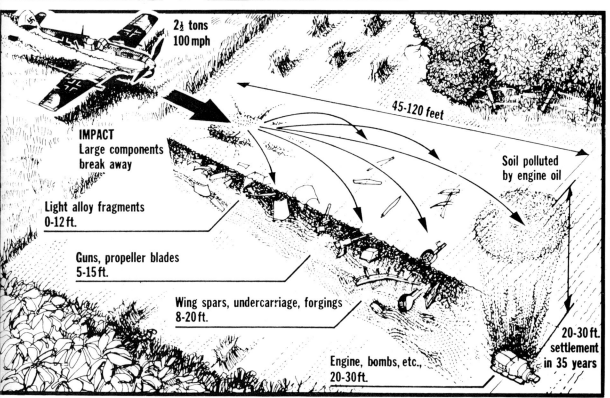

2½ tons
100 mph

45-120 feet

Soil polluted by engine oil

IMPACT
Large components break away

Light alloy fragments 0-12 ft.

Guns, propeller blades 5-15 ft.

Wing spars, undercarriage, forgings 8-20 ft.

Engine, bombs, etc., 20-30 ft.

20-30 ft. settlement in 35 years

Acknowledgments

The author and publishers thank all those who most kindly provided information on, and reminiscences of, the Battle of Britain. They are especially grateful for the help and advice given so generously by Charles Cain, Malcolm Bates and Jack Foreman.

The maps were drawn by Elaine Perrer and the statistical charts by Felicity Clark.

The artwork is by Peter Sarson and Tony Bryan, Peter Sullivan, and Michael Jackson.

The photographs of the Hurricane in the air today, on the title page and on pages 102–103, were specially taken by Tony Howarth (© Rainbird). Other commissioned photography is by Derrick Witty.

The author and publishers are also grateful to the following for permission to reproduce photographs on the pages indicated:

Aerofilms: 220. Associated Press: 106–107. R F Barclay: 94 above centre, 121, 122, 152 above, 191 top. British Aerospace: 46, 47, 171. BBC Hulton Picture Library: 37, 38 top left, 67, 82, 87 top left, 129, 134 below left, 193 above right, 205 left. Bundesarchiv: 78–79. Central Press Photos: 10 top, 12 right, 13 left, 13 right, 14, 23 top left, 23 left, 27 below, 33, 34 top left, 34 top right, 36 above, 62, 75, 84 top left, 94 centre below, 117, 130 left, 136 left, 137 left, 157, 152–153, 165 left, 176 top right, 177 below right, 178, 180, 181, 190 top right. J Foreman: 95 above centre, 95 above left, 95 above right, 95 centre, 95 below right, 147. Fox Photos: 107 below, 122–123, 142 left below, 217. Hamlyn Group Picture Library: 15, 143 top. R Hunt; 10 below right, 153 top right, 197. Imperial War Museum: 8, 11, 35, 63 below, 67 top left, 69, 72–73 below, 81 right, 86, 87 below, 89, 94 below left, 94 below right, 104, 114 above right, 118, 126, 134 top centre, 140, 146–7, 149, 156, 174, 188 below left, 189 top right, 193 above left, 210 below, 211 top left, 212 top left. Air Vice-Marshal Sandy Johnstone: 94 above left. Kentish Express: 221 left. Keystone Press Agency: 9, 26, 27 above, 58 left, 72–73 top, 114 left, 137, 153 centre, 165 right, 170–171 below, 171 top, 186, 190 top right. J. MacClancy: half-title, 53 left, 53 top right, 58 right, 91, 100–101, 105, 107 above, 112, 116, 124, 128, 135 left above, 135 left, 136 right, 142 above left, 144–145, 148, 151, 160, 161, 166, 167, 168 below, 176 top left, 187, 190 top left, 190 below left, 198. National Portrait Gallery: 94 above right. Photoworld: 142–143 centre. Popperfoto: 12 left, 13 centre, 93, 170 top, 177 below left, 189 below. Private collection: 30 top, 34 below, 146. Public Record Office: 67 below, 81 left, 162. Punch: 84 centre, 204 above left. RAF Museum, Hendon: 36 below. Rainbird Publishing Group: 102–103, 163, 219. B Robertson: 10 left. Rolls-Royce: 23 right, 59 left. Royal Aeronautical Society: 59 right. Sport and General: 38 top right. Stato Maggiore Aeronautica: 12 centre. Süddeutscher Verlag: 28–29, 38 below, 70, 74, 78–79, 95 below left, 114 below right, 125 top, 129, 130 top, 143 below, 147, 154, 155, 166 top, 188 top left, 188 top right, 188 below right, 189 top left, 191 below, 198 below, 200. Sunday Times: 221 below. Syndication International: 179. J Topham Picture Library: 65, 84 top right, 84 below left, 84 below right, 125 below, 130 below, 131, 134 top left, 140, 153 below right, 193 below, 204, 205 above, 208, 210 top, 211 top right, 211 below, 212 below left, 212 below. Vickers: 43.

The painting of Sir Winston Churchill by C J Orde on page 219 and the painting of the aerial battle by Roy Nockolds on page 163 are reproduced by permission of the RAF Club, London.

The author and publishers are grateful to all those participants in the Battle of Britain whose words are quoted in the book and especially for permission to reproduce extracts from the following published works:

Fighter Pilot by George Barclay (Kimber 1976)
Spitfire Pilot by D M Crook (Faber 1942)
Nine Lives by Alan C Deere (Hodder and Stoughton 1959)
The First and the Last by A Galland (Methuen 1955)
Arise to Conquer by Ian Gleed (Severn House 1975)
Clouds of Fear by Roger Hall (Bailey Brothers and Swinfen 1975)
The Last Enemy by Richard Hillary (Macmillan 1942)
Enemy in the Sky by Sandy Johnstone (Kimber 1976)
One of the Few by J A Kent (Kimber 1971)
London Observer by Raymond E Lee (Hutchinson 1972)
Ack-Ack by Sir Frederick Pile (Harrap 1949)
Duel of Eagles by Peter Townsend (Weidenfeld 1970, Simon and Schuster 1971)

Index

Page numbers in **bold** type refer to captions to illustrations.